FOREWORD

Most cricketers know the story of the Kentish lar early 1800s, practised his cricket in a barn, to tl fielding of his dog. In those under-arm days, Wi ferocity of his sister's round-arm deliveries that he became determined to perfect the action for himself. The story ended in 1822, when Willes took a team from Kent to play against the M.C.C., at Lord's. He was no-balled so often that he hurled the ball to the ground, mounted his horse, and rode out of cricket for ever.

By a strange turn of fate, it was Willes's sister's son, Edward Hodges, who became the first cricketer to describe his life in Torquay, before any meaningful cricket was played here. Whilst reminiscing about his uncle, in 1907, he wrote "In the late 1830s, I moved to Torquay, and I can still remember how impressed I was to see the whole British Fleet under sail in Torbay. There was no cricket played in Torquay at that time, so I used to go out with a bat and ball on Daddy Hole Plain, and play alone. Later I went to Newton Abbot, and was fortunate to get some good cricket there".

Edward Hodges's story was a sad one, but all clouds have a silver lining, and the 1840s saw the birth of hundreds of cricket clubs throughout the length and breadth of England. The great new railway network enabled teams to travel economically, for the first time. The Penny Post enabled fixtures to be made, and reports to be filed. In 1841, the Commander-in-Chief of the Army, Lord Hill, ordered that cricket grounds should be provided for every garrison in England. Since there were few towns, of any size, without a garrison, this order provided thousands of cricketers with the last piece of their jigsaw.

Just like Cinderella, Torquay Cricket Club was a little late to the Ball, but, well before midnight, it arrived in all its finery. In 1851, the Great Exhibition was held in Hyde Park, but, on July 9th. of that year, a much smaller exhibition took place, in a far lovelier park. Torquay Cricket Club pitched its wickets at Windmill Hill, for the first time, and the thirty founder members reaped the first rewards of their labours.

Windmill Hill provides the breathtaking backdrop for Act 1, Scene 1, of Ray Batten's story. Forget the cold, wind-swept summit of the hill, which is all that remains today. Imagine, instead, the lower wooded slopes, which now extend down to Hele Village, and picture a gently sloping meadow surrounded on all four sides by mature woodlands. Listen to the chatter of the men, as they, joyfully, climb the hill each day to maintain their special ground. Peep into the kit box, and wonder at the cloth batting gloves, sewn on to tubular India rubber, with palms exposed. See the buckskin leg-guards, buttoned at the back, and the bats with one-piece handles. Smell the meat cooking, and taste the ale which cemented a club spirit so strong that it has lasted, unbroken, ever since.

The story of Torquay Cricket Club is an endlessly fascinating one. It is a battle for survival which becomes a drama. It is an ongoing soap opera which, at times, becomes a farce.

And it is a love-story for those special few whose absolute dedication has known no boundaries. Its pages tell of those players who spent their whole careers in the club's colours, and it tells of the meteors, who burned brightly and then vanished. It remembers the countless professionals whose livelihoods depended on their runs, or their wickets. Some loved, some admired, some despised, and some who simply failed. And, in its later pages, it breathes life back into the many colourful overseas players, who had just one season to leave their marks on the scoreboard, or in the bar.

But if clubs earn local esteem from the deeds of their members, they only earn national significance from the calibre of their visitors. No other cricket club, in Devon or Cornwall, has hosted the Test teams from Australia, South Africa, Pakistan, New Zealand, and the West Indies. How many local grounds have been graced by Old Clarke, Hammond, Bill Edrich, Ames, Tyson, Statham, Sobers, Worrell, and a hundred other Test cricketers? Torquay Cricket Club has earned a fine reputation throughout the cricket world, and its Official History is long overdue.

Lord Harris once said "I see fifty good players before I see one good umpire, and I see fifty good umpires before I see one good club secretary." He might have added "I see fifty good club secretaries before I see one good biographer" For they are the rarest of men! After all, how do you ask a Torquinian, who has retired to the English Riviera, to spend four years of that retirement in the bowels of a Public Library?

Ray Batten is a man who confronts issues, and then sets out to tackle them. Some years ago an A.G.M. was told that the cricket club had no caterers for the coming season. The gathering was stunned to hear Ray's voice, from the back of the room, announce " Well, if no-one else will do it, I will have to do it myself!" And what a fine job he did! After the Club's 150th.Anniversary, he decided that the Club needed a comprehensive History, and, with no further hesitation, his four year sentence began.

This is a man with clear, concise views, and an intellect that is razor sharp. He is a critic with a heart of gold, and his story is told with the same waspish sense of humour that endears him to all who spend a sunny afternoon at the Recreation Ground.

This biography reflects Ray's deep respect for Cricket, and for the Cricket Club which he has served for so many years. I am honoured to commend it to you.

ROGER MANN

INTRODUCTION

Employment took me away from Torquay for almost all of my working life but on frequent visits to see my parents there was always time for footsteps to the Recreation Ground. Cricket and Rugby memories from my youth were largely associated with that area, as they must have been for many thousands of other followers who had passed through the gates, and yet no one appeared to have committed facts or even reminiscences to paper.

As a consequence, when I returned to my birthplace to retire, I spent years at the local library copying old paper cuttings relative to the respective clubs, and their past history, intending "one day" to do something about them! Lazy as ever I was, the impetus came when the Torquay Cricket Club published their 150th Year Brochure. Beautifully produced but only touching on a few facts I knew then I had to try and relate a history of my "town's club". The following "potted" version with my own personal interpretations, impressions and factual observations is dedicated to all those, on or off the field, who have over the years contributed to the Torquay Cricket Club history.

Special acknowledgement and sincere thanks are given for the assistance provided in helping to produce this account and for the photographs provided, to Torquay Central Library, Herald and Express Publications, J.E.Dickinson, Roger Mann, W.G.Traylor, I.Western, B.M.Matthews, J.H.Edwards, A.H.Kingdon, K.Creber, P.Twose, H.G.Baker, John Haly, R.Gerard, Arnold Dean, K.V.Hosking, J.Kirby, B.J.Sewell, John Parry, R.Gibson, Mrs. J. McMurray, Darren Cowell, Jack Critchlow, T.Stephens,

Special Note. David Thomas and Conrad Sutcliffe are present day local cricket reporters. Normally factual, rarely lyrical and never poetic, so hence the comparisons with writers of yester year!

REFERENCE PAGES

THE EARLY YEARS

The Torquay Cricket Club is able to trace its formation in 1851 as the original Minute Book is still safely preserved. A book entitled A Chronological Record of Events by R. Dymond and J.T. White mentions that in 1828, "through the exertions of Captain Pearce a cricket club had been established at Torquay, with weekly meetings, and the member's bid fair to become powerful rivals to their crack neighbours the Teignbridge Club". After a few years there is no further mention of that club in the papers that have been researched. A further publication, The History of Torquay has a section devoted to clubs and quotes the opening dates of the Victoria Club, Manor Club, etc, and it goes on to mention the nucleus of a cricket club formed in 1848, although no records were to be found. Interestingly the Teignbridge Club has been recorded as the first cricket club formed in Devon in 1815. In the Torquay area the St. Marychurch club had been in existence, before "our " club was formed, but in its initial formation it only lasted a few years.

Faithfully recorded by W.H. Kitson, who became the first secretary and treasurer, the Minute Book states how letters were sent out to people who were thought to be interested in forming such a cricket club. The inaugural meeting was held at the Hearders Hotel in June 1851 and R.S.Cary was the chairman. After establishing the need it was decided that Windmill Hill would be the ideal site for the ground initially.

E.B.Julian was elected the captain and two teams were chosen to play each other from the thirty odd persons who were present. Following that initial game it is recorded. "A man, or men, must spend time to water, mow and prepare the ground for the next match. Orders are to be placed for two pair of batting gloves, one pair of wicket -keeping gloves, two pair of leggings, a paint pot and whiteing for the creases, a box for bats and a square".

At a subsequent meeting the secretary stated he had been in contact with Mr. Mallock asking permission to use a field near Torre Abbey but this had been refused. In 1851 the Squire of Cockington owned vast areas of land, including most of the fields along what is now the sea-front, and it was years before the local authority became involved in development, facilities and amenities.

The Minute Book states, "The first game against South Devon on August 8th. 1851 etc.etc....after the match Torquay paid for the dinners of thirteen of the South Devon members", presumably the eleven players, umpire and scorer.

While there are no details in the Minute Book of the teams or scores, every fact the writer now relates has been researched from papers of the time. They show that Torquay had South Devon out for 47 in their first innings and 54 in their second. In reply Torquay scored 74 runs and in their second innings 29 for 3 which enabled them to win fairly comfortably. A return match, again on the South Devon ground was arranged for a few weeks hence and after the first result created quite a lot of interest. South Devon introduced a newcomer in the second game, Fyfe, who was the top scorer with 24 in a total of 98 and he had 15 in the second innings when no one else obtained double figures. This game Torquay lost, they were out for seventy in each innings and failed by fourteen runs to pass the home team's combined innings total of 154.

The concluding game for the season was played at Windmill Hill between two sides composed of the club members. After which some forty members attended a dinner at the Hearder's Hotel. Following the meal a bat was presented to the Secretary, W.H. Kitson, subscribed to by members in appreciation of his exertions to "get the club up and running".

In the October of 1851 a meeting was held to discuss another ground and, despite members being informed that the area the committee were suggesting would need money and time spent on it, the decision to go ahead was given. While the new area was approved the club decided to still retain Windmill Hill as a temporary expedient.

When the 1852 season began members were anticipating the opening of their new ground, which in those days was known as Chapel Hill Cross, and is now called the cricket field in Barton Road. Huge press advertisements announced the opening on the 16th August with a match against the Officers of the Garrison of Plymouth. The game was to be followed by a "Soiree Dansante" in a large marquee with a "well boarded floor for dancing", since at that stage there was no pavilion. The advertisement gave admission to the ground as being one shilling (5p) while for the entertainment the charges were to be, ladies four shillings and gentlemen five shillings. Special trains had been arranged from Exeter and Plymouth with a return journey at 9-30 p.m.

Actually, the ground was first played on by the members on 21st July when the club made up two sides for a game amongst themselves. A further match was arranged against South Devon and took place just a week before the official opening. Torquay managed to total 62 after bowling the visitors out for just 26, and following a meal South Devon were then bowled out again for 34 leaving Torquay winners by an innings and two runs.

The weather spoilt the planned opening and as a consequence the game did not start until after lunch had been taken. With that protracted event restricting the time left for cricket, it was impossible to complete the game. The officers were all out for 92 and in reply Torquay were 66 for 3. The reporter mentioned the presence of His Imperial Highness the Prince of Oldeunburg, the superb food and the dancing "until a late hour".

As already stated the oldest cricket club in Devon, Teignbridge had for two successive years arranged an Eleven of All England to play on their ground against Twenty-Two of Devonshire. During August 1853, just two years after the club was formed Torquay were going to host the game. A special sub -committee had been appointed to ensure the necessary tents, marquees, and refreshments were arranged while everyone hoped for three fine days. At the end of the first day the Twenty-Two of Devon had been bowled out for 106 with Capt. Fyfe top scorer with 26 and the Eleven were 22 for 1. On the second day the Eleven took their score to 172 while the Tinley brothers, famous professional players of that time, took all the wickets between them. Clarke and Hillier then ran through the Devonshire batsmen and had them all back in the pavilion for a mere 54 forestalling any thought of having to bat again.

Other than the cricket, mention was made of, "the illustrious visitors now in the town and attending the game including Their Imperial Highness the Grand Duchess Marie and Grand Duchess Olga of Russia with the Crown Prince of Wurtemburg".

In the April of 1854 a meeting was held at the Hearders Hotel to make arrangements for another game against the England Eleven. The report said it was "a lengthy conversation of the subject". Prior to the first meeting of those two sides numerous tradesmen in the town, who were interested in cricket, had subscribed £70 towards the cost of staging the venture, which had in effect been over £140. Soundings had already been taken again and this time there had been much less interest and only £30 had been promised. Going through records there are only accounts of games against, Exeter, Paignton, South Devon and Instow so presumably the monies could not be raised and the game never took place. At this same meeting in 1854 it was announced that a proposal, of the 1853 meeting, for a pavilion had come to fruition. The money needed had been raised by selling £5 shares and while the original cost authorised had been £130 the actual expense was £30 more and this had been covered by selling further shares. It was further explained that the "handsome and spacious marquee" previously used had been donated by Mr. Palk, son of Sir Lawrence.

Researching, the writer could find only accounts of four or five games a season during the clubs early years and the number was confirmed at the Annual General Meeting of 1855 when the results were given. "Games played during the 1854 season 5, won 1, drawn 3 and lost 1". Mention was made that a professional, King had been engaged for one game and the committee were recommending that he should be engaged permanently, "although no funds can be voted for such a purpose". The secretary went on to tell the members that the club had lost the tenant at the pavilion and had secured another who would be responsible for the ground. Sir Lawrence Palk was no longer going to charge for the ground but, the pavilion rent was to rise to £5 a year. Even at that early stage the club was already in debt as receipts for the year were £66-10 and outgoing costs over £76 while the original debt of £75, and over two years interest, had not been cleared. The committee suggested, "exertion to increase the number of members and rigid economy in expenditure"!

Advertisements found in the papers of that period show the club must have had some income. The Archery Club were holding their meetings on the ground every Tuesday and Thursday at three o'clock and were inviting people to "come along". There were also mentions of matches between St. Marychurch and Bovey taking place on the Torquay Ground.

The Rev. G.T.Warner brought sides to Torquay in the 1850s which were either under the heading of "Pupils" or Highstead and he invariably had a professional in his side. In one instance Bentley was named and on another occasion the previously mentioned pro, King, but neither were able to provide victories for the Reverend on every occasion. Regular visitors were South Devon, Paignton, Totnes, Culm Valley and Sidmouth, who all defeated Torquay during the 1856 season.

Throughout the 1850s, except during the month of August, there appeared to be very little cricket played by the Torquay club whereas there were a few matches reported as, Mr. Almond's Side v Mr. Reed's Side, Mr. Marshall's Side v Mr. Almond's Side, etc. A Torquay Town team played on the ground as well as St. Marychurch and Montvidere School on odd occasions, while the Rev. Warner's Pupils and Highstead were frequently reported as having played.

A report on a Torquay v Culm Vale game caught the eye,

"the fielding was good on both sides, but barren of any extraordinary feat, unless we exempt a 'run out' by Mr. Patch. Suddenly he changed his action from delivery of the ball to put down the wicket at his own end, and cut short the career of a promising young player, guesting from Cheltenham College, who was backing up too eagerly and thus increased his experience of the Game"!

Each year the club appeared to have home and away fixtures with Boconnoc and it was only in a report of 1857 that the writer discovered their ground was near Lostwithel, always a two day fixture.

During the August of 1858 Torquay entertained a Cheltenham College X1 and while the score card was given, showing a victory for the club, the report was scathing. "The ground was well attended by spectators, and during the afternoon some donkey racing was started to the annoyance, and be it said also, of the cricketers. We were pleased at seeing foot races last Christmas, but we hope the Torquay club will not again permit donkeys to run during a game of cricket. The name of the club stands well in South Devon and we hope it will long remain so."

Later in the month the first of the North Devon v South Devon games was held and sowed the seed for future County matches. South Devon were represented by A. Hawes(Plymouth), T. Were(Sidmouth), R. Martin and J. Edwards(Totnes), J. Green(Brixham), J. Carpenter(Tavistock) and while the only Torquay player invited had been G. Warner, because of refusals and cry offs, H. Almond, E. Ford, J. Kitson and R. Reed, all of Torquay, had been seconded. R. Bagg of North Devon scored 112 not out, which alone was more than the South Devon total of 79, and ensured a handsome victory as the second day was washed out. The evening saw a soiree at the Baths Assembly Room to entertain the visitors and guests.

At the end of season dinner W.H. Kitson said, prior to the North v South game the seasons finances had been satisfactory, but after that match the club now had a deficiency. However, "he thought that was of little consequence considering the importance of the game to the club"!!

During the 1859 A.G.M. Mr. Kitson told the meeting that the original debt had been brought down to £150 and the committee were advising that the best way forward for the club was to offer life-membership to the shareholders in lieu. Two members, on the committee, had already given their shares to the club. He went on to explain that Bentley had been paid by the club for looking after the ground but the 'Professional Fund', to pay him for games played, was entirely supported by voluntary contributions.

The first game of any note in the 1859 season was a Western counties side which played a school's X1, selected from Eton, Harrow, Rugby and Winchester. Actually the so called Counties side was a collection of players from the best in South Devon, with individuals from Exeter, Plymouth and Teignbridge included. A charge for admission was made for this game and the press reported a good attendance over the two days. Percival, from Plymouth, was the top scorer with 44 for the so called Counties and while Bentley took seven wickets in the two innings the Schools X1 won by seventeen runs. This became a regular game for many seasons under the title of Public Schools.

Another game between the gentlemen of North Devon and South Devon took place at the ground in late August. With fine weather, a fete on the ground and a dinner and dance arranged to complete the evening, yet another event became part of the club's history. This time the North returned well and truly beaten by nine wickets. After the last game of the season, when the teams were selected from only amongst the club members, a dinner was held at the Union Hotel. W.H.Kitson did a quick review of the season for the assembly and stated that of the 9 games the club had played 3 had been won and the rest drawn. He felt the heavy expenditure during the season, for the North v South and the Public Schools game, would see a debt overall and he expected having to increase subscriptions at the annual meeting.

Annual General Meetings, for many years, were given newspaper coverage as were the club dinners and at the dinner of 1861 it was stated, "It is desirable that a Devon County Cricket Club be formed with its Headquarters in Torquay". Great aspirations! At the following A.G.M. members were informed, "The past season has seen the formation of a Devon County Cricket Club originated at your annual dinner".

The Queen's Hotel saw the meeting for the 1861 A.G.M. and Kitson reported a shortfall of over £24. After a lot of discussion it was decided to hold another meeting, at the same venue in a month, when the proposed increase in subscriptions and the negative balance would be the subject. He said the agreement with Bentley had run out and the committee had decided to take over the management of the ground itself. Bentley had made an offer of his professional services for the season for £50 and the committee were still considering it. While no details of the agreement with Bentley could be found an understanding must have been reached since his "benefit game" was reported on later in the season.

During the 1861 season Torquay invited the Tor cricket club to use the ground and also the newly formed Meadfoot club, as well as renewing the agreement with the Archery Club for participation. Researching the writer rarely found accounts of Torquay games in May or June but Tor and Meadfoot quickly made use of the facilities offered for their matches. The Public Schools game against the so called Western Counties was to be for Bentley's benefit game and it was interesting to see that six members had promised a £1 each, eleven 10 shillings each and five, 5 shillings each with the hope that many more members would participate. On this occasion the Public Schools were defeated by some ninety runs.

The Annual meeting in 1862 began in the usual way by announcing to members that the financial state of the club was in need of "serious attention". A sum of almost £23 had been spent on ground draining, which had become imperative, and the income was not meeting the club's needs. The wooden fences around the thorn hedges were in a bad state of repair and something had to be done fairly quickly or they would not be able to let the field for the grazing of sheep. In those far off days, before any kind of grass cutters were in use, the sheep were a necessary evil to keep the grass low, as well as bringing in some revenue. In the committee's opinion the subscriptions would have to rise in the near future. It was stressed the 1862 season had seen the formation of the Devon County Cricket Club as planned at the dinner.

When the season began Torquay's first match was not until late June, away at Plymouth, and they were beaten on the first innings score as time prevented any further play. During the July Exeter were defeated by just eleven runs and the Royal Artillery were also beaten.

Devon's first game was played at Durdham Downs against Gloucester and the side lost by an innings and seventy seven runs. The Rev. G. T. Warner made the top score of 19 but the report said more about "the beautiful ground", and the three Grace brothers in the Gloucester side, than it did about the actual game. Mention was made of, "Mr. Grace's slow balls were most fatal!", and this was the famous W. G's elder brother, E.M. However the paper did give liberal coverage to Devon defeating Cornwall at Plymouth by an innings and 199 runs while for the game at Exeter, against Somerset, snide remarks were made regarding the state of the ground and the fact the visitors arrived with only nine men.

The beginning of August saw the first match against Deddington from Oxfordshire, the club made it quite an occasion with the band of the 32 Regiment playing throughout the game. Lunch was taken at two o'clock but play ended in time for everyone to retire and change ready for the evenings dancing. Torquay winning the match by an innings and over a hundred runs. Later in August when it was advertised that Torquay were to play "An X1 of Oxford and Cambridge" the papers reported the Plymouth Garrison team coming to Torquay to play the Combined Universities and winning by six wickets. The same week Torquay did have a match and beat Exeter at Chapel Hill Cross by nine wickets.

Well into September the Torquay club arranged a game between the Gentlemen of Devon and the Players of Devon. While the press related where the Players came from, no mention was made regarding the Gentlemen, for the record the team was,
    Abraham of Exeter, Iles of Haldon, Odell of Tiverton, Haig of Devonport, Mountford, Manley and Staddon, (all of Bovey), Newham and Parsons (Plymouth) Bigg and J. Bentley (Torquay).
The Players won by nine wickets and the Rev. G. T. Warner, who led the Players, was the outstanding batsman with a 39 and 57 not out. A separate paragraph to the account of the result mentioned, " clubs wishing to contact Bigg could do so at the Union Hotel", indicating the professional was available for odd matches.

As was usual the season finished with an inter club game and then the annual dinner, which at that time was held at the Union Hotel, President, the Rev. Wolfe, taking the chair. Following the meal various toasts were covered and for the first time mention was made of the Bentley family. Father had had an accident and for the later games the son John had been doing the work on the ground under his father's instructions. After W.H.Kitson had gone over the financial difficulties once again the assembly were told the annual subscription was going up to a guinea.

1863 began with a fixture in mid-May between the Rev Warner's pupils from Highstead and the Tor club, who included John Bentley, and won quite comfortably. A number of individuals made up sides, and the team played under the organiser's name. Matches were noted against Highstead, The Braddons, etc. but the first account of a Torquay team playing was in July, when they defeated Plymouth and then Highstead. The so called Western Counties were also reported playing their annual match with the Public Schools X1. Torquay began August with a two day game with Bentham, which turned out to be a side from Cheltenham under the captaincy of Mr. Bentham, who had been a Torquay player and had arranged a short tour. His side managed a drawn game since two innings each was not completed in the two days.

The Gentlemen of Devon beat the Players on the Torquay ground before they were themselves again defeated by Gloucester in a match at Tiverton.

August saw Torquay thrashed by the Royal Artillery X1 and Toogood, a more than useful player, was noted as turning out for Paignton when Torquay had no game. The Oxford and Cambridge X1 fixture with the club was cancelled on two scheduled occasions during the season and eventually played in September. A rather one sided game saw the visitors winning by an innings. Following the last game the usual club dinner was held after which W.H. Kitson produced some plans which had been drawn and ready to present to Sir Lawrence Palk for permission to enlarge the pavilion. With the more important games, the increased following and the social events, it had been evident after certain matches that there was a lack of adequate facilities. The original tender for £470 was accepted and passed by the members. The proposals included gas lighting, an American type bowling alley and a stable. The latter was needed on occasions for the horse hired to pull the roller and for individuals who rode their own horse to the ground before playing. Later reports said the finished product cost nearer £800 but was "the best in the county".

The Rev.S.B.Warren was elected captain for the 1864 season and that year Torquay actually had a match in late May and defeated their opponents, South Devon. All other games on the ground had seen Braddons play Highstead and H.M.S.Brittania, Highstead play Montvider etc.

During June Torquay entertained Plymouth and Exmouth, while the ground was also used by Braddons who had games against Teignmouth, Highstead and H.M.S.Britannia.

Torquay's two matches during July were both in Plymouth where they were beaten by the city side and the Garrison.

A new name appeared on the team sheet for the Highstead encounter, Hutchinson, who went on to make 102 runs and later reports of his batting quoted him as being a captain in the Royal Artillery, guesting for the club.

During the season work had been going on to complete the extension to the pavilion and it was finished early in the August ready for entertaining the Plymouth Garrison. Arrangements had been made to ensure the entire week would be memorable from the cricket and social aspect. At the end of the first days play there was a dinner at which Sir Lawrence Palk presided with "the elite of the cricketing fraternity, resident gentlemen, visitors and leading tradesmen present" the papers reported. During all the toasts to one another there were some sensible words spoken and reference was made to the Canterbury Week in Kent, and other places in the North. Palk told the assembly that they should go ahead and take over the adjoining field to enlarge the playing area but Kitson replied it was a little early for that and finances did not allow!

Following the second days play a Ball was held in the specially decorated pavilion and the reporter was quite lyrical regarding the "promenading to enjoy the cool night breeze", very "musical" with all the detail of the tunes played by the band during the day, but with very little copy about the actual play!

During Wednesday and Thursday of the week Devon played Dorset and each evening parties went off to the Lyceum where the Histrionic Club put on entertainment. More will be written about this club who did so much to try and save Torquay's cricket team. Devon beat Dorset by over one hundred runs and then it was the last game of what had become "The Week". On Friday and Saturday Torquay entertained Boconnoc although it was not really polite entertaining! Having run up a total of 300 all out before the evening Ball, Torquay bowled out their visitors twice during the Saturday to complete a very satisfactory six days, and nights!

The opening of the new pavilion, and the cricket arranged for the week, had been such a success that certain individuals in the town proposed that in future years each August, the week prior to the Yachting Regatta, the club should do the same again as regards games and the entertainment. Torquay was becoming a well known resort and the Regatta was now attracting sportsmen from far and wide. Thus began, for a number of seasons, what became officially known as "The Week" and on occasions stretched into two.

The success of the venture was emphasised at the 1865 A.G.M. although the topic that evening which caused so much discussion, and heated argument, was the 'American type bowling alley', or rather the lack of it! It transpired space had been allowed, but it had not been fitted!! Many members who had contributed to the overall cost of the pavilion extension resented the omission. The committee estimated the cost of putting the bowling alley operative at £130 and felt they were not in a financial position to do so. Members pointed out that monies had been contributed on the understanding that the bowling alley was to be installed. Secretary Kitson referred to the minutes regarding the Pavilion and quoted, "embracing IF possible a bowling alley". After heated discussion and various arguments a proposal was suggested and it was passed by a majority vote, "It is expedient to fit up the bowling alley with as little delay as possible and the attention of the committee be requested".

(Even in those days members had to keep an eye on the committee they elected!)

A dinner held at the end of the season in the pavilion saw the opening of the bowling alley "at considerable cost". Mr. Tayleur who proposed the health of W.H.Kitson, absent because of sickness, went on to say "what with cricket, archery, quoits and bowling the Pavilion would be the centre of attraction for the town". Mention was made that those gentlemen who came to Torquay for the winter would have somewhere to go on inclement days apart from the players being able to entertain on wet days when play was stopped.

Later mention will be made of the Festivals of the 1950 and 1960s but reading of The Week or August Occasion and, letting ones imagination take over, those far off days had to be something special. To mentally picture "up to fifty horse drawn carriages waiting at one end of the field and a band playing near an enclosure packed with spectators", as papers quoted, is like something out of a modern television production. Mention is made of the notables present when the Home Fleet was in Torbay with the names of Admirals, Vice-Admirals, Commanders, Captains and Flag Lieutenants very much to the fore. The writer tends to wonder how the reporter found the time to gather the fifty or sixty names often listed as "in the enclosure" as well as report the game and include the titles of the various pieces of music played !

The A.G.M. of the Torquay Club held at the Queen's Hotel in 1866 was immediately followed by the Devon County Club's annual meeting. At the latter a letter was read from the Plymouth Cricket Club asking if the County would share the expenses should Plymouth be able to fix a game with the Eleven of England. The meeting decided that Devon were in no position to promise any subsidies whatsoever.

An account was found for that season of the M.C.C. game against Devon at Lord's with Devon winning by seven wickets and Bentley taking seven wickets in the two innings and a couple of catches.

During the Cricket Week in August of that year J.F.Scobell playing for the Gentlemen of Devon against the same from Dorset hit what was, at that time, the third highest score ever recorded, 269 runs. The report said that on leaving his wicket after being caught he received "a perfect ovation and was presented with a bat by the County". That was a little piece of history on the Torquay ground and by a Torquay player!

Throughout the 1866/7/8 every speaker at dinners or meetings were consistently mentioning economies that were necessary and yet at the 1867 meeting some of the committee were pressing for the two Bentleys to be professionals for the club! With fewer Torquay Club games being played on the ground attendances were suffering and only the special occasions of August appeared to hold any appeal.

Sir Lawrence Palk speaking at the 1868 dinner was reported as follows,

"He had great satisfaction in putting the field at the disposal of the Torquay Cricket Club and he was proud to say it was one of the prettiest in the country. There were many people who regretted the destruction of the Old Wood on the other side but he would take the opportunity of saying that he had done it on a plan which he hoped would be of considerable advantage to the place. A great many trees had been left and it was his intention to make a park for ladies and gentlemen to drive in .He had done much already and a lot more had to be done and he supposed it would be some years before he could carry his plan into execution. When that was done there would be a large place for the youth of Torquay to disport in and he trusted that however large the town might grow there would be a place wherein the youth might enjoy themselves."

Yes, a digression from the cricket but an interesting insight in to what some of the landed gentry thought about for the good of the community, but all too sadly the plan never came to fruition.

Research has shown that the Bentley name, glibly mentioned now (2000) as "the first pro" was a member of a well known cricketing family. C .Bentley, Charles, was the player for Torquay, accompanied by son John on occasions, while newspaper reports refer to C and C.A. umpiring during the August Week. A report covering the 1873 Week mentioned that after seventeen years service one of the two day games was to be his benefit match as his employment would cease at the end of that season. As the attendance was poor donations made the amount up to "about £50", however without explanation he did appear to play further games in later years. What the relationship was of C.A.Bentley or A. Bentley, who were occasionally quoted, the writer has been unable to find out.

In the late 1860s there are various accounts of Croquet taking place on the Torquay cricket ground and in the September of 1869 one week was given over for the West of England Croquet Tournament.

Throughout the 1870s the seasons were rather mixed as games became fewer for the Torquay club and numerous private schools were allowed to use the ground. The August Week remained the highlight of the fixture list although one year there was no mention of the usual first night dinner and the dance was reported as being held at the Royal Hotel. During the 1876 season two of the best players, Rev. Warner and A.F.Fortesque appear to have played more games for Teignbridge than Torquay. The one thing that did not change at any meeting was the call for economy! Dropped for period of three years, what had been "the annual end of season Sports Day" was revised, as the income from same had been badly missed.

Since the game, or rather 'part game'! , took place on the Torquay ground, an incident in the 1875 season makes interesting reading. From time to time the local paper reported games of an Apsley House X1 and in this instance Newton Town had written for a fixture. They received a reply suggesting a date and saying, "Shall we suggest 2 p.m.? but come earlier if you like, but we are very weak and that should give you time to finish us off". On the appointed day a flower show was being held at Apsley House and the game was transferred to the Barton Road ground. Half of the Apsley House X1 were not members of that club and included Torquay players', there was also one J.H.Hodson, a member of the M.C.C. on holiday! He actually opened the batting and scored 139 out of the 239 runs the Apsley team made. Newton Town feeling they had been "taken in" and treated unfairly changed out of their whites when the fielding was completed and left the ground saying, "you're welcome to claim the victory if you want to"!

At the A.G.M. of 1872 W.H.Kitson told the members that having served them for 21 years he was resigning. Eventually he was persuaded to continue as the Treasurer but J.N.Whitehead took over as club secretary. No reports could be found regarding Mr. Whitehead but within two years a C.W.Kitson was being quoted as the treasurer.

1875 appears to have been a bad year for the club. Having been due to play the Plymouth Garrison on June 5th the club was informed that as so many of the officers had gone up to London, for the Derby, that the garrison had been unable to raise a team. Gill of Newton College had managed to assemble a side and took over the fixture. Throughout the June and July there are brief accounts of various college and private school teams using the ground and only in August did a Torquay X1 play a side from the Plymouth Garrison. Later in the same week Devon played Hampshire and won. Devon scored 141 and 296, Hampshire 136 and 82.

As already mentioned accounts of the A.G.Ms were given some press coverage and to the writer were quite fascinating and deserve mention in the history of the club. The 1875 A.G.M. was held in the Queens Hotel and Mr. Delafield presided. One of the oldest members, The Rev. Prebendary Wolfe, requested permission to discuss the Gun Club and then began to remonstrate against the ground being let for their pigeon shooting. He quoted a Highway Act of the day regarding the distance from any road for the firing of a gun and felt that too often the participants were acting illegally.
His three main objections were,
1. Passing the ground with ladies when the firing had been going on they had become alarmed and frightened and none of Her Majesties subjects should be put in that position.
2. The ground is rather exposed and the number of children perched on the hedges to see what was going on was not a spectacle for children.
3. His biggest objection however was that the cricket ground was too close to the cemetery. While he gave the Gun Club members credit in that they stopped firing

when a cortège passed by to the cemetery when he conducted the actual burial service at the graveside the noise was incessant and jarred on the feelings of the mourners.

C.W. Kitson, Hon. Sec., explained the Gun Club paid ten guineas for the use of the ground and that amount would be quite a loss of income. Rev. Davis then wondered if he lease allowed the ground to be used for anything other than cricket. The first X1 captain then reminded the meeting that most of the members were members of both clubs! Numerous other remarks were made before the Chairman decided the committee would meet the Gun Club and "talk things over". Following that report it was always the Clay Pigeon Club that had further mention in the accounts and, while there was no reference whatsoever to them for several years, in the 1880s they were back again with a reduced rental in 1895, and those who were not members of the cricket club were made honorary members!

At the same venue a year later the A.G.M had to be adjourned .The Hon. Sec. C.W.Kitson began talking about the accounts and told the members there were outstanding debts of £176. He said things were not as bad as they appeared because £37 had been spent on pavilion repairs. W. Hearder asked for a copy of the accounts so that a discussion could take place, but was told by Kitson he had not prepared them. Hearder then told the meeting he felt the position the club was in had to be put down to bad management. After several members had made their respective feelings known it was agreed the committee should examine the results and bring a balance sheet to the next meeting. So, two weeks later the members met again and it transpired that Hearder and Grimshaw, the caterers during the summer months, were owed £80, their account not having been paid for five seasons! Rev. Boyle said in the past a committee member had gone around to the members' houses to collect their annual subscriptions and that had not been done for some years. Mr. Hall-Plumber said things could not just be left to the secretary to collect monies. W. Fortescue made his feelings known in no uncertain manner. He told members it was time to discontinue the Free List which included wines at meals for certain visiting teams. While all the discussion continued John Kitson said the bank would allow the club to overdraw their account to the extent of £100, whereupon C.W.Kitson thought it best to borrow the money and by the end of the season they should be able to repay £50.

W. J. Lyon, a Cambridge 'blue' in 1861, played occasionally for Torquay as did W.S.O.Warner, another 'blue' of 1867/8. Of all the numerous clergymen who were associated with the club in the 1800s the Reverend G.T. Warner was the most famous and, long after he finished playing, went on to occupy different positions on the committee. He also became President of the Devon Rugby Football Union.

Reading various papers of 1880 one does tend to wonder just what was going on in the club. A weekly article headed, "Chit-chat" by Atlas caught the writer's eye while researching and from the articles appended below it does appear the club's 'high days' were very much in decline.

May, "I am repeatedly being asked for the whereabouts of the Torquay Cricket ground so I went down the other evening to the field I thought to be the right one but only found a net erected behind three stumps. There was no one on the ground and I felt these things must have been forgotten in changing their locality. Can anyone give me the address of the new field ? "

June, I have received the following letter. "Sir, I was officially connected with the Torquay Cricket Club some years since. The field was granted on the supposition that it would be used for cricket and the ground rent was nominal. Sir Lawrence Palk would have, had he foreseen the collapse of the object, undoubtedly hesitated to grant the field. At present the club is a combination of youths, under the aegis of a few of the old, and therefore incapable cricketers, who while away their respectability and their hours , by throwing a ball at a bat placed in front of a net"…

12th June, "Looking through the cricket fixtures of the year I regret to see that there is not a single match worthy of particular mark arranged .Torquay not only ought to possess a cricket ground, but also an efficient club that would offer attraction to the townspeople and the neighbouring public. It is not yet too late for some loyal and enterprising lovers of the game to take steps for arranging at least one high class match".

26th. June, Scarborough is claiming superiority over Torquay in the matter of cricket and no wonder! The Torquay club is badly off for members, the very few matches arranged are simply the outcome of previous, annual visits. If the managers would think more of the sport they were elected to promote they would offer inducements to lovers of cricket to join the club. At present the only object seems to be to maintain its holding of the field and pavilion by placing boys once a week on either side of three stumps. The Scarborough Mercury has written, "Complaints are being made in Torquay that there is no efficient cricket club there. Scarborough is especially fortunate in this respect, very few, if any, watering places have so good and so attractive a cricket club and ground as Scarborough".

These extracts tend to show that although the club had existed a long time it was anything but flourishing and certainly needed organisation.

The 1880 season results showed that 17 games had been won out of the 30 played but the biggest number of matches had been with sides selected by individual members within the club and not against other organisations.

The Torquay Times/South Devon Advertiser for many years had a column "Places of Interest in the neighbourhood". Listed along with Kent's Cavern Pomeroy Castle, The River Dart, Dartmoor etc., was the Torquay Cricket Grou constantly engaged in matches during the summer, good ground, well kept ᵢ ..ɔ situated in the Barton Road about a mile out of Torquay."

However by 1883 the club were dropped from the list .Fewer games were being played and at each Annual General Meeting the accounts showed the financial difficulties the club was experiencing.

During the December of 1882 a special meeting was called and members were informed that the season's debt was "well over £300". Subscriptions were to go up from £1 to £1 and ten shillings (an extra fifty pence) and the extra would go directly into a "debt fund". Many members, men and women, also belonged to the West of England Histrionic Club and during the August Fortnight would put on shows at the Abbey Road Assembly Rooms. While the club was in such dire financial straights they arranged to put on entertainments at the Bath Saloons during January and April.....two years later, at the 1884 A.G.M., it was announced the debts had been cleared. Thanks were given to Mr. R. Kitson for his "careful handling of the monies received" and to Mr .F.A. Miller for "the zeal and energy he had put in to organising the various shows". Miller was in the main the one committee member who was forever warning against the expenditure on meals and wine.

Every cricket season finished with a sports meeting open to all members and their families. Unable to obtain any photographs of participants the mind tends to wonder what was the dress of the day. Details printed in 1869 said the "high standing jump was won at a height of four feet" "the high jump with pole was won by Mr. Shelton who cleared eight feet and one inch". "The Chapel Hill Steeplechase, over about a mile and a half on the surrounding fields that were mostly ploughed, was completed by the winner in ten minutes". "A ladies race of about one hundred yards over eight hurdles was won in nineteen seconds".

For the reader to have a little idea of the cricket during this period the following is an extract from the report of the opening game in 1887:
"The opening match of the season for the Torquay Cricket club was played in delightful weather and resulted in an easy victory by an innings and 43 runs. Winning the toss and electing to bat Torquay had the assistance of Rev. G.T.Warner, the county captain. Starting at half past twelve the score was 64 for 4 by lunch and the total of 99 was reached before Torquay were all out. St. Marychurch were all out for 20 and were asked to follow on, etc but the result of the second innings was not much more satisfactory. The underhand bowling of Warner and Gibson proving nearly as destructive as the swift, overhand deliveries of Jarvis and Curtis etc .In the first innings Jarvis took 6 for 7 and Curtis 4 for 13. Warner, with his Lob bowling in the second innings took 4 for 10 and Gibson 5 for 12". Lob bowling was quite legal in those days. Following on was requested if a side were more than fifty runs adrift.

Annual General Meetings and the season's debts have already been mentioned but in 1889 and 1893 they were extremely blunt affairs. Members were told "unless there is more interest in the club it will not be able to continue". Various people put forward suggestions and F.A. Miller said he had two friends, who were prepared to buy the ground for the club, providing existing rules and conditions were changed and pointing out the subscriptions were far too high. Miller, later to become the club Vice-President, worked hard on the club's behalf and who knows what might have happened had the ground been purchased. While the paper reported all the proposals it mentioned that the only one passed was "ladies were allowed to become members on payment of half a guinea yearly". The following year the members were told the club was clear of debt, "thanks are entirely due to the Mayor who has gone around to his friends with his hat, and not due to the amateur theatricals".

Throughout the 1890s various articles in the Torquay Times and South Devon Advertiser give an "insight" into the casual way the club was run and the indifference to suggested changes. During the Devon v Cornwall game in 1894 the reporter commented on the poor attendance and wrote of his interview with the Cornish secretary, Mr. J.Bray. He was told "ordinary games in the Duchy attracted crowds of about five hundred and when Devon went down to play at Truro gates of about two thousand were expected". Organisation and any kind of advertising of the fixture in the area had been completely missing at Torquay.

The press were refused entry for the A.G.M. of 1895 and the report, obtained second hand from a disgruntled member, read. "It is not the way to go about obtaining additional support and popularity, which are so badly needed…was it wise to be dispensing with Anscombe, the pro, after his successful season, just because the club was to be run on more economical lines?". Wise or not in 1897 the secretary, Mr. Shrubb told the meeting the season was beginning free of debt, "a position only attained by dispensing with the professional for the last two years".

Anscombe, who had been the club professional for some seasons, was engaged by Leopald Rothchild's private cricket club at Escott in Buckinghamshire very quickly once his availability was known.

1897 saw the end of the Devon County Cricket Club and when it was revived it was due entirely to members in the Exeter area. A sad reflection on the efforts of those earlier Torquay members who had initiated its conception but indicative of the state the club had reached. At the opening of the 1898 season it was announced the new professional was Mr. Spencer from Nottingham. The following is an extract from the South Devon Journal for the first week in June. "Spencer has had a very short innings as the Torquay pro. Although he only started work, or should it be play? May 11th he has packed his traps and departed. To succeed him Mr. Shrubb has engaged Huish, the South Devon pro."

During the August of 1898 in a game against South Devon, which w
fixture in "The Week", Torquay had the assistance of Ernest Smith, a
county player who deputised as captain of that county when Lord H
unavailable, and a Scott-Smith who were staying in the district. Having wo
Torquay batted first and at the end of the first day had reached 324 for 3, both of
the guests had scored a century. The following day Smith continued his innings and
when the declaration came at 401 for 6 he had 152 not out. This was the first
account found of two men having centuries in an innings and then Smith went on
to take eleven wickets when the visitors managed just 182 runs in two visits to the
stumps! Another paper reported how, "South Devon went into the game missing
several players while Torquay had a very strong eleven in the field".

Following the M.C.C. tour of the Westcountry in 1898 the Rev .G T. Warner, who
had at one time been secretary of the Devon County Cricket Club, wrote to the
South Devon Journal saying,

"During my recent cricket tour of Devon, with the M.C.C. I could
not but help feel there was a great blank in our not playing an eleven of Devon
County. I had heard the club had been dissolved, but until I came to Devon I did
not realise how sad it was to find the supporters of the game so apathetic to the
honour of the old County in the cricket world."
He went on at some length about the Devonians, who leave the County and
organise dinners, meetings and dances for other county exiles throughout the
entire country, "because being away Devonians were even more keen on its good
fame". He was sure the attitude to cricket could not be due to lack of money in
Devon as there were so many good supporters but he did feel that so many "big
towns were standing aloof because they could not all be the headquarters of the
County Club". The entire article had a headline, "An appeal to Wake Up", and the
entire article was certainly that. Warner suggested that Colonel Fellowes, as the late
secretary of the Hampshire County Club, would be an ideal man to take on the task
of uniting parties as he was settling at Exminster in the near future.

Since this was to be the last season Peyto Shrubb was to hold office at Torquay, as
he was leaving the area, his wife held an "At home" in the Pavilion after the M.C.C.
game. An article in the Torquay Directory covering the event and the names of
those attending was twice as long as the report on the actual game itself. The writer
counted the two hundred names actually printed, to which had to be added the
teams and officials!

In the July of 1899 a mention is made of a Russian playing for South Devon against
Torquay when the game was transferred to Cricketfield Road because of the state
of the Newton ground. The following game saw F.A. Zezspanski, the Russian, in the
Torquay team against the Newton Blues but he only appeared to have played for

Torquay during the July of that one season. With the number of games taking place a book was placed in the Pavilion and players were asked to sign what days they were available to play each week. Since various captains spoke of the help and success of this method the writer feels that perhaps discipline, or desire, was greater in those days! Even all those years ago there were holidaymakers who came and played the odd game with instances of tourists staying on, after their team went home, to play more cricket.

When the fixtures were printed for the 1900 season Torquay appeared to have a large number of games but very few of them were attractive to the supporters or indeed the players. Playing the two school sides, Weston and Montpelier, each twice plus home and away matches with Newton College and Newton Blues along with Torwood and Marldon there were few days to look forward to until July when Exeter, South Devon and Teignbridge were due.

Throughout 1898/9 Montpelier School and Weston School played the majority of their matches on the Torquay ground and the respective staff members played games for the club once the schools closed for the holidays.

The first game reported in May 1900, against the R.N.E. College, read "Torquay were poorly represented", and, "the display given by the home team is best described as feeble". Four days later the side lost to Montpelier School and the first victory was eventually gained against Kingskerswell.

Some statistics found at the end of an indifferent season showed that the club had played 27 games, against varying strength opposition, and had won 12 while losing 14. C.W.Crowdy, who had captained the side through most of the season, had played in 22 of the games but over 70 men had gone to the wicket, many of them on just one occasion! Sixteen different bowlers had been used and five of those had not even bowled ten overs each throughout the season. Two professionals, Russell and Pepall, never mentioned before, were included in the compilation of averages. Several of the games due to be played were cancelled as either the club, or their opponents, were unable to raise a team on the appropriate day.

The following is an extract from a letter published in the Torquay Times in November 1900.

"TORQUAY CRICKET CLUB"

At a special meeting of the Torquay Cricket Club held on September 25th. It was decided that the club should be dissolved forthwith. It may interest your readers, and the public generally, to know the reasons that have lead to this radical step, they may be summarised in a few words, to the totally inadequate support given to the club. Subscriptions have been getting less every year while the cost of

maintenance of the ground has increased despite the closest ec
expenditure. The total income for the year is a little over £90 while the
are about £150. In the circumstances the Committee were reluctantly (
to advise the dissolution of the club on the expiration of our yearly
consequently it will cease to exist on March 23rd. 1901.
It must be a matter of the profoundest regret to all lovers of cricket that so
beautiful a field, with a quaint pavilion, the admiration of all our visitors, should
pass out of our possession after an existence of fifty years".

As will be seen the special meeting took place in the September but, until the Vice
President's letter to the paper in November, there was no notification of the drastic
step that the Committee had decided to take. Mr. F.A.Miller, who had signed the
letter, went on to explain the outstanding debts, the finance needed to run the club
properly, and, even so long ago, the good publicity and monies that had come into
the town through the annual visits of the cricketing tourists who made Torquay
their headquarters.

 Mention has already been made of the warnings Miller gave the club on the
expenditure, and his work with the theatrical shows to offset various debts, and
sadly he was not to live to see the "rebirth" of his beloved cricket club. During his
time as Vice-President of the club he took his daughter, who later became famous
as Agatha Christie, to help him score on occasions. Many years later, in her
biography, she mentions making her chauffeur detour to see the cricket ground
and where she used to live, when returning to her then home on the River Dart.

So, after fifty turbulent years, which had seen the formation of the Devon County
Club through the instigation of the Torquay members, the advent of touring sides
and the beginning of cricket festivals in the West Country our club went out of
existence.

Within a week of Mr. Millers letter there was an announcement under "Editors
Jottings" which read,
 "We are pleased to learn that the picturesque cricket ground in Barton Road is not,
as was feared might be its fate, to be given to a speculative builder, at least not at
present. The tenancy of the Torquay Cricket Club expires on Lady Day but, Mr.
Little, of Weston School at St. Marychurch, and Mr.Bennett, of Montpelier School,
Paignton,have with much public spirit , agreed between them to take over the
ground, and this most desirable pitch, a long way the best of the very few to be
found in the neighbourhood , will not be lost to the national game etc. etc...I am
pretty certain that if the club was worked on proper business lines, and made less
exclusive, it would prove successful. I was in favour of a second team so that those
not competent to figure in the first team would have had the opportunities to take
part in a secondary game."

REFORMED

The 1901 cricket season opened in Torquay with the Babbacombe and Upton clubs getting the press coverage and "Looker On", the reporter of the time stated,

"The cricket season of 1901, as far as Torquay is concerned, will be memorable in a sense not creditable to the town, in as much as the Torquay club which was started in the early fifties will have ceased to exist. For several years past the premier club of the town has gradually been dwindling, through lack of support and financial difficulties ".

He went on to praise the work done by the captain, Mr.Crowdy, and Mr. Miller during the last season and the difficulties the captain had in "inducing men to play".That explained to the researcher why there were no reports of games marked down for the following week, they had never taken place.

Mr. Little, who owned the Weston School, had been the King's College, Cambridge cricket captain in his younger days. When he started his school he had played occasional games for Torquay but always captained his own school team. Several of the masters he employed were cricket players and figured in the school side.When he took over the Barton Road ground teams such as Babbacombe, Upton and Bovey arranged fixtures with him and he included one or two of the ex- Torquay players to strengthen his side.These matches could only take place at the end of July, and through August, when the school term had finished, but were looked forward to by the visiting clubs because it was the best wicket in the area.

Throughout the seasons of 1901 and 1902 people were asking "when the town would have a cricket club again?" One has to use the imagination when reading this to get the "feel" of the situation and understand, all those years ago, just what the club meant to certain people. Here were all sorts of ordinary people enjoying their cricket with Babbacombe, St. Marychurch, Torquay Athletic etc. and so many of those that employed them no longer had a club to go to. The loss of Devon fixtures since the demise of the Torquay club also caused resentment and this grew through the seasons.

Eventually, in November 1902 a meeting was held in the Torquay Town Hall, presided over by the Mayor, for "The purpose of considering the desirability of forming a cricket club for the Borough of Torquay". YES! that was the title of the meeting, and note, the Mayor was in the Chair. In those days the Torquay Times and South Devon Advertiser were large papers and the report, printed on November 21st,,covered two complete columns.

The Mayor, Councillor Taylor, opened the proceedings and stressed from the beginning it was imperative for the town to have a cricket club but, "It had to be run on more popular lines than before and subscriptions should be fixed at a level so that it was open to all who had a love for the game". With that plain opening he set the tone for the meeting and asked Mr. Little to speak, reminding those present that Mr. Little held the lease on the ground where the club once played.

Mr. Little then explained the conditions he would let the ground to a Torquay Club if one was formed as a result of the meeting.

a. The ground could be used every Saturday throughout the cricket season.

b. One Wednesday in May, two in June, and every day during August and September.

c. Montpelier school had the ground each Wednesday, except those quoted, and Weston school would occupy the ground on Thursdays. .

He would let the ground for £12 up to the 29th. September 1903. There would be no rates or taxes to pay up to that date and the club would have the use of the rollers and other appliances. Mr. Little went on to say that the existing lease ran until Michaelmas 1908 but it could be broken in 1904 or 1906, and he would give the new club the option of taking over in 1903, if they wished to do so. He was willing to employ a man two days a week on the ground up until the end of the year, but after that he felt the club should be responsible. Little stressed, "That it is important the club is run on popular lines, no class distinction and anyone who behaved properly on the field should be allowed to join".

 He then told the meeting he had persuaded Colonel Fellowes, the County Sec. to attend and introduced him (the ex- Hampshire sec. mentioned by Rev. Warner). The Col. referred to the days back to 1864 when he came to Torquay and acknowledged that "clubs in those days were run on different lines which were not possible now!" He went on to say that if a club were formed, and found a professional who would qualify to play for Devon in two years, the County would pay one third of his wages throughout the summer months!

After listening to the opening discussions and the various promises of monies, Mr. V. Andee proposed, "a cricket club be formed and called the Torquay Cricket Club". This was duly seconded by H. Terry, but not before numerous speakers had reiterated that there must not be any class distinction or prejudice in the new club. The motion was overwhelmingly carried and the Mayor was elected as the first President. He suggested that members should pay ten shillings subscriptions and players five shillings, after which a steering committee was formed and they were charged with bringing rules to another meeting that would be arranged when they had completed their studies.

The Mayor again took the Chair at the second meeting which took place in mid-December and the selected committee announced as, A.G. Dineley(hon.sec), H.L.Mackenzie(hon. treasurer), C.Rivers(auditor), Rev. Northey, Messrs. Hooman, Grogan, Andee, Terry, Fogg, Narracott, Crockwell and Wyndham-Robinson. J.F.W.Little had been selected as the first captain.

When the new Club Rules were presented for discussion the "fun" really began! .Despite all that had been said at the inaugural meeting, and the Presidents suggestions for subscriptions, the committee had come up with their own ideas. They had decided that members should pay ten shillings and sixpence but playing members subscriptions would be one guinea with youths ten and sixpence. The Committee also wanted to have the power to admit a limited number of playing members for five shillings, but such members would not have the privilege of voting, or indeed being able to introduce friends into the pavilion!

The Reverend Cheatle was the first to speak, saying that it was invidious that such a rule should be suggested and would create a distinction which should not be allowed if the club was to be run on the democratic lines as had been suggested at the original meeting. Speaker after speaker referred to the "democratic lines" stressed previously and said that every member should be able to take their friends into the pavilion. On behalf of the Committee Mr. Little told the meeting that they did not want people who could afford ten shillings becoming members for five shillings. After numerous speakers aired their respective views, with many recalling the last meeting and the "class distinction and democratic lines", votes were taken. The no voting and pavilion privilege was rejected along with the five shilling membership.

A "mathematically minded" Mr. Cockayne pointed out that 200 members at ten shillings and sixpence would only amount to £105 and the meeting had been told it needed a minimum of £150 to operate the club properly. Mr. Little then said there were already eighty paid up members and many had given from one to five guineas rather than the ten shillings and sixpence that he had asked for. He went on to ask those present to back his suggestion that Mr. D. Potts-Chatto was asked to become a Patron of the club since he had already subscribed £10.

Before the meeting closed Mr.Little announced that he had, since the November gathering, arranged fixtures for the 1903 season. Matches had been confirmed with South Devon, Bovey, Exeter, Paignton, Babbacombe and Teignmouth. He would see what he could do about some games for the August Week but, after a two year gap, a number of touring sides had made other arrangements.

1903.

Prior to the start of the 1903 season the reporter covered a meeting with the new club secretary, A.G. Dineley. A professional had been engaged, Sandiford, from Kent. Two masters at Mr. Little's school, Woodford and Patterson, had become members of the Torquay club, having previously played for Newton College, as had another new comer S.G.Crockwell. H.Butler along with two other players from the defunct Upton club had "thrown in their lot and joined" so from a playing point of view things looked quite promising.

The first game reported in any detail was against Brixham where one of their bowlers, Arlidge, took 7 wickets for 37 runs. However Torquay's opening bowler Narracott, eventually took all ten wickets .While his statistics are not recorded, and since Brixham were all out for 27 with only four extras being mentioned, it had to be good bowling. The captain thought so and wrote to the ball manufacturers, Quaife of Birmingham, and on the Wednesday morning Narracott received a brand new ball from Quaifes.

While researching the year of 1903 the formation of the Early Closing Association Club was noted and they were so fortunate in being able to play on a good ground immediately. It should be remembered in those distant days many employees only had a half day off during the week and for many in the retail trade in this area it was Wednesday. Since the Recreation Ground was only used by the rugby clubs cricket team on a Saturday it was free for mid-week games.

Mention has been made of the games arranged against ships officers when the Royal Navy were in the bay and in 1903 , when the Home Fleet was at anchor, similar matches are recorded. Mr. Victor Andre, who was by this time the captain of the Home Team, was responsible for such games since he appeared to be able to arrange same at short notice and to be able to call on the necessary players, one of which was always the professional. Whether these games were of importance to the town, or the club, the author is not sure but the reporter always faithfully noted all those in the enclosure. Admiral of the Home Fleet, Sir Arthur K. Wilson, Commanders, Flag Lieuts, Captains from the various warships, all by name and then the Mayor and Mayoress plus other civic dignitaries.

Press coverage has certainly changed over the years and only in certain circumstances is one able to follow the movement of players from club to club in those far distant days. What would not be tolerated now though is the personal reporting where names were quoted for "slovenly fielding" and "is so and so really worth his place?" Throughout the season Sandiford, the pro, had been out l.b.w. on many occasions and the following is an extract from a report. "Sandiford has quite a knack of getting his legs in front of the wicket and on Saturday he was once more given out. There was no doubt about the decision in this case". He was later selected to play for Devon against the M.C.C. and took five wickets but not Sir Arthur Conan Doyle's who frequently toured with that side.

At the end of the resuscitation season Torquay had played 22 games, won 13, lost 4 and drawn 5. It was announced that Morrison, who had kept wicket so effectively all the season, was not going to be available for the next season as he was taking up a new post in Egypt. Mr. Little had recruited yet another school teacher, a cricketer no less, who would be joining the club. There is no doubt the Torquay club owed a tremendous amount to Little, not only for maintaining the ground for the two years the club was dormant, but for the energy he displayed in recruiting players and ensuring good men were available throughout August. Whenever he spoke he always remembered the groundsman, Palmer, with praise for his wickets and, if the benefit day for the pro was wet he changed it for another worthwhile fixture. These aspects endeared him to all who played for the club at that time.

1904 began with an article saying that Mr. Layland Barratt M.P. and Mr.Lopes, the Conservative candidate for the next election, had both asked to become vice-presidents. Many spectators who had frequented the ground the previous season had already been along to Barton Road and paid their ten shillings and six pence. The report went on, "one of the standing rules, strictly adhered to, was that subscriptions had to be paid before use of the ground, or playing, was allowed."

The first game was the time honoured encounter with Bovey, the papers never printed the full Bovey Tracey for many years. A statement was issued that the Monday and Tuesday of the opening of the August Week was going to clash with the start of the Torbay Regatta but, "it was hoped that all lovers of the game would, if unable to be present at the ground, send their monies to the club treasurer". The first game of the Week was scheduled to be against the M.C.C. tourists but as was reported at the time, "torrential rain prevented any play on the first day and very few spectators turned up for the second".

During the September two teams of the lady members played each other and it was judged to be much more satisfactory than the previous year when the ladies had played against a men's side that had to bat and bowl left handed.

A pre-season report on the ground of 1905 said, "considerable repairs have improved the appearance of the pavilion with the roof re-thatched in several sections, a piece of the iron roof has been replaced with thatching and new railings have been erected". Mention was made of the outfield looking better despite the fact that a portion had been used during the winter for "a field of play for the Torquay United Club". Little was to be the captain again while Sandiford had been retained as the professional. Narracott was joining the new club of a private firm, White, Chatton & Co. while new men who had joined Torquay included Fulham, the Devon and Exeter player, Fulcher from Kingswear and a fast bowler A.Codner. T.Fogg was taking over the secretarial post from A.G.Dineley but the latter would still be available to play.

No apologies are made by the writer for including the following 'snippet' taken from the Western Morning News of June 1905, from a book by Ashley Cooper, entitled Devonshire Cricket and Cricketers since it does reflect on the Torquay history one is trying to record.

"The Devonshire Cricket Club was originally formed in 1861…three years later it was stated there is no county ground, no subscription is necessary to enable anyone to play for the county BUT, all who play are compelled to only receive only second class railway fares. Member's annual subscription is one guinea and life membership £10…Headquarters are at Torquay. The county side first appeared at Lords in 1864….August 1864 saw the opening of the new Torquay pavilion with a dance floor, dressing rooms and an American type bowling alley at a cost of over £600... Among the best known members of the county team in those far off days were the brothers Warner, both of whom entered Holy Orders.....At the time of the formation of the county team the central figure in Torquay cricket was Charles Bentley. He was the nephew of Henry Bentley, who published a book of scores in 1823, (a score book) and a son of John Bentley who looked after the scholars of Westminster School. Charles Bentley was born at the Inn on Lords Cricket Ground on February 28th. 1819 and settled in Torquay 1852, a fast round arm bowler and a brilliant slip fielder (this is the Bentley who dispensed the beer). The Reverend J.F.Scobell who often played for Devon was playing for the Gentlemen of Devon, in 1860, against the Gentlemen of Dorset and scored 269, composed of two 6s, three 5s, twelve 4s, thirty six 3s and twenty six 2s on the Torquay ground. At that time 269 was the third highest individual score recorded anywhere, in the next match he failed to score in either innings"... (Seek, and history can be found anywhere if one looks hard enough)

Torquay finished the season having won 23 of the 33 games played, drawn 6 and lost just 4. Gerrish had headed both the batting and bowling averages although Fulham had scored 1207 runs after joining from Exeter. The decision to retain the pro had proved a success since he had taken 148 wickets at an average of 9:8 and was a close second in the batting average. "Onlooker" the reporter, invariably referred to the sunshine as "King Sol", and stressed that the "King" had been much kinder that season and hence a bigger percentage of games had concluded with a positive result.
The account of the final game, a ladies match with the ladies of Dawlish and the only one recorded, was a victory for Torquay by 101 runs against the visitors 42. While the reporter had been allowed 'free reign' with his derogatory remarks as to the ladies bowling and catching he was a man of vision. He went on, "having seen this week a woman riding a horse like a man (normally in those days a woman sat side saddle) there is no doubt that the fair sex are pressing men hard in every vocation of life. They mean to get to the top and they will, but it will take time, such a thing may happen but not in the near future, as a Test Match between the Ladies of England and those of Australia. The fair sex are persevering and, when its members get the hang of things, gracefulness in execution will come". As much of a prophet as my friend John Pelosi!

Long before the next season the club was in deep trouble. In March 1906 the pavilion was burnt down and the press account read,

"About 9-25 yesterday morning the ivy covered, picturesque pavilion of the Torquay Cricket Club in Barton Road, caught fire and was practically gutted, nothing but the bare walls remaining intact. The largest section of the building is unoccupied, except during the actual cricket season .However several rooms at the end of the building are inhabited by the groundsman, Mr. Palmer, who with his family, live there all the year."...The article went on to name all the people who rendered assistance in saving the Palmers furniture and it said the ground and pavilion was owned by Mr.Tredenham Hugh Spry of Cornwall. While there was Insurance for £200 the estimated damage was put at about £500.

Just after this tragic happening a local paper ran an article saying how it had come into possession of an American publication which showed, "a lovely photograph of the picturesque pavilion accompanied by a quite glowing account of its charms". It then went on to say,, "The Torquay Cricket Club suffered a severe loss on March 15th, when its pavilion, with cottage attached, was destroyed by fire. We appeal to all who are interested in the great national game, and all who are interested in Torquay generally, to help in providing the sum necessary to erect a worthy pavilion for the cricket club". Following this appeal a statement went on to say that the Committee had made a great effort on the site but the remains were an "eyesore". It was envisaged that the groundsmans premises would be rebuilt as it was, but the pavilion would only be a one storey building on account of the expense.

With no chance of having the pavilion rebuilt before the opening of the season fears were expressed regarding changing facilities, catering and even whether some members might leave the club. As it happened the season went quite well from reports found, tents were erected for the respective teams and teas were taken under cover of a marquee.

Bovey opened the season at Barton Road and it was reported that Torquay would parade their new professional, Stuart, but on the day supporters were told he had a knee injury. He was not seen for some weeks and then the club announced "his services had been dispensed with ", no explanation whatsoever.

At the end of May the Torquay Times announced the arrival of a new vicar for St.Marychurch, a Rev.T.W.Little. Actually the brother of Torquay's captain and from the details it was noted that whenever he previously came down to play for his brothers team he had been travelling from Stampford Courtenay, his original stipend.

During the June the first team had no fixtures for two successive weeks so the reporter followed the Home Team to the Plainmoor area where they were due to play St.Marychurch. Apart from the game he recounted the days when St. Marychurch would play and sometimes beat Torquay, South Devon, R.N.E.College and other front rank local sides. Describing the spacious tent erected for that particular day he waxed lyrical about the "air of a real old country cricket match", and his overall account was almost poetic.!.

1907
Just prior to the opening game it was it was announced the pavilion rebuilding had been completed and Mr.Fogg was happy to say, "there will be no more "picknicking on the ground, the old world picturesqueness has gone but the ivy

will grow again and the building weather in the course of time". A new professional, J.Mantell had been engaged, and a Mr.W.S.Dobson had joined the club. Big things were expected of the latter as he had been playing for Durham, but Mr. Fogg, nor anyone else, could have envisaged just what a great part Dobson was to play in the history of Torquay Cricket Club. The firm of White, Chatton had disbanded their club team and P.T.Narracott was returning to the fold and had persuaded the Bailey brothers to join him at Barton Road. The article then added, "this news is distinctly cheering etc. for although we may at times criticise the clubs constitution and wish for it to be run on more popular lines it is THE club of the district"…One can read what inference one likes in such reporting but it does appear there were reasons behind the scenes why the club rarely received the support it required.

Over several seasons the cricket reporter would compare the fortunes of Frank Harry and C.G.Deane when they were playing respectively for Lancashire and Somerset. Harry had played for Torquay in the late 1890s and had also been a most successful rugby player for Torquay Athletic, so much so that he was enticed by Broughton Rangers to turn professional. Eventually he qualified to play cricket for Lancashire and between 1903 and 1908 played 69 county games. C.G.Deane, also a good Torquay all-rounder, played as an amateur for Somerset prior to the 1914 – 1918 war, and lost his life in India. Harry returned from the conflict and played a number of games for Worcestershire as an amateur. Two of the clubs successful players, forgotten in the passage of time!

In the April of 1909 a special meeting was held to present T.H.Fogg with a gold watch and the clubs sincere thanks for all the work he had done as the secretary during many years. Leaving the area to take up a new appointment in Chippenham, he expressed his thanks to everyone for the enjoyment he had while playing and working for the club. The new secretary elected to take over was A. G. Dineley.

In 1910 "Longstop" had taken over as the cricket reporter for the Torquay Times and his comments were, to the writer, much more interesting than the games he was apparently sent to cover! He continually asked why half day matches could not start on time, and since they rarely did, why on earth a tea interval was necessary in such circumstances,, the spectators suffered in that they rarely saw a result! In June, in his coverage of the games against Paignton, he was asking questions about form and attitude. Quoting a week when Paignton were all out for "a miserable total of 18 runs and then two weeks later obtaining a respectable total of 156 against exactly the same bowling attack". The inference as to whether he was getting at the Torquay bowlers or the Paignton batsmen one could not be sure but there was little reporting about the actual play .With no first team game to report on he went to see the Home Side play Kingswear..His report read "There must be something rotten in the State of Denmark, otherwise the Torquay Home Team,, what is the matter with them??.They seem unable to win a game unless it is against third or fourth rate sides and for the second time this season they went under to Kingswear, a truly inglorious display". (shades of David Thomas or Conrad Sutcliffe !). However two weeks later, headlines.

"See the conquering heroes come,
Blow the bugle, beat the drum"

"No doubt about it either! Just fancy! 168 for 8 and able to declare! Verily the Home Team has achieved great things the shepherd has returned to his flock and led the valiant lambs to victory"!

What had happened was Dobson, the ex-Durham, now Devon and first team player had dropped to the Home Team to shake them up. Having scored his 68 and then taken 6 Bovey wickets for 16 runs it had been rather a one man show, but Longstop certainly made the most of it in his "copy".

There was an interesting item relating to the game between the first teams of Bovey and Torquay. The latter's umpire was the old stalwart Harry Terry and as a Bovey batsman hit a ball to leg he also broke his wicket with his foot, as the last man everyone began to leave the field. Mr. Terry called everyone back saying it was "not out" on account that the actual stroke had been completed prior to knocking off the bail. There was so much discussion afterwards that Terry wrote to the journal of the time 'Sportsman' and the editor answered, "June 15th 1910, the umpire must decide on the facts before him. If in his opinion the stroke had been completed before the bail dropped NOT OUT was quite right". A great sportsman was Terry, having played cricket and rugby for Ellacombe and then joining both the Torquay rugby and cricket clubs, where he played before serving on both their committees.

The club announced, prior to the first game of 1911, the ground would no longer be open to the general public and the press announcement read.

"The Barton Road cricket ground will no longer be open to the general public. The Committee have wisely determined to eliminate the youthful and somewhat noisy element that have, at times, made things lively by indiscriminate football and noisy horseplay. A charge of two pence is now to be made and entrance will only be obtained at the main gate. Decidedly a move in the right direction and though inconvenient to members who usually enter at the bottom end they will put up with this".

While J.F.W. Little was again the captain for the season it was revealed he would not be available to play for sometime as his health had suffered badly during the winter. The Home Team captain was to be W. Dobson but, "they were likely to lose his batting skills since he will doubtless aid the first team most of the while". (the author suggests, another Phil Bradford!)

During the June while playing at Chudleigh the home teams leading batsman ,Dr. Walters, was called away to do an emergency operation .Little motored over to see part of the game and hoped to be fit enough to play very soon. That same week yet another vicar joined the club, Reverend Lake who had taken over the parish at Stokeinteignhead. After a short spell in the Home team he contributed many runs for the first eleven that season as did the Reverend Turpin.

At the end of July Mr. Little had his first game for the season against Hampstead Itinerants. As the captain Mr. Little, included his vicar brother in the mid-week team and after his teams innings of 200 for 7 and then bowling the visitors out for 185 declared, " he was well pleased with the match".. Throughout the years there have been so many games against our neighbours around the Bay that defy understanding and 1911 was no exception. The account began about the "true and fast wicket" (a la Boycott inspection perhaps?) but later the questions.. "why were the spectators only able to see 132 runs in the entire afternoon?, Longstop went on,, "It could not be the fault of the wicket since the Torquay openers, Dobson and Deane, had been responsible for 62 of the 98 runs the team had scored, Mr. Extras had contributed 15 with May and England taking all the wickets. 20 runs were scored by the Paignton opening pair before disaster struck and they were all out for 34 with Deane and Dobson taking the wickets". This reporter did not mention the names of those who failed but he was very caustic on occasions.

A certain amount of the so called 'sledging' appears to be acceptable in the modern game, except when it becomes too personal, and numerous individuals have been held responsible for its beginnings. However it is definitely a practise that has been in the game for a very long time as the following will confirm. This is a digression from Torquay's history but certainly of local interest.

"The match between Babbacombe and Kingswear was marred by an incident regrettable in its character as it is, fortunately, in its infrequence of occurrence on the cricket field. Words between Shorthouse, of Kingswear, and Harper, of Babbacombe, developed into blows and a stand up fight. It was only brought to a closure by the intervention of the umpires and other players."
Reported in the South Devon Advertiser of July 1911.

From old records available one of the visiting sides that invariably defeated Torquay was the M.C.C. and the report of the 1911 game was typical of cricket coverage at that time.
"It is not intended to give anything like full details of the match but only one or two salient features of the game. Torquay had got together one of the most powerful sides it has put into the field for a very long time. "Rabbits" were conspicuous by their absence and as a batting and bowling side no fault could be found with it. On the result of the first innings there was just cause for jubilation for the locals headed the M.C.C., 187 to 175.. The second day was rather different, Torquay were all out for 108 and when stumps were drawn the M.C.C. were 122 for 2."

Salient features! The report certainly was but individual names would have been better. Time and time again sides went on batting until the time quoted for "close of play" irrespective of already passing the required total.

While it was announced at the A.G.M. that the playing results had been satisfactory the statement regarding the accounts was definitely not. It was the "old story", expenditure outstripping income and the adverse balance was £18-10 shillings. Members were told it was "imperative steps were taken if it was the desire that the club should continue to exist." It was moved that the accounts should be approved, and they were, whereupon the Chairman, Potts-Chatto said he would arrange for his wife to stage a concert on behalf of club funds. Councillor Towell, the Mayor, was elected President and A.G.Dineley took over the dual positions of Secretary and Treasurer. Little was again elected the first team captain and Dobson suggested Tom Kerslake as the man to be in charge of the Home team, this was approved. T.H.Kerslake over many years was the driving force behind the club and held numerous positions on the Committee. These, together with his occupation as the agent for the Cockington Estate are remembered by a plaque on the wall of the old school building right in the middle of Cockington Village. That building, like every other in the village, is now a commercial outlet and the tenant was told by the Corporation that he had to erect a No Parking sign that they provided in the early 1990s which he did, and covered the plaque! Mr. Wilfred Hore, almost a life long member, noticed this when back in Torquay on holiday and steps were taken to advise the tenant that he must "uncover history" or else! Within days the Kerslake Momento was once more on show for those who had the time to read it. Rev.T.Little was voted on to the Committee and the bat he had given for the best batting average of the season was presented to C.G.Deane, 1301 runs at an average of 54.2.

During the 1912 season the Torquay Times began a new feature and listed the best ten batting and bowling performances every week. On many occasions the names came from the junior sides such as, Y.M.C.A., G.P.O., Wesleyans and the Pupil Teachers who had just formed a club. However one week the list started with C.G.Deane and continued with Rev.Little, Rev. Turpin, and Rev.Lake all of Torquay and all against Paignton!

Rather sadly Bert Griffen, who had played for numerous sides in the Torquay area, was killed in London in a freak cricket incident. In a practice match he was keeping wicket and coaching when a fast ball rose and struck him on the temple and within minutes he died in the arms of the fielders. Griffen had worked locally on the now defunct Torquay Standard newspaper.

Despite the presence of so many clergy in the club Torquay had little luck with the weather that season. During the August Week both two day games against Chiswick Park and Incogniti were completely spoiled without a result. The Reverends Little, Turpin, Payne and Lake were all very much in form and fourteen of the twenty eight games were won while, mostly due to the weather, eleven were drawn. The season was deemed a success because no Devonshire side had beaten the first team.

At the A.G.M. of 1914 various congratulations were made regarding the playing exploits of the club but the accounts came in for much criticism and Harry Terry was very forthright with his comments. He said, "Second rate clubs in this town are able to make ends meet and for the premier club to show an adverse balance every year is a serious and critical state of affairs". Terry went on to reiterate a previous statement that he had made, feeling the ground was too far out of Torquay to get support in great numbers.

A member of the Home Team told the meeting they had had a discussion about the newly formed South Devon League and the majority were in favour of joining. A few of the older members, who had occasional games, felt they might be ignored in favour of the younger and more agile players, whereas the younger men felt the entire fixture list would suffer if they did not participate, since the teams joining were all much about second side standards.

For the record the league was divided into two divisions.
First Division Babbacombe, Buckfastleigh, Haytor Vale, Kingswear, Paignton Home Team, Wesleyans and Torquay Home Team.
Second Division Babbacombe Seconds, Brixham, Kingskerswell, Galmpton, Torquay Post Office, Torquay Y.M.C.A, Kingswear Seconds, and Wesleyans Seconds.
A Newton Section was expected to include Ashburton, Abbotskerswell, Teign Village, Berry Pomeroy and Ipplepen.

A short article at the beginning of the season in a Torquay Times read, "Babbacombe, noted for their optimism said they were more than hopeful of winning both divisions" Very few people would have envisaged they would do just that before the outbreak of the Great War.

From the few records found only the two divisions were up and running throughout the season as there is no mention of the Newton Section results. Torquay Home Team and Brixham, in their respective divisions were second to both Babbacombe sides at the end of the season.

Torquay's first X1 had their opening game in the traditional way against Bovey and, for the first time the Moorland town was quoted as Bovey Tracey. Both Torquay sides lost but the excuse for the Home Teams performance was understandable, they had to provide the first team with five men to replace last minute 'cry offs'.

With the first team away to Paignton the reporter covered the Home team encounter with Babbacombe on the Barton Road ground. Lyrical reporting and to appreciate colourful coverage the script read.

"It was a glorious afternoon and no mistake, one wanted nothing better to do than to stretch out full length in the sun, or to smoke quietly under the shade of the trees and lazily listen to the swish of the willow and the thud of the ball on to the bat. The rivalry of Torquay and Babbacombe had attracted quite a sizeable crowd. As one had grown to expect, the enthusiasts from "up there" were present in great force, far outnumbering the Torquay supporters and, from the applause that frequently disturbed the peace of the afternoon, one might have been forgiven for imagining oneself one of a large gate at an exciting football match. How one could get so excited on such an afternoon I don't know, but, those Babbacombe chaps did!! Etc.etc."

Crockwell had returned from his over-seas post at the beginning of the season and apart from playing for Torquay had assisted Paignton during mid-week games as had Arden and the Leleu brothers.

The last recorded game before the 1918 war was a two day match against the Old Bristolians which Torquay won by eight wickets. Winwood-Smith getting a 92 and then a 54 not out, in his best performance of the season.

GROUND SHARING AFTER THE WAR

When peace was declared in the November of 1918 and men began returning to the U.K. the desire to get back to normal life was uppermost.

During the conflict the Corporation had obtained the Barton Road land and had designated it for the Secondary School (now known as the Grammar School) playing fields. During the winter months a number of cricket enthusiasts had got together to discuss the next season and in the March of 1919 held a meeting to re-form the Torquay club. The Mayor, Alderman Cummings was elected President but he had to work in close co-operation with Mr. W. Jackson, the school principal, since the club would now be sub-tenants of the school. Mr. Palmer, the groundsman still lived at the ground, and tended to same, so the playing area was in quite good order. In consultation it was decided that intoxicants could no longer be served at the bar because of the law and restrictions regarding youths on licence premises. .Subscriptions had been agreed to be set at five shillings for those under twenty one and ten shillings and six pence for older members. Boys attending the school would automatically become members and have the opportunity for practice, plus the benefit of coaching from senior players. Should any of the schoolboys show the necessary ability they would be given places in the respective teams.

Charles Dear, formerly the Babbacombe player and secretary, came and joined the club and ex-members of Torquay at the meeting included Dobson, Ford, Bruce, Matthews, Rev. Lake and Harry Terry. Since all the clubs original equipment had been disposed of and members were advised it would be expensive to replace, it was hoped that every cricket lover would give generous support towards the purchase of replacements.

From the records found only one side was run during that first season, under the captaincy of the Rev. K. Lake who had been a pre-war player. The first game was in June against Wesleyans and was won by fifty runs. Later in the same month the team played an Australian army side that declared at 154 for 6 and had Torquay all-out for 102. A game against Exeter did get space in a paper with Torquay scoring 316 for 5, W. Dobson being the top scorer with 111. When stumps were drawn Exeter had 217 for 5, "but did not have as long at the crease as their opponents", the reporter stated.

So after a lot of hard work on the part of numerous people, the resurrected Torquay Cricket Club was up and running having got through its first season without too many difficulties. Great credit was due to those who had persevered in such times as it was quite an achievement. Those of us who were involved after the 1939-45 conflict remember the difficulties then and heaven knows what it was like all those years earlier.

Following the clubs pre-war practice a meeting was called in the March of 1920 and was in effect the first A.G.M. after the war. Held at the Town Hall the Mayor was unable to be present so General Caunter took the chair. C.S.Parr, Sec. & Treasurer, gave a brief report on the season and congratulated Rev. Lake on his captaincy and the wonderful sporting spirit he had enjoyed with his team. Thanks were also given to H.Walker, C.Hore, F.Luxton and Dr.Boucher for all their efforts on behalf of the club and to the schools headmaster, Mr.W.Jackson, for all his helpful suggestions.

While during the first year they had been unable to play mid-week games except in August, when the school was on holiday, for the 1920 season there would be fixtures against the Naval College and the Mental Hospital. During August two day matches had been fixed with the M.C.C. and the Old Olavians.

Mr. Parr was delighted to tell the meeting there was a balance in hand of £9, and the writer imagines the members were happy to hear that at the first meeting !!!. However he went on to say that it would be spent preparing the ground for the coming season. He further told them of meeting at Newton Abbot he had attended regarding starting up the South Devon league. A proposal was put to the meeting that Torquay did enter for one season as an experiment, but the captain, Rev.Lake, opposed and was seconded by Peter Saunders. Following much heated discussion a vote was taken and the opposition was carried by nine votes to eight…The writer was more than puzzled by the result since eighteen people were mentioned by name as speaking during the discussion, and the covering overall report said, "there was a good attendance"

The meeting closed after a proposal by Frank Luxton, seconded by C.Hore, that the name Home Team be done away with and the side referred to as the Second X1. This was carried unanimously.

The first two games of the season saw both Bovey Tracey and Paignton defeated by the first team but the seconds came off second best in their matches.

Statistics at the end of the cricket season showed that the first team had actually won eleven of their twenty two games played with five lost and six draws, Ford and Chatton had managed to play in twenty one and the Rev. Lake nineteen. Dobson and Ford headed the bowling averages and Crockwell and Dobson the batting.

Throughout the late 1800s and up until the 1914 war, the few individuals responsible for the clubs finances had repeatedly said that the club was too far out of Torquay to be well supported. In modern times it is difficult to picture what members had to contend with to get to Barton Road. Many of the roads of modern times were non-existent then, or were lanes and not in very good state of repair. Well into the 1900s tollgates were in existence and it was possible that members would have had to pay for more than one on their way to and from the ground. In those circumstances it is understandable that cricket lovers tended to follow their local side at Babbacombe, Ellacombe, St.Marychurch or Cockington.

Odd rumours began, sometime during the late 1918 and repeated in 1919, that there was a possibility of moving to another ground and it is worthwhile explaining exactly what happened. Remember that the rugby club had a ground adjacent to the station near the sea front from as early as 1902, and their cricket club played in that very convenient position. Putting things into sequence the local authority had discussed the need for leisure facilities and gardens on the seafront in the 1890s. While they talked for almost two years the "town's bright boys" formed a Company, sold three thousand £1 shares and leased land from Squire Mallock, thus starting the Recreation Ground Company. It came into being with a cycle track, big business in those days, and a football field in the middle, the home of Torquay Athletic. All sorts of entertainments were held including concerts by Torquay's famous Italian Band and there are accounts of even pony racing being held. Only when the Recreation Ground Company fell into financial difficulties in the early 1900s did the council take over the facility.

The rumours were as a result of the Chamber of Commerce's forward looking attitude. What a paper of the time described as an "influential delegation" had approached the Steward of the Cary Estate with a view to obtaining the use of part of Torre Abbey Meadows. Yes, in those days they were just that and cattle grazed there. During the Chamber's discussions it had transpired that the land was on a long lease to Mr. Brockman who owned a large hotel in Chestnut Avenue where his guests had a wonderful clear view to the sea. Brockman was prepared, if consent was given, to sub-let the meadow to the corporation for the purpose of bowls, croquet and tennis. The Chairman of the Chamber of Commerce announced this at one of their monthly meetings and had invited the Mayor Alderman Cummings to hear the news and said, "he had no intention of treading on the Councils toes and hoped that the Town Council would then persue the matter for the town's benefit".

As said before, little changes with the local authority and it was not until the summer of 1920 that the Authority made application to "Borrow £8500 for the purchase of a portion of Torre Abbey Meadow, Walls Hill, Babbacombe Downs, the Babbacombe and Oddicombe beaches, plus a further £1900 for the purchase of a motor fire engine on the Westhill Estate.". At that time £166 a year was being paid for a pair of horses for the fire appliance and it was felt a motorised fire engine would be more reliable for the hilly district.

Eventually the Ministry of Health held an Official Enquiry into the request for the money and a Mr. E. Dodley conducted same. The Torquay Times with endless columns of print reported the Enquiry with Mr. P.H. Almy, Deputy Town Clerk representing the Corporation. Reading the whole account and the acid comments by the Inspector it did look as though the application would be thrown out, but at the end of the year it was announced that the sanction had been approved.

While there was to be no land for a cricket field it does illustrate that on occasions the Corporation does act for the benefit of rate payers.

The Rev. Lake presided over the 1921 A.G.M. in the absence of the Mayor and with the Secretary/Treasurer announcing another £9 and fourteen shillings profit the meeting got off to a happy beginning. Interestingly the groundsmans wages were £21 & fifteen shillings a year plus his accommodation, ground rent £10, and new equipment £27 & seventeen shillings. Rev. Lake announced he had had his fiftieth birthday during the summer and he now asked for a younger man to take over the first team. Dr. Boucher was elected and Harry Walker captain of the Second X1.

Winning 14 of the 22 games played during the season and only losing six was judged most satisfactory, Crockwell, Dobson, Ford and Chatton had again been the mainstay of the first team. The one game that received proper press coverage was against Exeter, who having won the toss batted first and scored 138 runs. Boucher and Ford gave Torquay a good start and when Ford was out at 70 things still looked good. Boucher lost his wicket on 30 and it was ten runs to win with six wickets in hand. (the writer feels even John Pelosi would have had a bet then!!) Wickets began to fall and then Light took a hat-trick for Exeter which saw Torquay all out for 132 and losing by six runs. The wonderful game of cricket.

1922.

During the next A.G.M. it was disclosed that for the first time the wives of members, had made themselves responsible for the teas during the 1921 season and it had proved an unqualified success both financially and socially. Mr. Parr said more ladies had participated and there was a balance in hand of well over ten pounds. A Mr. Gillard was announced as the new groundsman and credit was given for the work he had done ready for the 1922 season. When the election of Officers took place it was decided that due to the work involved the post of Secretary/Treasurer should be separated and eventually A.R.Hayman became the new Hon.Sec., while A. Shepherd was appointed the Treasurer. The Mayor, Councillor Williams, was confirmed as President.

The 1922 playing record was extremely poor with only six games won out of the twenty five played by the first team. The Second X1 fared little better losing eleven of their eighteen fixtures. There were numerous complaints about the state of the ground and the Corporation and the School Governors agreed to spend £50 to put the field in better order before the 1923 season.

W.G.O'Donoghue was the first team captain for 1923 with G.H.L.Easterbrook his vice-captain while the seconds were under the jurisdiction of the Rev. Worthington.

Several reports covering Devon County games that season made mention of O'Donoghues bowling and against Dorset he returned figures of 7 for 40. The one match of the season that really had a big press was a game against the Officers of the H.M.S.Queen Elizabeth, "play being enlivened by the ships band", the report ended.

'Umpire' in his weekly report in the paper had the following suggestion.

"The cricket club is handicapped by the distance of the ground from the town itself but, it ought to be more generally known, especially to any visitor keen on cricket, that a tram to Torre Station will put the visitor within easy reach of the Barton Road ground either by the path through Chapel Hill or by St. Michaels Road. Five minutes walking would bring him to the ground and further, if last years arrangements are carried out, he or she can then obtain tea. The Torquay Cricket Club Committee might do worse than co-operate with the Tram Company and advertise their fixtures".

During the season Devon County advised various club committees that Devon were to establish stronger links with the smaller clubs and had arranged to play games at Newton and Exeter, in order to find potential county players. Torquay were asked to get the best local players together and play them at the end of the season. In September a newspaper article reported.

"The curtain has at last fallen on this season's cricket fixtures at Barton Road where an X1 of the Torquay Cricket Club tried conclusions with a District X1 captained by Mr. Morrell. The visitors were successful by 53 runs."

When the actual composition of the Torquay team was found it did not appear that the club had taken the request from Devon seriously since the secretary, treasurer, club umpire Harry Terry and a number of second team players made up the team. There were no more final fixtures of that nature.

It was at the 1924 A.G.M. that the Mayor, G.H.Iredale, announced that the Corporation had opened the new tennis and bowling greens at Torre Abbey and that further land had been purchased from the Devon Rosery. This land adjacent to the Recreation Ground was going to enable them to enlarge the ground, and abolish the steep banks at either end that had been essential for the cycle track. A new cricket ground would be ready for the Torquay Club to take over in 1925 and he went on, "we hope to give you a ground that will be worthy of your inviting the best players from all over the country to play on. No doubt when you do occupy the ground you will have an increase in players and the additional assistance of being able to charge for admission".

In the light of this information there was much interest in the proceedings and J.K.Aikman told everyone he had arranged 32 first eleven games for the season and it was up to everyone to ensure the last year at Barton Road was a success. The Committee had decided there must be a professional for part of the season, with a view to coaching some of the younger members and to be available during August, as there were so many games in that month. He went on to say he felt that when the club had the new ground a professional would have to be regularly employed. The meeting closed with the announcement that,, "the genuine patron of our sport, Mr.G.W.Hinds has placed the Palace Hotel ballroom and a specially augmented orchestra at the disposal of the club for a big dance on May 2cd. Special cars will run to Newton, Teignmouth and Paignton at the conclusion of the dance".

Checking reports, heavy rain throughout the area washed out any cricket until late May when the club did get away to winning start against South Devon. A newcomer took the eye with 47 not out and then obtaining five wickets for thirty one runs. F.G.Potts certainly was a great asset that season but in this day and age there would have been details of his background to record.

Of the 32 games arranged for the season ten were washed out completely, 12 were won, five lost and four drawn. While there were no financial records for the year to see just how badly the weather had affected things there was a report that Warwickshire County C.C. had launched an appeal to raise £3000 to alleviate their financial difficulties.

1925. DISAPPOINTMENT.

Despite the previous years announcement regarding a move to a new ground it was not to be, and the club had to endure another year at Barton Road. At the A.G.M. of 1925 there was yet another heated discussion on leagues. This time the Secretary explained that the South Devon Cricket Club had put forward a proposal to form a South Devon Cricket Association, in effect another league. It was eventually resolved that since the majority of the clubs considering joining such an organisation were mainly junior sides and did not include Plymouth, Exeter or Paignton who were attractive fixtures, and like the touring sides, of a higher standard of play, Torquay would not participate. Mr.Aikman announced one fixture had been lost, after many years Exmouth had decided that Torquay was too far to travel for a half day game. Mid-week games tended to commence at 11 or 11-30a.m. whereas the Saturday match were usually 2-30 affairs. Digressing, but interesting,, there are accounts of travel to Starcross by train and then over to Exmouth by the ferry.

Mr. Iredale was re-elected as President and all the Officers were voted in en-block although O'Donoghue had a new vice-captain in H.A.Hield.

With two games washed out at the beginning of May and then losing to Bovey Tracey by one run, the 1925 season did not get off to a good start. It is rather amazing the way the name Mountford crops up year after year in the score books of Torquay v Bovey from the early 1920s to the present day., of which more later. After losing at home to South Devon the club did get revenge before the end of the season, and very much to the surprise of most people who expected another defeat by the Newtonians. However, with Crockwell performing well with the bat and Potts excelling with the ball Torquay managed an unexpected victory.

During the July an Exeter and District League team arrived at Barton Road for a game and a report found, compiled by "Umpire", the papers correspondent of that time, wrote.

"Spectators had the opportunity of estimating the value of League Cricket and judging whether it is likely to raise the standard of cricket in Devon. Frankly speaking, etc. etc. etc, the fielding was patchy, dropped catches were so conspicuous and there was nothing to indicate a coming county player amongst them. Torquay were able to include V.H.Riddell who was home from Cambridge, where he had had a very successful season, and in this game was top scorer with 42. The game was drawn with the League side fifty runs behind and the last man at the wicket when stumps were pulled."

Looking at the records for the clubs last season at the Barton Road ground the spectators must have been rather disappointed. The first team only played a total of 19 games, winning ten, losing 4 and drawing 5. However the second X1 had even less cricket and won only three games out of the thirteen played. Seven were bad defeats but they did finish on a 'high'. Playing Brixham at Barton Road Dr.Ward and C.Pugh opened the batting and each scored 51 runs and then retired. Nothing like that had ever happened before with the seconds and eventually the side ran out winners by a hundred runs.

A New Home At The Recreation Ground

1926 arrived and at the A.G.M., before the season opened, plans were discussed for the future. Headmasters of all the local schools were to be approached and be asked to recommend lads for coaching. During the time at Barton Road few of the schoolboys had availed themselves of the facilities but it was now felt, that away from school influence, in the new Recreation Ground H.Q., lads might join. If this did work out a third team was envisaged that would have evening games.

G.H.Iredale retained his position as President, F. Potts as Hon. Secretary and T.H.Kerslake Hon.Treasurer for the first season in the new home. W.G.O'Donoghue was to be the captain of the first and C.S.Parr the seconds.

At this point the writer was completely staggered to find what a quiet beginning it was to a new season in a new ground that the club had hankered after for years! After all the fuss to obtain a new ground it opened with a second team match, OR DID IT? Despite extensive searching no report of the game could be found and the weekly article covering local cricket stated,

"Torquay Cricket Club commenced its season last Saturday with two fixtures against Chudleigh, the first away and the seconds at the Recreation Ground. The weather at Torquay held little promise of any cricket but at Chudleigh the conditions were good, no rain and the afternoon bright but cold".

Having scored 111 Torquay bowled Chudleigh out for 64, and the main point of recording this game is, it was the first mention of a name that became a legend at Torquay. G .S. Butler, who opened the innings and scored just 18 runs.

The first account of the first X1 playing at the Recreation Ground was two weeks later when the return game with Chudleigh took place. Another victory with the honours going to the captain, and Potts, they bowled throughout with O'Donoghue 4 for 27 and Potts 5 for 34. "Umpires" report said very little about the game but his comments regarding the field itself were interesting. He mentioned that, " the Town council must ensure a lot more grass cutting and heavy rolling, the latter especially where the rugby players had occupied the area. The wicket was noted as hard but contrary to expectations the ball never rose to a dangerous height". Stressing the fact that there might be county games there in the future and that Torquay were hoping to renew many of the touring clubs fixtures, " the Town council must take steps to materially improve the ground as a cricket field". Mention was made of the fact that the ladies supplied teas not only to the players but the general public as well and there were far more of the latter at the ground than had been seen at Barton Road on a normal occasion.

Since there are no well documented club records one has to rely on old paper clippings for many items and when one comes across such as the following the mind does tend to wonder.

Torquay Times 11th June, "What on earth is going on in the club, for the second week in succession there were no fixtures for either team at the Recreation Ground. Being of no disposition to allow a fine day to pass without a game the first team played fourteen of the second X1.G.S.Butler, who had not played in the return match against Chudleigh, opened and scored 52 and Tom Kerslake got 34 in the first teams total, which was far too many for the 14 men who were all out for 78". The following week there was yet another blank day for the first X1 as the Isle of Wight team cancelled their tour. Dawlish thrashed the second's.

At Exminster, against the Mental Hospital, a side that had beaten Torquay on many occasions, Butler scored 114 out of Torquay's total of 160 runs which became the first of many centuries he was to obtain for the club. Donoghue and Potts had the home side all out for 55.

Well into July, following a report against Harbourn Somerville there were further remarks as to the wicket. "It was like concrete, in spite of the fact that it was supposed to have been prepared by an expert, etc. etc., the Town Council will have to take up and relay the playing pitch before next season".

The same month the Atlantic Fleet anchored in Torbay and another of the Officers games was arranged .While the result was a draw, Torquay 192 for 6, the Fleet 160 for 3, the headlines were all about the thief who posed as a member of the visitors, went into their dressing room and proceeded to steal £25.

A name that was to become well known in local cricket circles joined the club in 1926, A.V.Twose. Having been a great star of the Torquay Athletic Rugby Club, when he came down from Wellington, "Rocker" as he was affectionately known, eventually turned professional for Wigan. On his return he quickly established himself in the first eleven and in the ensuing years his son, Paul, and grandsons Rick and Roger also played. Roger played county cricket and eventually represented New Zealand at international level. A very sporting family as Paul's wife, Pat, is also to be seen in the Ladies Team photograph enclosed in this publication.

Exeter were beaten both home and away, much to the supporters delight, with Riddell getting a century at the Recreation Ground and Arden doing likewise up at the County Ground.

Looking back on the first season at the Rec. the President, G.H.Iredale, said it had been a bold move. There had been some initial expense but thanks to the gate receipts there was money in hand. Spectators now had better facilities, on a dull day they had the rugby stand to sit in, and with a few sundry improvements he could see it becoming a first class ground where county games would be enjoyed. However, unlike Barton Road where games could take place in September the cricket lease finished on the last day of August and one report at the end of the 1927 season said;

"No sooner had the cricket game between Torquay and South Devon finished, South Devon 166, Torquay 131 for 9, than the rugby posts were being erected for the first practice match and the rugby followers were beginning to invade the ground."

The A.G.M. of 1928 must be mentioned since the first honary life member was appointed, W.S.Dobson. Tributes were paid by numerous individuals as to the work he had done for the club and by Dr.Ward to his outstanding abilities as a cricketer and clubman.

In time honoured fashion the season began with the fixture against Bovey Tracey. Having won the toss Dr.Ward sent in his opening batsmen but Butler and Kerslake were back in the pavilion without a run on the board, thanks to the Mountfords. Price and the Doctor stopped the rot and the total reached, what appeared a very inadequate number of runs, 113. Butler however was a different cricketer this day, his bowling was most accurate and he had 8 wickets for 33. Bovey were all out for 64, with the two Mountfords obtaining half of that score.
Back at the Recreation ground the seconds had suffered defeat at the hands of Kingsbridge and the game was only noted for the first appearance of one, George Emmett. He later went on to become the club's youngest professional, then a Gloucestershire player, and an English International with a cap against Australia. In this game however, like so many stars, he began with a duck but did take two wickets with his bowling.

On the Thursday, before the return game with Bovey, a J.Rasa was noted as playing and was chosen for the Saturday team. Torquay began well with Price and Butler getting 39 and 31 respectively before five quick ducks. W. Mountford, 6 for 28, and Torquay all out for 96. Apart from A.Mountford 26 not out Bovey had no answer to Butler and Rasa, 5 for 15 and 4 for 20 respectively. These are the only occasions found when J.Rasa played for the club, but obviously a useful player.
L.Vaughan, a left arm bowler who had been on the ground staff at Lords, played for Worcestershire and had been engaged as the professional, really showed his worth during the August. There were no explanations but numerous players were not available that particular month, several reports covering the games played said, "Vaughan carried the batting and bowling of the side". Butler's absence throughout most of the Augusts he was with Torquay was due to the fact that he went off to play county cricket for Wiltshire. Born in Malborough, where he attended the famous college, he played for the county from 1920 to 1939 although he did have one game, as an amateur for Somerset in 1920. George S Butler made several appearances for the Minor Counties and played against the various Commonwealth touring sides. Later in his career he did play for Devon. .

While the club had been getting a yearly lease of the ground, the Committee decided, in 1929, to write to the Parks and Pleasure Grounds Committee requesting a further lease, but for three years and not just one. A balance sheet was enclosed with the application showing that while there had not been a profit there had not been a loss either. The letter also pointed out that a professional had been engaged and his work with the junior members had been a great success. This information was obtained from a newspaper account of a Council Meeting which reported, "it was resolved that the club be granted a lease of three playing seasons. Rent to be £80 per season, less a rebate of £20 on condition that the club continue the services of a professional who will undertake to train the younger players during the whole of the three seasons".

The writer has been unable to find out when the rebate ceased, and does feel in those days the club "sold" itself to the local authority by stressing what it did for the local youth.

During this season an un-named London newspaper began offering a bat for the best all round performance of the week. There were many entries from all over the country and of interest to Torquay was the fact that G.S.Butler won on one occasion. His performance against Paignton included an innings of 138 not out and bowling figures of 7 for 27 were adjudged the best of the week. A further application was made on his behalf some weeks later, after a game against Keyham where he had another century and 8 for 26, but there is no record of him receiving another bat!

In the same season there is an account of the first known coloured player, V. Kumar. He was a member of the first team playing away against Chudleigh. 'Umpire' in his report expected it to be a high scoring game and with Butler and Price opening for Torquay with fifty and twenty respectively, spectators thought he might be correct. Wrong, a collapse followed, no one else got double figures and Torquay were all out for 101. Chudleigh however had no answers to the wiles of Vaughan, 7 for 18, and Butler 3 for 14 and were all back in the pavilion for 32. With so much of a lovely afternoon left the Torquay captain, Ford, asked Chudleigh to bat again. Amazingly worse was to follow, Ford used two different bowlers with Binmore taking 5 for 8 and Kumar 5 for 13 in a game Chudleigh were pleased to finish.

In a final flourish to the season Torquay easily beat the U.C.S.Old Boys, just managed to hold out for a draw against Exeter and finally lost badly against the long time tourists, Old Olavians, even though Vaughan returned figures of 7 for 70.

When the season's results were collated the first X1 had won 19 of the 33 games they played, losing and drawing seven apiece, the seconds only recorded six victories although they had played eighteen games. Nine were lost and three drawn.

At the 1930 A.G.M. Tom Kerslake resigned from his position as Treasurer and, after many tributes were paid to his playing for and working on the clubs behalf, he was made a life member, Mr.Yeo then took over the financial position. Secretary W.H.Nickels paid tribute to the work of the professional Vaughan and the great improvement there had been in the standard of play of the younger members. The club had been pleased to help two junior sides during the season, Strand C.C. and Torre C.C. by allowing them the use of the ground for home games. Strangely there was no report of the financial position but mention was made that there had been two successful dances held which had shown a profit of £30. Ford was again elected the first X1 captain and G.S.Butler his vice-captain.

No sooner had the 1930 season commenced than the county selectors were searching for potential future county players. Formerly the Dobson, Crockwell, Lake, Ford, Chatton and others who were useful cricketers, and had time to spare, were quickly chosen from the Torquay club. Now, in a changing environment, the county were casting a wider net to find talent. A trial was arranged for the 14th.May, at Exeter, and to local members disgust there was only one man from the Torquay club. The reporters actual remarks were, "a youthful member of the Torquay C.C., who showed some good form last season and, with appropriate training, should develop into a useful player, G.M.Emmett". While there was only one locally based player, it did appear that the selectors had travelled widely since, there were players from Exeter, Devonport, Exmouth, Cullompton, Sidmouth and the Holsworthy club.

Another trial game was arranged which was played at the Plymouth College ground and with the exception of a naval officer, Lieutenant Shorto, George Emmett was the only player to get a second chance. This trial was the beginning of what was to become a successful cricketing career in due course of time. Following the trials a Devon team was selected to play Surrey 2d.X1 at the Oval in June. J.H.Amery was to be captain but only one new face was in that team, E. Goldie of Exeter.

While mentioning G.M.Emmett reference should be made to the whole family and the difficulty the writer had while researching. Time and time again while going through old papers the reporter, the typesetter or printer appeared to confuse the C or the G. and the first game was a good illustration. Torquay's first eleven were playing Kingsbridge where Butler and Ward opened the innings. Then came G.M.Emmett followed by C. M. Emmett, checking the names of the second team on the same day against Babbacombe, there was yet another Emmett, C.A. A telephone call to their sister Joyce, to whom one is very indebted explained. Charles W, not C.M, Arthur was the A. and S for Sidney. These two brothers came home for holidays from India year after year to play cricket, and there was yet another to graduate from the Grammar School, Richard, or "Dick" as he was more widely known. Five very capable cricketing brothers that could hold their own in most sides but only one, George, pursued a cricketing career.

Still trying to stimulate interest from the public, and as motivation towards a better standard of cricket for the players, Devon arranged to play a Torquay and District X1 at the Recreation Ground late in the season. A.R.Shepherd, the county wicket-keeper at the time, was to captain Devon and the District team were to be led by Torquay's M.Ford. The Mayor and various members of the Corporation were present and entertained both sides to lunch on the Friday. During the course of numerous speeches the Mayor said the Council would do all in its power to ensure the ground was suitable for county matches in the near future.

In reply the County Secretary, Major Campbell, was equally definite in stating that his Committee would allocate county fixtures to Torquay if the playing area was brought up to standard. At the end of the first day's play Torquay & District had scored 171 all out, Wainright and Riddell scoring 64 and 55 respectively. Peagram of Paignton had 25 runs to his credit .Devon were bowled out for 181, a slender lead of just ten.
Peagram and Vaughan did most of the bowling and had taken the wickets. On the second day Ford sent in Peagram to open the innings and he was the top scorer with 28 in a poor total of 109. Much to everyone's surprise Devon actually lost nine wickets before the winning runs were hit. Ford did not bowl Vaughan at all during the second innings but Peagram was extensively used and took a further three wickets. He was acclaimed the 'find' of the game, which had been the original idea to see what local talent might be capable of when playing in a better grade of cricket, and under the scrutiny of the County selectors.

One could understand the comments made, during the luncheon speeches, regarding the playing area, after reading accounts of earlier matches. On several occasions during the season the matches were reported as late starting. The players themselves, having decided that the wicket had not been prepared properly, proceeded to roll another before the game could commence. By the end of the season poor wickets had seen Torquay dismissed for 30 runs by the Cotswold Tourers who in their turn had only managed 42, the lowest scoring seen up until then. Gloucester Bohemians were beaten, having only scored 54 runs in reply to Torquay's 74. The last game, against the famous Stinchcombe Stragglers, to everyone's embarrassment, was another occasion when the players felt the wicket prepared by the Corporation was unsuitable. A new wicket was cut and rolled whereupon the Stinchcombe Stragglers proceeded to score 194 for 8 and then bowl out the Torquay batsmen for just 72.

Mr. G.J.Lee-Barber took the chair at the 1931 A.G.M. and on this occasion the treasurer, F. B. Yeo did have some details to report. There was a balance in hand of some £14, thanks he said "mainly due to the ladies hard work". Mrs W. McKinnon who was in charge had provided the lunches for the all day matches and to those who knew the Recreation Ground years ago this is a mystery in itself.! There were no catering facilities under the rugby grandstand then, only the changing rooms which the cricket teams were using! While W .S. Brockman became the President for the first time all the other officers of the club retained their posts. The Secretary W.H.Nickels, made great play of the unique record the first team had created during 1930 by never having been defeated in a Saturday match. 33 games had been played during the season and twenty had been won, eight lost and five drawn, several of which were on a Saturday. He went on to say, "now that Tom Kerslake and Bill McKinnon are doing such sterling work on the Devon Committee the authorities are beginning to realise Torquay does exist". Reference was made to the Devon and District game and thanks were passed to the ex-Mayor who had entertained the sides to lunch. Vaughan and Price had each taken over a hundred wickets during the season while George Butler had once again headed the batting averages. He went on to say the "big game" for the season was to be between Devon and a Sir Julien Cahn's X1 who always toured with a number of International stars and this would be the first time at Torquay. The third X1, first proposed in 1927 had come in to being and it was announced that a number of games had been arranged. After the A.G.M., E.J.Smith,'Tiger' as he was known, the ex-England and Warwickshire wick-keeper, gave a short talk and it was said he would play during the August.

After reporting some successful, for Torquay, games in the May there was reference to a new fixture at the Exeter University. It had only a brief mention and no wonder, as Torquay had been thrashed. Butler had scored 47 runs and Extras totalled 5 in a score of 64, seven men had not troubled the scorer except for their names.

Although there were few reports of the third X1 games it was interesting to note the local junior teams they were playing and most of the matches were taking place at the Recreation Ground. Paignton Manor Office, Torbay G.W.R. Torquay Co-op, Midland Bank, Torquay Electricity and Wicks. The last named was a large furnishing business in Torre and at one time George Emmett had actually played occasional games for them. J.and G.W.Wicks both played for Torquay when their firm's side folded and many years later another family member, Mike, also joined Torquay. He was better known as a rugby player with the Torquay Athletic, turning professional with Huddersfield and eventually becoming a Wembley finalist. In that era, with no cricket pavilion, all the facilities of the rugby club were used and the stand was a superb viewing area. The far end of the ground, where cars are often parked nowadays near the present pavilion, became the thirds playing area. Many years later, after the pavilion was built, the junior sides played on what became known as "the sea end" down on the rugby field. Following the rugby season, the grounds man usually had a wicket ready for the first week in June and play was allowed until the second week in August, when the area had to be prepared for the rugby season again.

Early in the season all clubs received an appeal from Devon County Cricket Club for financial support, without which it would not be able to remain in the Minor Counties championship. A "shilling ticket fund" was launched with clubs, and distributors throughout the county selling same. The first prize was a 15 guinea portable wireless. NO, the writer did not find out who won it!

Throughout the season the weather was anything but kind to the game and its players, too such an extent that the principle of attaining a decision was copied by clubs as well as county sides. The outstanding local instance was when Torquay played Paignton and close of play had arrived. It was a draw and Paignton were entitled to register it as such but, in the spirit of getting results irrespective of club records, their captain allowed Torquay to bat on for the ten runs needed to win. The captain was not named but with H.L.Peagram and D.C.Coulton in the team it could have been one of those sportsmen.

Despite the wet summer the two day game between Devon and Sir Julien Cahn's X1 was blessed with sunshine. Sir Julien brought a strong side with R.W.V. Robins (England & Middlesex), J. Gunn (England &Notts) backed up by county players from Essex, Kent, Notts and Hants. Devon was represented by R.G.Seldon, C.D.McCarthy, P.G.Kingsley, R.W.Bovil, W.W.Hoare, J.S.Poynder, W.T.French, F.W. Midgley, J.W. and L.P Price and G.M.Emmett.

Batting first Cahn's side were all out for exactly 200, French taking the first four wickets with only twenty six runs scored, but Rhodes and Summers gave the total a boost with 87 and 50 respectively. Devon struggled against the bowling of Robins but saved the follow-on with Emmett top scoring with 32 valuable runs. In their second innings Cahn declared at 210 for 4, with Summers 97 and Heane 68 not out. McCarthy and Seldon got Devon away to a good start, 31 and 38 respectively and when stumps were drawn Devon were 156 for 5. The press reported that the attendance over the two days had been good and the Torquay C.C. had made excellent arrangements for the game. The huge score board, with every detail provided, was a great and useful addition and Torquay may reasonably expect county fixtures another season. The report concluded, "Devon must now consider young Emmett a permanent county player since he was top scorer in the first innings and over the two days he had taken seven wickets for eighty seven runs against very good batsmen".

During the early 1930's a few new names were noticed in the score books, including Ralph Haly, who went on to eventually become the club secretary after playing, umpiring and encouraging his two sons who are to be seen supporting the club to this day. Another was G.L. Plumb who also played both rugby and cricket at the Recreation Ground.

Newspaper articles were scathing about the county team and when they lost badly to Dorset, by ten wickets, and with the poor response to the appeal for funds people began to wonder whether they could survive.

During the 1932 season the club did defeat the M.C.C. thanks mainly to John Price who was having a great summer with the ball along with the pro Vaughan. Exeter had beaten Torquay at the County Ground but the return game at the Rec. was a different story three weeks later. For the first time the writer could find, A and G Emmett opened the batting together, and with Binmore and Crockwell adding runs, the total eventually reached 203. Price and G.Emmett with 4 for 13 and 5 for 28 then ensured a victory and an early finish which really pleased the home supporters.

Whatever had gone on during the 1932 season will never be known and the press reports of the 1933 A.G.M. could only hint at the troubles. Solicitor, G.J.Lee-Barber who chaired the meeting was reported as saying, "It is idle to disguise the fact that the financial state of affairs which the Committee have discovered is a great shock. Having given a great deal of time and thought to avoid it happening again, and if re-elected, they would be given the chance to re-organise the internal economy of the club".

Reading between the lines it does appear things were "covered up". Ford, a first team member, actually questioned £15 payments to the scorer and the gateman and that was a lot of money in those days! From the press account Ford did not receive an answer and Tom Kerslake was reported as eventually saying, "least said soonest mended". A vote was taken and the committee re-elected, whereupon Mr. Lee-Barber then reiterated that a firm of accountants would be appointed to manage the finances of the club. Secretary Nickels said they wanted a Rule changed to allow ten committee members and not the eight as at present. A vote was taken and carried but Mr. Kirkham pointed out, "alterations to the Rules could not be considered unless prior notice had been given", so that vote was declared to be void! G. S. Butler then asked that the A.G.M. be held in October or November rather than March and that too was also squashed. Club rules were upheld in those days! The one thing that did go through was the amendment that, "subscribers of £1 and upwards" would be vice-presidents of the club rather than "of £2 and upwards" that had been the rule in the previous season. This was due to the financial circumstances of the area and probably very difficult for younger readers to understand. In the 1930s there was mass unemployment and not the benefits of today's Social Services. Various organisations set up soup kitchens where some people had their only hot meal of the day, in fact probably their only meal of the day!

Due to the clubs financial position Vaughan was not retained and he was quickly engaged by Paignton and proved to be a thorn in our side as results will show later. Butler was to captain the side with Price as his second in command, Tom Gower the second X1 captain and Haly his vice-captain. For the first time a third eleven captain came into being and the honour was John Grahams.

The season of 1933 began with two blank Saturdays, washed out because of the weather. With the seconds off to Plympton several players were withdrawn and first team men took their place. Totally unfair of course, the excuse being "they wanted to get their eye in". George and Arthur Emmett took all the Plympton wickets for a mere 86 runs and then took Torquay to 137 for 4, scoring 103 between them.

The first eleven opened their home games with a match against Bradnich and then there was an encounter with one of the numerous colliery sides that used to tour, Griff Colliery. One of the last to visit Torquay on tour was Glapwell Colliery in the 1980s and since the decimation of the National Coal Board they now only use the village name of Glapwell.

As has been stated Vaughan had not been retained as the professional, reportedly due to the financial state of the club, but he had been quickly engaged by the Paignton club. However from score books found he was noticed as playing for Torquay in a few mid-week matches when not needed by his new club. During the June G.S.Butler went off to play for the Minor Counties in their game against the touring West Indies team, leaving Torquay to be hammered in his absence by Taunton.

Being a member of both clubs it was interesting to note that in 1933 the Cockington Corinthians then recently formed, had obtained fixtures with the clubs Third X1 and had won as they were to, years later against the Seconds and even the First X1s.

Weather again affected games during the season and most of the two day matches arranged for August became one day affairs. One game that month Torquay did not want to remember was that against the touring National Provincial Bank. Having knocked up 192 runs against first team bowlers the Bank then whipped out Torquay for just 30 runs. Supporters' sympathies were with John Price since he had taken 6 for 60 and had then scored ten of the thirty runs.

Early in 1934 the Torquay Club came in for a lot of good publicity when the Brockman Cup Competition was given permission for all the games in this knock out competition to be played at the Recreation Ground. Badly hampered by suitable grounds this was regarded as putting all teams on a level footing. At that time all the games were on the wicket at the sea end and only the final was played on the main square, which attracted hundreds each year. Mrs.Brockman was the President and usually presented the cup on Final Night.T.H.Kirkham was the Chairman and each club entering the competition had to pay five shillings and sixpence (27p). Matches consisted of one innings a side or one hours batting, only later did it become twenty overs a side.

George Emmett, who had become Torquay's youngest professional, had a trial at Lords that season and it was announced that he had been chosen to fill one of the two places for professional cricketers for the M.C.C. at Lords. Applications had totalled 79 but a paper report said," Plum Warner having seen Emmett in a trial at Lords had recommended him". Members were naturally elated. Sometime later it was disclosed that Don Welsh, a footballer on Torquay United books, who played mid-week cricket for Torquay was to take over as the pro. Welsh the footballer was eventually transferred to Charlton Athletic and became an England international. Another regular player from the football club at that time was Percy Maggs the goalkeeper. Over many years footballers assisted the cricket club and the cricket club often had games with other sporting bodies in the town including the golf, rugby teams and the Torquay United Football Club.

Sifting through the 1934 season the writer was puzzled by the number of names that only appeared to play one, two or three games and were never mentioned again. A report in the Western Morning News of a game against Plymouth cleared the air.

"Torquay reinforced by a number of visitors who have become temporary members drew this match". There have been occasions over the last twenty years when regular holiday makers, who attend mid-week games, have brought their kit in the hope of getting a game.

Torquay's game with Paignton at the Recreation Ground was once more a topic of conversation since yet again it was a surprise result for the home supporters. Coulton and Motts got Paignton away to a steady start but then Hicks and Binmore took wickets and six batsmen failed to obtain double figures. Drew, with 39, held the innings together and Paignton finished with a total of 122. The old Torquay saying "with the strength of our batting" was once again proved unreliable! Oliver and Binmore with 12 runs each were the only batsmen to get double figures. The rest of the team had no answer to their "old pro." Vaughan who had 7 for 32 in Torquay's all out 75.

At the start of the 1935 season Mr.Munros balance sheet showed a healthy credit of some £62 while Captain Hart and Harry Snape had been made captain and vice-captain of the second team, a partnership that was to last some years. Charles Dear was elected to the Committee which began an administration career within the club for which he worked so hard, and for such a long time. The one new player who was mentioned as joining the club the writer got to know very well, since he became a great friend of my father. Charlie Beardsworth was a very good opening bat and an excellent wicket keeper.

This season saw the return of Sir Julien Cahn's X1 again, not to play Devon but a Torquay and District X1. Once again Cahn had a very strong side to tour including, I.A.R.Peebles (England&Middlesex) D.P.B.Morkel (S.Africa) R.C.Blunt (New Zealand) C.S.Dempster (New Zealand &Leicester) plus the usual Nottinghamshire county players. Torquay included D.C.Coulton from Paignton and both Butler and George Emmett were available for this game. In their first innings Torquay scored 176, with Butler 58 and Stoneman 38 not out, Peebles taking 8 for 56. Summers with 49 and Morkel 33, had the best scores in Cahns X1of 298 all-out. Sadler, with 4 for 89 returned the best bowling figures. Batting a second time Torquay & District fared even worse against Peebles, 7 for 37, and the side were all out for 116, Bowley almost carrying his bat for 55. The visitors were 52 for 2 when stumps were drawn with the New Zealand test star Dempster on 38 not out, Sadler had taken both wickets for just eight runs. Two most enjoyable days of cricket according to my father!

A newspaper report of," approaching one thousand people sitting in the sunshine" for Paignton's home game against Torquay for the benefit match of Vaughan only made good reading for the Paignton supporters. Torquay were heavily defeated with Vaughan taking 5 for 26 and Peagram 4 for 40.

G. S. Butler had that season played for the Minor Counties again, against the South Africans. L.P.Price and F.Campling had both played for Devon. Details of the season results, First X1, played 39, won 27, lost 8, and 4 drawn. Second X1 played 15, won 9, lost 2 and 4 drawn. No records were kept for the third eleven.

That particular summer the Recreation Ground was used, in conjunction with the cricket club, for two other events that brought the town quite a lot of publicity.
 On Saturday July 13th the cricketers cleared the ground quite quickly as on that evening the ground was to be taken over for a night of amateur boxing. A ring was erected in front of the main rugby stand, which became a first class viewing point for spectators. No mention was made in the reports found of any local boxer taking part but, several Welsh champions were on view, with English champions from the Bristol and Bath area participating.

A week later the cricket club really was affected, as there were a lot of preparations necessary before Torquay was to get priceless world and nation wide publicity. The "Miss Europe Beauty Competition" was being held in the town. The local papers were full of photographs of the gorgeous creatures, with numerous civic dignitaries or stage stars who were in Torquay to judge the event. The staging of the actual crowning precluded any cricket for a number of days with the preparations that were necessary. For the record Miss Spain, who was "crowned" Miss Europe was later killed in the Spanish Civil War.

SELF SUFFICIENT
OUR OWN PAVILION

Prior to the A.G.M. of 1936 the Torquay Cricket Club made an announcement that they were to try and raise £100 immediately to take advantage of a generous offer which would enable the club to build its own pavilion. During the A.G.M. Mr. Lee-Barber explained the club wanted to become its own master and, after discussion in committee, it had been decided to go ahead with a pavilion. This had been facilitated by the generous offer of a £400 loan, on very generous terms, by Mr. Charles Dear. Various difficulties had been encountered, but after long negotiations with the Town Council the lease had been extended for a further ten years. Reading accounts of the Council Meetings (as the writer did) one can appreciate why Lee-Barber voiced,"great thanks to Alderman Johns and Tom Kerslake for the numerous meetings attended to agree the site for the pavilion". The Corporation had been suggesting various areas for sighting the building that the cricket club did not approve of. Eventually the Parks Superintendent had accepted the club's proposed position for the new pavilion which was away from the rugby field and would enable members to sit in the sunshine. Since Mr. Lee-Barber also said,"Ald. Johns did his job as a Councillor and club member" one tends to think he eventually weaned Mr.Cousins to his way of thinking! Originally the committee had anticipated the building would cost £500 but another £100 had to be found and stress was made that every member should do his best to see that sum was forthcoming. Life membership was offered for a payment of ten guineas and a member, C.H.Grant, of the Midland Bank consented to act as treasurer for the fund.

President W.S.Brockman said he was resigning after his years of service and D. R. Riddle was elected to succeed him.

The offer of life membership for ten guineas will seem silly to the average reader in 2004 but the writer would point out that few men received a weekly wage of £3 at that time. Invidious as it is, the author takes leave to remind readers of the gulf that existed between the members at that time, the advertisements placed in the local newspapers are however quite explanatory.

"TWO MOST IMPORTANT FIXTURES"
(In aid of the new pavilion fund)

The Ball at the Baths Ballroom.   The Dance at the Town Hall
Tickets 10/6.   Tickets 5/s.
(spectators 1/s)

A famous band of the time, Ambrose, was engaged to come down from London for the occasions, which were held on successive nights, and clearly indicated officials realised that few of the ordinary members would be in a position to attend the Ball. Evening dress in those days was not part of the ordinary individual wardrobe.

While there were few games of real note that season it must be recorded that George Butler started in form. 133 against The United services at Mount Wise, 128 not out against South Devon and 130 in the defeat of Paignton at the Recreation Ground. In the return match at Queens Park during August, when Butler was away playing for Wiltshire, Torquay almost suffered a defeat. Paignton declared at 242 for 8 and Torquay were holding on at 140 for 8 when stumps were pulled, Vaughan again upsetting Torquay with five wickets for twenty five runs!

The long awaited cricket pavilion was officially opened in the August of 1936. The players and spectators had seen the work progressing throughout the season and wondered whether it would be completed that year. That it did was in no small measure due to the unceasing efforts of Tom Kerslake. While the club sneaked in a game before the official opening by the Mayor, the President made a joke of it in his speech. Welcoming Col. Rowland Ward, Dr. Riddle said, "the club have used the pavilion, furtively, but now you have come to put it right, with the official opening. It is a very nice building but unfortunately it has not been paid for and to clear the debt another £400 is needed". After the Mayors speech Mr. Lee-Barber thanked Alderman Johns, Chairman of the Parks Committee.

Players made comparisons of walking to the wicket from the new pavilion and to going out from the rugby dressing rooms. Spectators were much happier too since the position of the building enabled them to enjoy endless sunshine as well as the cricket. The enclosure was strictly for the members and the general spectators were very definitely not tolerated in that domain.

Devon had a very bad season and dropped five places in the Minor Counties table. Torquay had managed 28 victories out of the 44 games played, losing and drawing 7 with only two matches falling foul of the elements. Campling had played for Devon while Butler, with his form playing for Wiltshire, finished third in the complete list of Minor County batsmen with an average of 46:6.

After less than a year in office, the President, Dr. Riddle died. At the yearly meeting Mr. Lee-Barber paid tribute to the work done by Riddle and, after members had stood in silence, announced that with great persuasion by the committee,

Mr. Brockman was returning as President. He went on to thank the grounds man, Percy White, and then appealed for more people to help those few who always did the work! (things changeth not !) Members were told that for the summer, an awning would be erected over part of the enclosure, and teas would be available there. All the Officers retained their posts but Tom Kirkham (hon.sec.) said there were to be administration changes. An honorary steward was appointed, Mr.A.S.Rivers and Captain Hart, in charge of the second X1, would also become the mid-week X1 captain and deal with those clubs who were asking for fixtures the following year. It was becoming quite a problem for the Committee since so many clubs, having heard about the facilities in the South West, were writing for matches and the club needed to avoid any chance of duplication.

Before an early season game against St. Lukes College, Mr. F.G.Potts presented a new flag to the club via Mr. Aikman, who in return gave him the old flag to keep as "a momento of his own dashing displays in the past". When the writer first returned to Torquay the club flag always adorned the flagpole whenever there was a game, the then secretary, Harry Ball, and Bert Kingdon were most particular about that.

1937 being the year of the Coronation the Recreation Ground was commandeered for several events including a revue by the Princess Royal of some 4000 Girl Guides.

After a season or so Sadler, the professional, was beginning to show his real worth and at the R.N.E.College had taken 5 for 30 with Butler getting the other 5 for 39…All out for 80 and it looked like an early night, especially with Butler opening and having 20 before being cleaned bowled. However from then on it was a procession with only Hicks able to score double figures and Torquay were all out for 48.

The county match against Cornwall, a two day affair, saw Devon win easily. Having first use of the wicket Devon scored 304 for 9 before declaring, C.Kendall 62 and several others scoring 40s and 30s. Cornwall were bowled out for 178 and asked to follow on and only managed 162. The required twenty one runs were obtained without losing a wicket and the local hero, Torquay's F.S.Campling taking 15 wickets for 117 runs in the match.

The difficulties with touring sides, which still exist, have been going on for a very long time and were clearly illustrated that season. Courtaulds and Chiswick Park cricket clubs had both been coming on tour, annually, for a very long time and, while usually "quite useful" sides, they were games one expected to win. It was not to be that season and in both instances the Torquay team were badly beaten. Also the Good Companions usually succumbed to Torquay but this year they had the home team all out for 88 and were themselves 78 for 6, when heavy rain ended the proceedings. However things were completely reversed when the Wayfarers arrived, normally a very strong side which provided tough opposition and an interesting game. What had been intended as a two day match became two one day affairs. George Emmett was home and in a total of 296 had cracked a brilliant 158. Sadler quickly took five wickets for thirty two and even when the change bowlers came on the Wayfarers total only reached 64. The second day the batting order was changed and Campling had 83 not out in a total of 195 for 5. The Wayfarers again could only manage 73, Hicks taking 4 for 27 and Sadler 4 for 28.

There are many occasions when the hosts, with all their games, cannot field good teams day after day but more recently the visitors, who are getting less, cannot persuade many younger players to tour since there are so many other holiday attractions The writer is of the opinion that when Bill Traylor, and later, Barton Sewell were solely responsible for the mid-week sides, creditable teams were put into the field since both took the necessary time to ensure the visitors would be given a good game.

At Callard's Café in March 1938 G.S.Butler finally had his way. After a long discussion a vote was taken and the future A.G.Ms were to be held at the end of the season and before the Christmas. While some members wanted a change to the club's colours it was eventually agreed to adhere to the existing red and black. In presenting the secretary's report Tom Kirkham advised members that the Devon Committee had said Torquay's financial response with County games was far in excess of any other ground Devon played on. However the Club were not to be awarded a game for that season despite the good attendances. The explanation being that the Plymouth Corporation had spent £4000 on a new pavilion for that club and were making "great guns about it" so Plymouth would be hosting a match. E.W.Harrison said the gate receipts of £139 in the previous season was a record and went on to tell the members that £100 had been paid off the pavilion loan, some £40 had been spent on alterations and there was still a credit balance of £18.

Having made reference to the monies forwarded to Devon when Torquay were awarded a game the writer suggests the following extract from a paper later in the 1938 season is of interest.

"Devon County Cricket Club, which has not played a game at Torquay this season is faced with an adverse balance sheet. The County has enjoyed little support and officials complain that many people who actually live in Devon are subscribers to the Somerset County Club. R.H.Lock (hon.sec. of Devon) says, "It is most dispiriting to finishes up one season just as badly as another. I managed to get 20 new subscribers this year but this has been levelled by the death of 17 old members so our financial position is as pressing as ever. We are living from hand to hand and I do consider it is about time that cricket supporters in the County and in Exeter especially, should realise we cannot go on carrying the County Ground on our backs without more support. Run as cheaply as possible each home game costs the County at least £25".

So, even in those far off days, with few people owning cars, they were prepared to get on a train, very frequent and reliable then, and go off to Taunton to support county cricket.
Apologies to the reader for digressing but as mentioned before time changes little.

When the 1938 season began the fixture secretary announced he had arranged 53 games for the first X1 and no less than 44 of them would be at the Recreation Ground! Great from the spectator's point of view, but the poor devils who were regular members of the second X1 were not enamoured with all their away matches. Just to make things that little bit harder to take, on a Saturday the first X1 were travelling away to play their game, the Rec. was actually being let to the Devon Ladies X1, to play their fixture with the Gloucestershire Ladies.
This game actually took place in July when the first X1 were away at Exeter and the seconds did play at home. No report could be found of the match but the Torquay Times printed a photograph of the Devon Ladies and said they won 133 runs against 104, believed to be the first ladies game played on the ground. B.Hughes, the captain, scored 80 of the Devon total.

Richard Emmett was getting "fair copy" this season for his exploits at the Grammar School and for the various Torquay sides he played in, while Hilary Lee-Barber was another young player getting mentioned.
As regards the first X1 it was the same old story for the supporter, winning when it did not really matter and losing badly when the result was everything. Thrashed by Exeter who had Torquay all back in the pavilion for a mere 48 runs, then stunned and stuffed by Paignton for the lowest total of the season, 32! Paignton's stalwart, Peagram, taking seven wickets for just twelve runs.

The regular tourists for many years, Old Collegians, came and won, as was often the case, and this year they had W.A.Oldfield the former Australian Test wicket-keeper playing for them. In covering the game the local reporter also had several extracts from his conversation with Oldfield. He was pleased the selectors had finally recognised the talent of Edrich and Compton but he did not think the majority of cricket followers did appreciate the finer points of the game. An interesting observation and when one considers today's one day games that appear to appeal to the majority, it could still hold true.

The annual game against the Torquay United Football Club was quite a struggle and Captain Hart, always known by his ex-army rank for some unknown reason, made it known he did not feel he had been given a strong enough team for the occasion. With both goalkeepers, Maggs and Joslin, in great form the footballers scored 213 and had the club struggling at 164 for 7 when stumps were drawn.

The Gloucester City team arrived and spectators saw the most amazing over of bowling during the entire season, from R.Hicks. Butler and the professional Sadler had taken three Gloucester wickets but could not trouble Stevens, the opening batsman, so Butler threw the ball to Hicks for him to bowl an over. First ball and he cleaned bowled a batsman, second ball and Hicks had an lbw decision given, third ball and Sadler took a great catch. The hat trick did not frighten the next batsman and he clouted his first ball for six but was clean bowled by the next delivery. Yet another l.b.w. victim completed the over but Stevens carried his bat for 33 not out in the Gloucester total of 55.

Prior to the start of the 1939 season the Committee announced they had engaged a new professional. No explanation was given, and neither would the secretary respond to the press or to the members' questions, even though Tom Sadler had certainly earned his "corn" during the four summers he had held the position. The new man turned out to be F.C.Gamble, a right arm fast bowler who had been the mainstay of Surrey second X1 but only had a few outings for the county side. The actual announcement said, "he will be well known to footballer followers for his exploits as a centre forward for Brentford and Reading and he has helped Surrey Second X1 dismiss Devon for under 100 runs on two occasions at Exeter".

In one of the early games the young Richard Emmett was promoted into the first team and, following George Butlers early dismissal for only 9, went on to make what the report said, "was an excellent 47", backed up by the ex-Babbacombe stalwart ,Oliver, who got 61. Time and time again when checking old score-books it is seen that the side batting second in friendly fixtures invariably bat on until stumps irrespective of passing their required total to win.

While both Campling and Gamble were picked to play for Devon, G.S.Butler was once again representing the Minor Counties against the touring West Indies team. It was interesting later in the season to see that Torquay refused to release Gamble to play for Devon in home and away games against Cornwall. The excuse being that with Campling unavailable because of appendicitis, they needed Gamble to play for themselves. As it happened he did take 9 for 48 against Exeter and still Torquay lost. Scoring just 102 runs after their opponents had totalled 118.
Richard Hicks, a slow bowler, who season after season took his hundred wickets, had the last over against Wolverhampton and managed to win the game against the odds. With the last three balls of his over he took three wickets which gave Hicks yet another hat trick for the season.

Throughout the summer the newspapers were full of the threat of war. The Torquay Cricket club was first affected when the tourists from Cheltenham were unable to fulfil their August fixture because, "the demands of the militia mean we have insufficient players to tour". As a result of that communication the team arranged a game against a Mrs. Brockman X1 but it was no match for Torquay. Both Hicks and Gamble were in fine form and in looking at the players on duty one wonders why on earth the organisers did not ensure a fairer distribution of talent to ensure better entertainment.

WAR YEARS 1939 - 1945

With the declaration of war on September 3rd 1939, many sports clubs closed for the duration while others decided to wait before making a decision. Since the cricket season was already over as far as Torquay were concerned, they did not have to come to an immediate conclusion. Consequently when the summer of 1940 was approaching the Committee were able to see more clearly the possibilities of continuing.

Despite the number of men who were called to the colours because of their territorial activities, there were quite a number who had been available for selection for the rugby club and the same applied to cricket clubs. The coastline had been covered in barbed wire entanglements and a vast number of soldiers had been drafted into the area. Over a period of time numerous hotels were taken over to accommodate R.A.F. personnel, men who were undergoing initial training to become air personnel and officers. Their instructors were invariably first class sportsmen which included international stars and many household names.

Since the Recreation Ground had not been commandeered the Torquay Committee decided to carry on and invited servicemen stationed locally, who wanted a game of cricket to come to the ground. Invitations also went out to players whose clubs had decided to close down for the duration of the war. With almost all their first team players still available Torquay opened their season against Sidmouth and won easily. Butler commenced with a knock of 56 and then took four wickets for fourteen runs, Campling and Hick obtained the remaining wickets.

Another victory followed, over the Royal Naval Engineering College, Torquay 218 for 3, Butler 128. The college were all out for 88 with Vallis taking 8 for 32 including a hat-trick. Two weeks later the College asked for a return game and almost turned the tables. The College declared at 237 for 7 but with seven wickets down Torquay reached 243 in the last over. Games like this were great entertainment for the spectators during the war.

Included in the Physical training instructors and Officers stationed locally, were, L.E.G.Ames, England and Kent wicket-keeper batsman and W.J.Edrich(Bill) England and Middlesex batsman and bowler. These two were the first of many stars to play for Torquay and in retrospect it was completely unfair on many local clubs. Their first recorded game together for Torquay was against Paignton, and what entertainment it was for the home supporters, apart from seeing house-hold names in real life their abilities really did give the side an unfair advantage. Torquay declared at 250 for 6 after Ames had hammered a century in 47 minutes. Paignton were all out for 62 with Edrich taking 9 for 21.

The following week South Devon were to suffer the same fate, this time it was due to Edrich, 68 with the bat and then he followed with a bowling performance when his seven wickets were obtained for just thirty two runs. Ames had a poor day and only just managed a double figure innings. In a return game Edrich hit 102 while Rhodes, the Lancashire bowler playing for Torquay, took 4 for 22 and the local stalwart, Hicks, 4 for 11.

At the end of July it was arranged for a Torquay District X1 to play a Services X1 at the Recreation Ground in aid of funds for the Red Cross. When the event did take place it was a Royal Air Force X1 captained by W.R.Hammond which played before a "crowd approaching two thousand" the press stated. Batting first the R.A.F. scored 156.

Royal Air Force X1

W.J.Edrich (England/Middlesex)		bowled Ford	42
D.Roberts (MCC/Surrey)	l.b.w.	Ford	30
L.E.G.Ames (England/Kent)	l.b.w.	Lock	1
W.R.Hammond (England/Gloucs)	run out		19
D.W.Hocking		bowled Lock	1
V. Brown	l.b.w.	Lock	0
A.M.Camplin	bowled	Ford	6
H.Parkinson	St.Beardsworth	bowled Hicks	35
C.G.Macaulay(England/Yorks)		bowled Hicks	9
C.Rhodes(Lancs.)	ct. Clarke	bowled Peagram	1
D.Boothman	not out		6
		Extras	6
		Total	**156**

Torquay & District XI

G.S.Butler(Torquay/Wilts)	l.b.w.	Macaulay	45
R.G.Seldon(Blundell's/Devon)		bowled Bootham	14
C.C.Clarke(S.Devon/Derbyshire)		bowled Edrich	1
C.W.Ford(Exeter/Herts.)		bowled Edrich	0
C.Beardsworth.(Torquay/Devon)	l.b.w.	Macaulay	6
R.J.Oliver(Torquay)	ct. Boothman	bowled Rhodes	4.
A.E.Davey(Torquay)	run out		13
H.L.Peagram(Paignton/Devon)	ct.Edrich	bowled Macaulay	7
H.C.Lock(Exeter/Surrey)		bowled Macaulay	5
W.T.French(S.Devon/Devon)	not out		0
R.Hicks.(Torquay)		bowled Rhodes	1
		Extras	1
		Total	**97**

Bowling:	Edrich 2 for 26	Boothman 1 for 26
	Rhodes 2 for 9	Macaulay 4 for 35
Umpires:	C. C. Langley and L.G.Crawley.	

Having witnessed this game, and despite all the Test Matches I have ever seen, the one moment I shall never forget is the run out of Wally Hammond. The look on Hammond's face really showed his feelings and the poor devil responsible was moved from deep third man to the same every over when the R.A.F. were in the field.

As mentioned, Charlie Beardsworth was a great friend of my father and Pop was a butcher. Whenever Charlie knew he would be facing Bill Edrich he came to the shop for two small pieces of steak to go inside his wicket-keeping gloves since he said "over four overs that so and so is the fastest bowler I have ever kept to"…When Mother found out that was another story !.(meat was rationed and I think the weekly allowance at that time was one shilling, i.e. 5p.) Edrich is usually thought of as a batsman and remembered for the days when he and Compton were a formidable partnership in the Middlesex X1, however older readers will also recall his bouncers bowled at Lindwall in the 1948 Test at Old Trafford and will understand Beardsworth's precautions.

It was claimed that the gate receipts were over £100 and a further £12 was raised by raffling two signed miniature bats. Due to the success of this match another was arranged for late August and was to be on a Saturday. Very little could be found out about that encounter except that it was reported that Hammond, having been called away on the morning of the game, did not participate. Colby opened the R.A.F. innings and was not out 101 when their innings was closed on 220 for 5. A short report said neither Wooller nor Gilligan made much impact in the game and Torquay and District were 207 for 6 when stumps were drawn.

As more and more men were called up for duty in the respective services there were less reports of games at the Recreation Ground that featured Torquay and the ground was used by numerous local sides that were able to arrange fixtures. Cockington Corinthians v A Services X1, Great Western Railway v Slades & Son's (older readers will remember this firm who had premises at the beginning of what is now Fleet Walk) are two of the examples. The difficulties in arranging games, because of the men going into the services and fewer clubs playing, was exampled by Babbacombe and the Corinthians who, during the season, resorted to playing each other on no less than five occasions.

Prior to the commencement of the 1941 season the deaths were announced of the President W.S.Brockman and W.G.O'Donoghue who had captained the first X1 for many years before retiring. A Warwickshire second team player from the age of sixteen and one who took a vast number of wickets during the years he played for Torquay. At a meeting held in the April after numerous tributes were paid to Mr. Brockman, G. J. Lee-Barber was eventually selected to become the new President. Mr. C.Langley presented accounts for the past season and announced that while £250 had been raised for the Red Cross by the games with the R.A.F. X1 the outstanding debt of the Pavilion Account had also been cleared and the club were

£62 in credit. He went on to say that he felt the retiring Mayor had been discourteous to the club; he had left office in November and had printed a list of all the organisations that had raised monies for the Red Cross. Most of them with sums from £30 to £70 but had completely ignored the cricket club's large contribution. The big plus in helping to pay off the pavilion fund was there had been no wages to be paid for a professional player which had cost the club £138 in 1939. Amazingly all the club's officers were at the meeting and all available for re-election which was duly sanctioned.

Again an invitation went out for all servicemen in the area to come along for evening nets that were due to start in two weeks. It was pointed out that with the assistance of the services players the club had been able to put teams into the field on many occasions and the committee hoped to be able to raise a side for every Saturday in the coming season.

From subsequent press reports that hope was not realised and, with more and more men enlisting in the services, but rarely getting a local posting, raising a team became more difficult. George Robinson, a schoolmaster at Homelands Central School (now Westland's) was a useful bowler and an ex-captain of the second X1 who tried to persuade some of the better school players to go to the Recreation Ground, the one or two who did were quickly into the team. However within months George, or "Gandy" as he was known at school was on his way to take a headmaster's position at Tewkesbury. The writer will always be grateful to Mr. Robinson since, while not good enough to get a game, he did get sixpence a time scoring for the seconds before the war!

The first account of a game in 1941 was on Whit Monday against South Devon. Torquay declared on 150 for 6 with a team that was listed, Corporal Smith, Corporal Hayter, Aircraftsman Wilkins, etc.etc.plus the only recognised names, Beardsworth, Hart and Vallis. South Devon, in a drawn match, were 95 for 7 at the close of play and K.R.Bryant was one of those noted who did not bat. He was later to join Torquay as a player and then eventually become the club President, as well as a Councillor and later Mayor of the Borough.

Papers were small during the war, lack of materials and news that could actually be published. Consequently when there was little news readers letters got pride of place to fill in space. Bowlers, cricketers, footballers and tennis players were all at different times asking why golfers could enjoy their sport on a Sunday and not anyone else. Interesting to think that it was so many years before Torquay allowed Sunday, or even Good Friday, sport. Another "scribe" of the time complained that too often cricket games were far too one sided to watch and the "stars on parade" should be shared between the sides participating…actually I think he was correct!

By the start of the 1942 summer Tom Goddard had joined the Torquay club while stationed in the area. In the first game of the season against University College of the South West the students put on thirty runs against the bowling of Vallis and

Philipson but when Goddard and Hayter replaced them the collapse began. Goddard 5 for 12, Hayter 5 for 16. Torquay lost their first four wickets for five runs, including Butler for three, but went on to 124 all out. A strong Torquay X1 played a Services X1 a short while later and P.O. Tom Goddard was on the opposing side this time. George Emmett was home to assist Torquay and L. Vaughan was available. Sadly the account of the game merely said "Edrich, brother of the Test cricketer was in the Services side", so with no initials one is uncertain which brother. The Services X1 declared on 189 for 7 with Vaughan taking 6 for 98. Butler and Emmett got Torquay away to a good start, 33 and 38 respectively but the side were all out for 117, Goddard 4 for 25, Curtis 3 for 16 and Flemming 3 for 38.

When St. Luke's College Exeter was unable to fulfil their Saturday fixture a game against an Air Force X1 was arranged at short notice. Torquay batting first were all out for 104, and that looked very inadequate while Edrich was batting. However, when he was caught in the deep, off Vaughan for 60, the rest of the batting were unable to cope and the team were all out for 90. Vaughan finished with figures of 7 for 52.

The A.G.M. in April 1943 was actually held in the club Pavilion and while Tom Kirkham told the members that nine games had been won out of the fourteen played, four lost and one drawn, he went on to warn that the club did not expect to be as strong for the forthcoming season. Butler, the captain for so many years, had left the area as had Beardsworth and Kendall. Quite a number of the Prudential Assurance Company, who had been re-located in Torquay, and had become players and non playing members of the cricket club, had also been called to the forces. However, Mr. Lee-Barber assured the meeting that the Committee were determined to carry on and history would not be repeated, as in 1914, and there would be a club for the men to come back to. In G.S. Butler's absence M.G. Hart was elected captain and R. Hicks his deputy.

Opening the season in May Torquay had an easy victory over H.M.S. Dartmouth. Declaring at 221 for 5, with a young Peter Ely 35 not out, Torquay then bowled out their opponents for just 49. Ely was a local lad who went on to become a useful club player at both cricket and rugby.

There are accounts of matches against Services teams but the number of occasions when Torquay played South Devon, University College or the Royal Naval Engineering College indicated the lack of teams still being able to operate.

Prior to the opening of the 1944 season the death was announced of A.G. Dineley who, as already mentioned, was, after a successful playing career, a hard working member of the committee. A short press article in April 1944 has never been resolved, it reported, "Mr. Charles Dear, hon.sec of the Torquay Cricket Club states that arrangements have been made whereby the fixtures for the coming season will be played on the usual pitch at the Recreation Ground. The Pavilion and club enclosure will not be available but ample dressing accommodation has been secured".

Researching proved how hard behind the scenes certain individuals worked to get fixtures for those able to play and attract spectators. South Devon must have been just as pleased as Torquay were to have games, since during the season there are accounts of four matches with each other. Exeter Fire Brigade became regular opponents as were R.N.E. College and the Royal Artillery. C.Beardsworth was back in the town again and appeared frequently, as did Hicks, L and J Oliver, Ely and Waldron. Fifteen matches were played during the season, eight victories, with four lost and three drawn.

With the announcement in March 1945 that G.S.Butler and H.Snape were once again back in Torquay and available for the club, expectations for a better season were quite high. It is difficult to explain to those who never lived in the "Butler Era" just what his name meant to the average follower then, and the expectations when he went out to bat or took the ball when in the field.
G.J.Adye, for so many years the hon. treasurer retired at the A.G.M. and was made a life member for his services but he was to die during the season.
During the season Torquay played 16 games, 11 were won and only one lost. Some were very easy victories, against Service teams, when soldiers were just happy enough to get away from camp for a few hours. Others were very much a game to be won, as was an encounter against an Australian Service X1. As mentioned reporting has changed over the years and it was only through checking score books that one noticed the appearance of C.V.G. Haines(a member of the British Empire X1) in the Torquay side, then Derek Cole and Bert Whitehead, whereas in modern times each man would have had a paragraph to himself on joining the club.

The Australian game attracted quite a crowd and, batting first, Torquay declared on 186 for 9, Cole was the top scorer with 51. Initially the Australian wickets went down cheaply to Whitehead, but Dawson with 61, almost pulled off a victory. However a superb caught and bowled by Whitehead left the visitors three runs short of the required total. Once again it was great entertainment for the spectators.

During the Saturday when Torquay were playing Southern Districts, Sgt. George Emmett was at Lords playing for the Central Mediterranean Forces. Southern Districts declared their innings closed on 176 for 6 but, in great form Butler, had 74 before being run out, his partner Waldron, 74 not out, and later Whitehead 24 not out ensured Torquay's victory. When the club played the R.A.F.(Exeter) Butler, Waldron and Cole hit off the necessary 177 runs to win, Butler obtaining 93. The rest of the batsmen began wondering when they would get to the wicket again!

The final game, against the Royal Marines, was cancelled due to the weather and statistics for the season were. Played 16, won 11, lost 1. G. S. Butler played in 14 of the games and scored 932 runs with two centuries. Haines actually headed the averages with 85.5 but Whitehead with 44 wickets at 13:6 each and a batting average of 55 was adjudged the all rounder of the season. C.V.G.Haines, who had played as an amateur for Glamorgan, was a great acquisition for the club.

As demobilisation was taking place faster than anticipated, it was announced at the A.G.M., that while two sides would be operating for the season the club also hoped to arrange games for a third team, even if it was only for evening matches. Charles Dear, (hon.sec.) informed the assembled members "that after his exploits the previous season Bert Whitehead had been chosen as the club professional". G.S.Butler would resume his role as captain, while Tom Kerslake and Captain Hart would represent Torquay on the Devon Committee.

A proposal that, "a tablet be placed in the pavilion in memory of those members killed on active service", was passed unanimously. Whereas no accurate record of those who lost their lives in the 1914-18 conflict is too hand the following were recorded as killed in the 1939;45 war.

F.S.Campling. (Torquay and Devon, 1934 -39) died as a P.O.W. in Japan.

A.G.Gibbs (Torquay 1937-39) died as a P.O.W. of Japan in Thailand.

E.D.Comber-Higgs. (Torquay and Magdalene College 1938-39) R.A.F.

L.Dobson   (Torquay and Newton College, 1937-39)   R.A.F.

As an ex-service man the writer is deeply ashamed this plaque was taken down and never re-instated.

BACK TO NORMAL
AFTER THE CONFLICT

The season opened with the club playing Bovey Tracey at the Recreation Ground and while a lot of the familiar names were present, a Tolchard and a Croxford were making a first appearance in the Torquay team. Declaring at 179 for 7, Butler 84, Bovey were then all out for just 81. A long letter the following week, from a C.Barnett, was published in the Torquay Times complaining about the lack of competition in the match. "Strong batting clouting weak bowling at will, I left the farce to continue", one person wrote. The Editor printed the whole letter and then wrote his own reply, which to either a Bovey supporter or Torquay's is most interesting, and to the author, quite amusing

"Our correspondent is rather hard on the Torquay Club...He obviously does not know that the fixture with Bovey Tracey is one of the oldest on the card, for over 50 years the two teams have been accustomed to open the season against each other. Bovey would, we are certain, be the first to admit they are no match for Torquay, but, the fixture dates back to the days when Torquay were just an ordinary village side. The fact that the fixture has not been allowed to die out just because Torquay have become a strong side is one of those sporting gestures that have given origin to the phrase used of us in so many other connections that we "play cricket" etc.etc."

Dear reader, as you plough through these scribblings try and smile, the world is a changing place and I loved the Editors comments!

Two new players joined the club and after the Bovey game went into the first X1 for the match with the R.N.E.College. G.L.Turle came from the St.James Club in Exeter and had played for Devon, while R .Drennan, said to be a bowler, actually did take 4 for 26 in his first game, while Turle had 17 not out in the victory over the College.

The highlight of the season was a two day game between Devon and Lancashire. Devon were represented by, R.G.Seldon (captain), G.S.Butler, F.A.Parker, C.V.G.Haines, D.V.H.Cole, J.S.Ponder, L.Allen, C.W.Ford, C.Beardsworth, A.Whitehead and L.Butters. Lancashire. N.Howard (captain), W.Place, G.A.Edrich, F.Cooper, E.H.Edrich, T.L.Brierley, W.Philipson, R.G.Garlick, W.B.Roberts, H.Price and R.Alderson.

With five Torquay players in the side Devon had a lot of local support and the press estimated some 1500 present when play began. At lunch Lancashire were 106 for 4 and later at 201 for 7 Devonians were feeling quite relaxed. The break did the batsmen good but not the bowlers, in less than an hour the later batsmen added some eighty odd runs and were all out for 296. By the close of play Devon were 97 for 2 with Butler out for just 22. Resuming on the Monday, no Sunday play allowed in Torquay on the Sabbath, Devon declared at 201 for 8 trusting for a sporting declaration from the Lancastrians. Howard and his colleagues went after the bowling from the start and added 122 for 3 before they called a halt, Nigel Howard having scored 51 in less than thirty minutes. Devon were left to chase 218 in two and a half hours but after 41 from Butler none of the others were able to cope with the county bowling and were all out, ten minutes before stumps were due to be drawn, for 132.

Both teams had been entertained to Sunday lunch at the Grand Hotel by the Mayor, Alderman T.C.Bowden, who commented that, "Devon did not seem as cricket minded as some of the counties but the visit of Lancashire had been a big step to popularise the game". The Devon captain, R.J.Seldon, expressed the view that after the splendid support Torquay should get more county games. Knowing Tom Bowden very well he was no cricket lover but did his Civic duties superbly.

Later estimates of the two day attendance said it was a record for the county and that some five thousand people had seen some part of the game. There was a "pat on the back" for Bert Bellworthy for the excellent wicket he had prepared and the very tidy outfield. He really was a caring grounds man all the years he was at the Recreation Ground. A Torquay committee member reported handing out two deck-chairs to a visitor who offered half-a-crown and when told they were free with his admission charge said, "first seaside I have ever found where chairs cost nought"!

Looking back on the 1946 season, the first complete one following the war years, the club were very lucky to have had such a hard working, and efficient, secretary as Charles Dear. Not only had his organisation been first class for the Lancashire game, but the manner in which he had so quickly fixed matches with old friends of touring sides who were ready to come to the West Country again was amazing. Barnes, Bolton and Stinchcombe Stragglers were among the visiting sides and eventually 28 games were played during the season. 17 were won and 3 lost. From the records found only C.V.Haines had obtained a century during the season and headed the batting averages with 42. Whitehead and Kelly had borne the brunt of the bowling, each having turned the arm for more than three hundred overs and Whiteheads 70 wickets had cost only 709 runs. Drennan had only been able to play occasionally but had obtained 30 wickets for 403 runs proving he had been quite an acquisition for the club.

Probably the strangest happening at the Recreation Ground that summer, and nothing at all to do with the Torquay club, was the Brockman Cup final. Taking part were Babbacombe and Narracott's. The latter, batting first hit 100 runs off their 20 overs for the loss of 8 wickets, R.Parker making 56. Babbacombe scored four runs off the first four overs and then went to 44 for 3. After a bowling change Nickels and Ross were quickly after the runs and took the score to 98, Nickels was then caught out and after two runs were added another wicket fell. With one ball to go in the last over, the wicket-keeper standing well back, a bye was run for the winning score, or so the crowd thought.

Then the respective scorers were in disagreement, one showed the not out batsman Ross on 36 but his individual hits only totalled 35! The other book had 40 runs hit off the bowling of Higgins while the other scorer only had it as 39! The Brockman Committee had a special meeting on the Monday night and, after what the press described as "a lengthy session", Babbacombe were awarded the cup. It was an exciting finish at the time, but rather unsatisfactory and especially to the Narracott team.

1947 was to begin a new era for the Torquay Club, firstly there was the bad news. After being appointed vice captain to Butler the paper reported that C.V.Haines had left the town and would not be available to play again. J.Kelly, the bowler who had so strongly supported Whitehead the previous season, was appointed in his place. Then an article in the Torquay Times related how two Midland sportsmen, George Watson and Ted Dickinson, had opened a sports outfitters business in Belgrave Road. It went on to say how Watson had won an England amateur international cap when playing for Charlton Athletic and had been a county cricketer for Kent. In 1931 he had qualified for Leicestershire where Dickinson had also played as an amateur. Dickinson a scratch golfer had also been on the books of Derby County until an injury had cut his soccer career short. The article went on to reveal that these two sportsmen were looking for further premises to start an indoor cricket school which they felt the district needed.

Little did anyone realise at that time what a great part the all round sportsman J.E.Dickinson, or Ted as he became so well known to all cricket lovers, was to play in the future of the Torquay Club. Actually, as he explained later, all by accident as he originally went across to Queen's Park, Paignton since he had been recommended to join them by someone in the Midlands. There was no one at the ground so he came back to the Recreation Ground where Bert Bellworthy, and it is believed Charles Dear, were about, and the rest is history.

After just one season Leslie Turle left the club to join the Cockington Corinthians but with Sidney and Arthur Emmett home from Ceylon, and Dickinson available, the batting appeared strong. However as the Bovey ground was unfit the first X1 had no game, while for the second week the Paignton ground was unfit, and the second's had their match cancelled because of it. It was noted that for the first time, the press announcement of teams, was also including the scorer and umpire. .Mentioned for Torquay was, Umpire J Aikman, Scorer R.J.Haly, both ex-players and committee officials.

A game of note that season was played on the Whit Monday when Torquay entertained the Devon Club and Ground X1. Batting first the visitors were 48 for 6 at lunch with Whitehead having figures of 6 for 10, and that was after Oxley, the Paignton player, had cracked him for two fours! After lunch the debacle continued and Whitehead had all ten wickets for twenty runs, whereupon the Rev.Girdlestone went around the crowd with his hat and collected £10 for the professional. Real entertainment for a Bank Holiday crowd but it was not to finish there because the Devon C and G had such a bowler as Whitehead. C.Morris, no club given, took 7 for 10 in 15 overs and Torquay were all back in the pavilion for exactly the same score of 62. It was a Bank Holiday, and there were a lot of spectators, so the Devon C. and G. were invited to bat again and were 83 for 7 when stumps were drawn, Dickinson having taken 6 for 19 in thirteen overs, six of which were maidens.

The reporter who covered the afternoon wrote about the "96 year history of the club and the first all 10 wicket haul" but was corrected the following week. John Price had returned from holiday to learn about the reporters claim and wrote to the paper referring to his ten wicket performance in 1931. He had taken all ten wickets against the Good Companions Cricket Club and he still had the actual ball, with the inscription, which had been presented to him.

Torquay actually won their first game for the season against the annual tourists Glamorgan Nomads, and that in the last over of the day thanks to a "good catch" by the Torquay United goalkeeper, Phil Joslin.

Early in July two teams were selected to play a trial match at the Rec. to choose a side for the Southern Area of the Devon Club Cricket Association.
"A" Team.   G.S.Butler (Torquay, captain) C.Beardsworth (Torquay) S.Oxley (Paignton) G.Rowe (Bovey) I.Edwards (Barton) R.Spurway (S.Devon) A.Crang (Brixham) L.Harris (Bovey) W.Scourfield (Corinthians) A.Poulton (Paignton) T.Rosenburgh (Babbacombe)

"B" Team.   H.L.Peagram (Paignton, captain) W.Binmore(Paignton) K.Drennan (Torquay) C.Heath (Buckfastleigh) H.Harris (Corinthians) J.Bovey (Dartington) K.Pascoe (S.Devon) D.McMorran (Torquay) E.Davey (Babbacombe) W.Jackson (Narracotts) F.Greener (Torquay)
Reserves: E.Knapman (Corinthians) Chave (Kingskerswell) R.Williams (Narracotts) Umpires: Cheesman (Paignton) and Aikman (Torquay).
The sad thing is that despite endless research the writer could not find any record of the scores but many names will recall memories for older readers and several players did go on to play for the Devon team, including Cyril Heath, who also played for such a long time that he became a legend in his own lifetime.

C.J.Barnett of Gloucestershire had a benefit year in 1947 and his organisers elected to have a game at Torquay against a Devon side. Unlike so many modern benefit fixtures this was a two day match and thoroughly enjoyed by a good crowd, including holidaymakers. Devon reached 164 in their first innings with C.W.Ford top scoring with 71. Parker bowled well for Devon taking 6 for 43 and Gloucs were all out for 115. Ford again top scored in Devon's second innings with 60 before declaring at 193 for 8. At the close of play Gloucestershire were 230 for 5 so a drawn game was recorded. For the record, charges for admission were two shillings with boy's half price while a note on all the advertisements found stated, "no car parking at the ground".

Devon also played a Surrey Second X1 at the Recreation Ground but this match held little attraction as there was an Athletics Meeting at Queens Park Paignton. Arthur Wint and Macdonald Bailey certainly drew the crowds and papers of the time reported, "that while the meeting began at 2-30, gates opened at noon and hundreds queued hours before that". Stuart Surridge and Tony Lock of Surrey held little interest at that stage in their careers even though they did play very efficiently to ensure Devon's defeat.

In Devon's Minor County matches, Torquay's representatives were invariably D.H.Cole and A.E.Whitehead. Following the game against Dorset, Cole was awarded his county cap having taken 7 for 58 in the second innings and in the overall game 11 for 77. Three other Torquay men represented the County during the season, F.Greener, C.W.Beardsworth and for the first time, J.E.Dickinson.

Towards the end of the season Torquay encountered some very strong touring sides and were well beaten by Slough and, had time allowed, would have lost to both United Services and the Old Olavians. Butler and Whitehead, due to injury, were unable to accept Paignton's invitation to play for them against Cross Arrows but Cole and Dickinson did. A large crowd was disappointed that Sandham(England/Surrey) was run out before he had scored but Sharp(Middlesex) and Muncer(Glamorgan) provided great entertainment and the Arrows declaration came on 246 for 9. The Paignton side struggled against the Cross Arrows bowling and Cole was top scorer with 47 in a total of 162 for 5 when stumps were drawn.

Following Torquay's last game, a defeat by Middleton(Sussex), a tour was announced, and to the writers knowledge, the first for the club. One detected the hand of Dickinson since the games were to be with Ashby, Leicester and the Burton Gentlemen, the very area Ted came from. As the years went by numerous tours took place and all sorts of stories are still reminisced over when old players meet. During research the writer had several meetings with Ted Dickinson and others, so the following "snippets" are not in any sense of order. The occasion is mentioned when several members watched the tide roll in where Ted Dickinson and his wife Jane were fast asleep in their deck-chairs. As the chairs sank in the sand they had to rush and rescue the occupants since they could not get up in the wet sand. No one would name the individual who was pushed into the Thames during drunken horse-play on the boat, but everyone said later, "his hotel room was a picture". On his return he had strung string across the room and had pegged out all his currency notes to dry! There was the team captain who said he was arranging a pre-season tour for all the players to get to know him and each other. He was the only one to turn up minus his gear, since he intended it to be a "glorious booze up" and consequently had not arranged any games! Actually the writer's favourite, and thankfully Jane was very unsure on which tour the happening took place, but they were all staying at a hotel owned by one of Ted Dickinson's many relatives. After a couple of nights he complained to Ted that more people were coming down to breakfast than had been booked in, and most of them appeared to be female!

It was at the 1948 A.G.M. that Charles Dear explained to members that the club had negotiated an extension on the lease after being told by the Corporation the club must provide new sanitary arrangements in the pavilion. That requirement was obviously going to cost hundreds of pounds and the renewed lease the committee had obtained was a protection for the club. However, when the treasurer put forward proposals to increase subscriptions to help pay for the necessary expenditure, there was a lot of discussion amongst the members. Eventually, recognising the need, it was approved that subscriptions would be increased, vice-presidents £2-2shillings, male members £1-1shilling, ladies, ten shillings and six pence. Members were told that Bert Whitehead had accepted the position of professional again and there would be another "Benefit Game". Barnett had been so pleased with his excursion to Torquay that his Gloucestershire colleague Tom Goddard, had decided one of his games would also be held at the Recreation Ground.

W.Pike, an occasional player in the second X1, complained rather bitterly that the youngsters in that side were not getting the encouragement they needed and went on to quote instances when it was obvious the game was going to be won but the batting order was never changed. As for the younger bowlers it appeared they were only in the team to make up the number. The press reported G.S.Butler quickly onto his feet with,, "Our professional is always at the nets waiting for the younger players to turn up .The ones who do come to the ground play the fool, muck up the nets and its heart-breaking. It seems to me that the older people are the backbone of cricket clubs as youngsters have too many other attractions". (that in 1948 !) Mr. Pike did not press the matter after Mr. Butler had spoken, and members who remember G.S.B. will probably understand why. He was elected captain again and J.E.Dickinson .his second in command, Harry Snape taking charge of the second X1.

Cole, Beardsworth and Dickinson were chosen for the Devon side to play Glamorgan Seconds at Abergavenny under the leadership of Irish the Sidmouth captain. R.G.Seldon was teaching at Blundell's School so hence the change of captaincy, but on discovering this in research the writer, cynically, did wonder if that was the reason Torquay, for years, gave the School a fixture! Those games were hardly great watching for the real cricket enthusiast when Torquay put on 187 for 3, Cole 101 not out and then had Blundell's all out for 71, Whitehead 8 for 21 or similar, as happened.

A scathing Devon paper account said a "Go Slow" exhibition prevented Devon from winning with only the scores mentioned after that withering start to the reporters copy. Devon 114 and 280. Glamorgan 187 and 129 for 8. Actually by the end of the season it was interesting to see what had happened to Devon taking into account, "Dreams for the future" which will be explained when covering the 1949

A.G.M.12 matches had been played and Devon had won one, lost two, obtained first innings points on three occasions but lost them in five, and had slipped to 17th. place in the Minor Counties table.

When Torquay played South Devon on the Newtonians ground the reporter referred to a "bowlers dream wicket". Torquay were all out for just 89, with Marshall taking 3 for 12 and Thomas 3 for 11. However the home batsmen were unable to cope either, Derek Cole returned bowling figures of 6 for 26 and the South Devon players were all out for 51. The match between the respective second teams on the Torquay Recreation Ground was stopped, the sea mist rolled in and, while on many occasions it has made cricket difficult to play, that was the first report of "sea-fret stopped play".

A. E. Whitehead took nine Ashford (Middlesex) wickets for 34 runs in a victory that saw some big hitting by both sides. K.Miller for Ashford hit six 6s and six 4s in his 73 not out, while A.Snowden had five 6s and two 4s for Torquay but there was no mention as to how many balls were lost in the Kings Drive !
The annual match against Plymouth was usually a close and well attended game so Bert Whitehead decided to have same for his benefit. Plymouth were all out for 143 of which W.Rawlings had 63 not out while Cole returned figures of 5 wickets for 45 runs. Whitehead opened with Butler and was 51 not out when the game was won at 148 for 1. The other not out batsman being J.V.Rowley, who often appeared during the July/August period, a rugby "blue" and a good cricketer.

Long before the cricket season began in 1949 there were all sorts of rumours about the Devon County Committee. When Torquay held their A.G.M., and Charles Dear was asked to speak, the substance of the rumours was made clear and the "dream" already mentioned, was explained to the members. Devon County had been led to believe that the first class counties might be extending their competition. After discussions the County Committee were ready to resign from the Minor Counties because of the continual lost monies at grounds where the team were not supported. It was explained that it would be expensive to join the first class counties championship but, the County had budgeted as far as they could during their discussions. Their reasoning being, if the existing membership of 800 could be raised to 2000, the Committee felt that Devon could manage with eight full time professional cricketers and the amateur talent that was in the county. So, with the possibility of Devon going first class, as well as 1951 being Torquay's Centenary year, the A.G.M. at the Queen's Hotel was quite a lively affair.

As said before, this had to be one of the biggest "pipe dreams" of all times and it would be interesting to read the Devon County minutes of that time.
New players officially joining the club included Peter Borkel, a regular for Devon the previous season and A.W.Dobson who had previously played occasional games

for the club. Phil Joslin was back for the summer and another Torquay footballer, John Conley was expecting to play.

Throughout the May there were many letters in the press relating to Sunday sport. The lack of it was in no way a majority feeling, numerous writers made the point that so many hoteliers were "only interested in filling their pockets rather than maintaining Torquay's high standard of cultured civilisation" !.(Just over 50 years ago) After most Church Councils, and thousands of the local population had written to the Mayor, or their respective Councillor, a debate was held in Council. By 19 votes to 12 any hopes of Sunday games in Torquay in the near future were completely discarded. The writer, always a cynic, was most interested to see in the Council report those Councillors, for and against, and the Wards the Councillors represented. In this day and age the whole matter appears quite incredible.

A young schoolboy, who came through to the first team on occasions this year, had been having a lot of schooling in the nets by Bert Whitehead, and the pavilion pundits were predicting a good future for him. Robert Stainton, an Audley Park pupil, turned out to be a very good player at both cricket and rugby and. at that time, the youngest player at fifteen to get into the first X1 This left arm, leg break bowler had taken 8 for 38 for the Second X1 against a Plymouth side and was promoted to the first team to play the Plymouth Bohemians. In that match when he was asked to bowl, Bob Stainton took a wicket with his first delivery. During the season, against the Polytechnic tourists, who were well beaten, Stainton actually had 3 for 29 while the master Whitehead 3 for 14. A completely different aspect of his play was seen against the Old Olavians, Stainton and Pike managing a stand of 44 in a pathetic total of 67. The rest of the team failed miserably against a Cambridge "blue", Wait, who took 6 for 12.

When Torquay went across to Queen's Park that season the previously played Devon v Dorset game there, had seen big scores, 353 and 407 for 3, but the wicket did not suit Torquay. Soundly beaten by a hundred runs while, after so much success with the bat, G.S.Butler recorded his second duck in consecutive innings. That was a rare occurrence.

Probably the most exciting game at the Recreation Ground that season was the encounter between Devon and Kent Seconds who included a household name of the future, Colin Cowdrey. Kent hammered 321 in their first innings and Devon, with a modest 193 were asked to follow on. N.F.Borrett made 109 out of a total 223 and then the fun began. Mayes and Woollett opened for Kent and the first wicket went down for eight runs. Then it became two, and shortly afterwards three for eight. Ufton, who had made a century in his first innings was out for a duck and when stumps were drawn Kent were 39 for 6. The press reported it as, "a fascinating last three-quarters of an hour".

The first X1 won 16 of the 40 games played, lost 15 with 9 drawn, although it was not known at the time this was to be Whitehead's last season. When it was officially announced at the 1950 A.G.M. the President paid great tribute to his work, unfailing courtesy and devotion to duty .Mr. Lee-Barber said, "I have known several professionals and they have all been good fellows but I say, without hesitation, no has brought into effect an atmosphere of ready help exceeding that of Mr. Whitehead" and then went on to thank Mrs Whitehead for the yeoman work she had done. In those days the club did not make paid employees life members, irrespective of the work they did.

G.S.Butler was the only Torquay player in the Devon side that met Worcester at Paignton's Queen's Park in July, J.Wilson, the Exeter wicket-keeper, having replaced Beardsworth behind the stumps. Devon lost by six wickets but the large number of spectators pleased the authorities and Paignton was to have its first taste of Minor Counties cricket in the August by hosting the Devon v Dorset match.

At the end of July Torquay, strengthened by Irish (Sidmouth) and Fairclough (Exeter) played a Gloucestershire side that included Crapp, Graveney, B.O.Allen, Milton, GeorgeEmmett, Wilson, Cook and Goddard. With superb weather over the two days there was a good attendance and the gate receipts were given as "over £380". Butler set a declaration that left Gloucs .requiring 152 in ninety minutes and, with six wickets down, the runs were obtained with five minutes to spare. One brief report suggested that George Emmett had not fielded throughout as he was attending his sister's wedding.

Of interest in the August, when the Sun Life of Canada made their annual visit, playing for them was none other than R.E.S.Wyatt who had skippered the Worcester team at Paignton earlier in the season. Ted Dickinson took 5 for 33 in the Sun Life's total of 163 and the young Stainton hit the winning run for Torquay with nine wickets down.
Charles Dear always on the alert for improvement had a large board prepared and painted with a clock face. Each day of a game he put the hands to the time that stumps would be drawn.

Supporters really thought they were in for a treat to commence the 1950 season since the first game was a two day county affair with Worcestershire commencing on May 3rd. Whether it was because it was so early in the season or due to the number of new faces in the Devon team, it was a low scoring game won by the visitors by nine wickets. At lunch on the first day Devon were back in the pavilion for 58 runs, the new Torquay pro, Pierpoint, had managed 17 and Butler 15 but no other batsman had obtained double figures. A one time Cornish player, A. H. Chesterton had taken 4 for 14 and P.Jackson 4 for 14. Fortunately for Devon I. Skelton bowled well and took 5 for 36 including the wickets of L.Outschoorn and P.E.Richardson. Devon's second innings was a little better, thanks mainly to

J.H.Stallibrass (Sidmouth) 37, and K. N. Benton (Paignton) 35, but the all out total was only 115 and certainly not enough to give the bowlers a chance.

Once Torquay's season began F.G.Pierpoint showed why he had been on Surrey's books, mostly with the ball but on occasions with the bat. Going through the history of the club it is amazing how, as the saying goes, "history repeats itself". A strong Torquay side went off to Bovey but were quickly bowled out for a mere 78 runs, L.Harris 4 for 14 and S.Gribble 3 for 17. Pierpoint was the highest scorer with 23 and Dickinson managed 17. However, when Bovey went in to bat there was evidence that the wicket was not all it might have been. When L.Mountford went in at number five not a single run had been hit, eventually J.Crossley, with 7 runs, was the top score in a total of 32. Dickinson took 3 for 9 and Pierpoint's bowling, 4 for 18, really did decimate the Bovey batting. As memory fades one tends to think of Ted Dickinson as being a batsman but on this day he was a real all rounder.

One of the exciting games of the season was against South Devon, on their ground. Torquay bowled them out for 175 and began chasing that total in fine style but it was more than a shock to find it was too many. All out for 172, with Peter Cassells the hero for South Devon, with 7 for 59. It was disappointing for the Torquay supporters who made the trip but worse was to follow in the Paignton match. Declaring on 166 for 9, Paignton had Torquay back in the pavilion for 80, Benton returning figures of 5 for 31 and H.L.Peagram, Paignton's oldest playing member, still in good fettle.

Two new faces to appear part way through the season were H.G. and W. Uren of the Plymouth family. H.G. was a schoolmaster in Scotland and came down for the August holiday to play cricket, both excellent players and called up by Devon on occasions.

In order for the reader to appreciate Torquay's standing in the eyes of the County the writer now includes notes from the Counties A.G.M. of 1951. "It is committed for 1951 but from 1952 we are going to reduce the number of Minor County games in order to economise, and will only play Dorset, Cornwall, Berkshire and Oxfordshire all both home and away." No Devon Club and Ground matches would be envisaged but the long honoured game with the Royal Navy would be kept. No professional would be employed and the hon.treasurer,G.H.Hollis went on, " the estimated expenses of games at Paignton and Sidmouth were some £205, having to pay travelling and hotel bills for four nights, plus drinks! Estimating receipts at £150 the loss would be at least £50. Mr. Cath, County Sec. said, "Similar arrangements had been made for the Somerset and Surrey matches at Torquay, BUT, Torquay Cricket Club had made itself responsible for the expenses of visiting teams"!

No wonder the County loved the Torquay Club in those distant days.

THE SECOND HUNDRED YEARS BEGIN

Celebrating its Centenary the Torquay Cricket Club held a dinner at the Grand Hotel in the April and a press report started, "Appropriately enough the club flag was on display together with a bat presented to the clubs first secretary, W. H. Kitson, in 1851". Herbert Cath, hon.sec of the Devon County, paid tribute to the Torquay Club and gave a lot of credit to Charles Dear for the work he had done. He went on to mention three cricketers of the period, G.S.Butler, A.H.Whitehead and J.E.Dickinson and their success on the field of play. The Torquay President, G.J.Lee-Barber spoke "of the unique occasion and how sorry he was that it was not all together thanks to the Corporation that the Club was still in existence! During the 1914-18 war the club had to cease its activities and the Corporation seized the ground, pavilion and equipment that nearly put paid to the Club". He did go on to say how the Town Council had made up for their "unkindness later" by allowing the use of the Recreation Ground .(This speech was made in front of the main guests, Mayor Ald. Adams, Alderman Ely, Alderman Bryant, who was then the second X1 captain !!.. a man after the writer's liking)

The season commenced with two away games, both victories, and then it was Taunton at the Recreation Ground. Bert Whitehead after one season at Paignton where he had been coaching came back to Torquay and announced he was ready to play again "as and where required". A newcomer to the area H. Hetherington, had joined the club and quickly established himself in the first X1. In the Taunton game Whitehead certainly made his mark, 57 not out and then taking 3 for 34.

Against the R.N.E. College both the first and second teams obtained victories, which had not been done for several years. While Butler was getting his numberless century Peter Ely was scoring his first, in and out of the first team he was never the less a useful club player.

Charles Dear had worked hard and long to ensure the Centenary Season would be remembered and by the end of May the supporters were praying for sunshine. The first big game was against Lancashire, joint County Champions. The Torquay side was to be strengthened by with the inclusion of guest players and when the names of the guests were announced, local cricket lovers were excited. F.Worrell (West Indies), Fairclough, Irish and Davies, all of whom played for Devon, E.Ingram (Middlesex) V.Ransom (Hants) and F.D.Ahl (Worcs). Sadly, as so often happens, rain, or at least over-night dampness affected the play. Torquay were asked to bat first and were all out before lunch for 46. Tattersall bowled ten overs and had figures of 6 for 19, while Hilton took 4 for 22. Irish and Ingram were the two batsmen to get into double figures. Lancashire lost Booth to Worrell for a duck but Ikin 58, and G.A.Edrich 89, soon made the score respectable. Skipper Howard 68, and Ken Grieves 30, further helped to Lancashire's total of 280 all out. In the second innings the crowd were given an exhibition of big hitting by Worrell who scored 72 before he was caught and bowled by Hilton. Sadly for the club, both Butler and Whitehead were out without troubling the scorers while Phil Joslin, who was allowed to deputise for Ted Dickinson, was last man out for 19. Dickinson had left the field on the reported death of his father. Lancashire won the match quite comfortably by an innings and Tattersall's bowling figures were 4 for 9 off 7 overs. Great entertainment enjoyed by a large crowd of local cricket lovers and holidaymakers.

With both Torquay and South Devon celebrating their hundred years it was interesting to see what was happening in the domestic field. Both sides played the majority of the same tourists, and while Torquay had been beaten, the press were still headlining, "S.Devon keep Unbeaten Record". So in June, when Torquay went to Newton, it was an interesting situation. Torquay were all out for a mere 93, Tom Dean, inevitably taking wickets, finished with 7 for 30. Ivor Murrin and Dean started the South Devon innings and at 61 for 2 it looked like being an easy victory. Runs began to come more slowly as a wicket fell and Torquay supporters had hope. Their hopes rose even higher when Cole took two wickets with successive balls, then he cleaned bowled Varcoe, South Devon's captain, the ball breaking the middle stump in two, causing somewhat of a delay and more tension. However, that was the end and at 96 for 7 South Devon still had their record!

Being the wonderful game of endless surprises that cricket is, Torquay played Mitre from Nottingham and had them all out for 59, Pierpoint taking 8 for 29 after Torquay had declared on 159 for 6. However, when the same Mitre team went to play South Devon the visitors had their hosts out for 69 and only lost three wickets in obtaining the runs necessary to win and capture that unbeaten record. The Mitre Club were pleased and to a degree, so were Torquay!

Two days in July the ground was given over to the Police Sports which at one time was an annual event. A large crowd attended but a number of spectators were disappointed since the star of the meeting, McDonald Bailey, was beaten into third place.

The County game that season saw Devon entertaining Somerset at the Recreation Ground. Gimblett and Lawrence attracted a good attendance and Somerset also included a young Pakistan student who, over the years, was to become well known to the followers of the Torquay club, Khan Mohammad. On the first day Somerset were all out by four o'clock for 238 thanks to some fine bowling by B.J.Hervey-Macleay, a Royal Navy officer who took 5 for 90. Khan Mohammad had been the top scorer with 58, including ten fours. While the press described his bowling as fast and accurate it was John Lawrence who did the most toward a Somerset victory by 105 runs. With 4 for 80 in the first innings and then 7 for 45 only the Devon captain N.H.Humphries was able to cope with Lawrence's bowling, scoring 74 and 52.

Before the Somerset game was forgotten Charles Dear's next big game was underway. This was to be a Devon team, composed of mostly Torquay members the other had been a Torquay side consisting mostly of guests. Surrey, led by skipper Barton was without Alec Bedser but included Jim Laker, Tony Lock, and Eric Bedser. Batting first Surrey amassed 400 runs, Barton 105, Whittaker 85 and Constable 62. Devon could only manage 163 with Bedser taking 5 for 22 and Surridge 4 for 42. Stuart Surridge was later to become captain of Surrey and began the run of seven successive county championships which Peter May completed. Surrey did not enforce the follow on and changed the batting order to entertain the crowd. Bedser and Laker opened but Cole and Pierpoint had them back in the pavilion for 5 and 7 respectively. Surridge was the next to go for 8, another Pierpoint victim and Barton eventually declared at 76 for 4. Faring even worse in their second innings the home team were all out for 143, only Stallibrass was able to cope with the bowling of Laker and Surridge and scored 67 runs to go with his 40 obtained in the first innings. Being fortunate with the weather the game was well supported and thoroughly enjoyed. (The writer was home on holiday for the match)

During the August Torquay were back to their inconsistent best, Pierpoint, bowling superbly and returning figures of 7 for 54, 7 for 66, 6 for 63, and still being on the losing side !

Thanks to the co-operation of the Torquay Athletic Rugby Club a two day game was arranged for September 11/12th against Warwickshire, under the terms of the ground lease cricket should finish on the last day of August. The home side were to be named Victoria Cricketers Country Club and was composed of Devon and Somerset players. After expenses had been paid it was hoped that Torquay Rugby Club, Devon Cricket Club and Torquay would be able to share a substantial sum. The Mayor, Ald. Ely, was to receive both teams and there was to be a dinner at the Imperial Hotel followed by dancing until 1 a.m. In this instance the weather did not behave at all kindly and one does tend to wonder if there were any proceeds from the game after the deduction of expenses.
Warwickshire, captained by H.E.Dollery included Hollies, Gladwell, Groves, Bannister and Townsend, in a strong side. The Victorian cricketers were led by N.H.Bennett (Surrey) ,who included in his side, amongst others, Tom Dean (South Devon), Khan Mohammad (Somerset) and a young A.E.Hitchman who was with the Exmouth club. Due to the heavy rain there was no play at all on the first day. When the match did get started Warwickshire batted first and declared on 169 for 6, with Gardner having scored 46 and Wolton not out 51. After just six overs, during which Grove had taken two wickets for five runs, heavy rain precluded any further play. A press report stated, "A crowd of about one thousand" and adverts found said, admission two shillings so the receipts would have been "thinly spread".

Early in 1952 Charles Dear gave notice of his intention to retire and behind the scenes the President, G.J.Lee-Barber began preparations. At the A.G.M. Mr. Dear gave his usual report including the playing statistics, 17 won out of 41 played, 6 lost and 12 drawn with bad weather accounting for a further six. Mr. Lee-Barber then rose to his feet and outlined the life of Charles Dear from the time "he saw the light" and left Babbacombe to join Torquay, elected to the committee in 1935, the tremendous amount of work he had done for the club and the vision he had shown in bringing almost first class fixtures to the Recreation Ground. He went on to say that thanks to the cricket contacts made more visiting sides could be envisaged, which also benefited the Borough. Mr. Lee-Barber then read a letter received from the Mayor, Alderman Ely.

"I learn with mixed feelings that you are retiring and I would like on behalf of the town and the Corporation to place on record our deep appreciation of your outstanding services to the community. We will always treasure the benefits of your far-sighted and bold vision on behalf of the town."
Mr. Dear was then presented with a television set and leather bound volume of the names of those who had contributed to his retirement presents.
After years as a player, committee member, and assistant secretary, Ralph Haly was then confirmed as Charles Dear's successor. J.V.Kerr was appointed to take over as Treasurer due to the ill health of A.B.Cripps. G.S.Butler announced that while he would continue to play he was handing the captaincy over to J.E.Dickinson.

During question time an unnamed member stood and asked why the club could not have a better score-board to save the "monkey like" climbing up and down. Another member told the meeting Exeter had an automatic one which cost about £500. The President quickly replied, "that answers the question as to why we cannot have one".

During the winter a new bar was fitted in the pavilion and this snippet of news in the press reminded readers that "only members and their guests" would have the benefit of same.

April, in 1952, was rather a wet month and while nets had been erected around the matting covered concrete wickets, officials had been unable to prepare a good grass practice area. This was always done in the old days but never seen in the last twenty years. Rain caused the cancellation of the first game, against Bovey Tracey, and most of the first team ended up at Plainmoor watching Torquay United. The following two weekends were also affected by the weather. Paignton lost a good money spinner when the local 'derby' had to be called off and Torquay's first home opponents, Devon Dumplings, celebrating their jubilee season, were disappointed when the Recreation Ground was unfit for play.

"Cricket at last!, and able to complete the game ".
Headlines in the local press after Torquay had managed to play Taunton on a wicket where both team's bowlers had a field day. Torquay were out for just 100 with Haines, Pierpoint and Hetherington mainly responsible for the runs. Taunton had

thirty runs on the board before a wicket fell but then it was a procession to and from the wicket. Cole, 5 for 19 and Haines, 4 for 16, had the visitors all out for 57.

Nothing to do with Torquay, but interesting at the time. This was to be Harold Gimblett's benefit season and the Lord's Day Observance Society was objecting to the Sunday games being arranged. To overcome the problem organisers allowed free admission and held a collection in the ground. Younger readers will never have heard of the organisation but in those days that religious society stopped many a sporting venture. The same summer Roley Jenkins was chosen to play for the M.C.C. at Lord's against the touring Indian X1. Worcestershire refused to release him and Malcolm Hilton of Lancashire took his place.

The continuing run of Gloucestershire players wanting a benefit game at Torquay was claimed by their old boy George Emmett. July 9/10th was set aside for the game and members were told to expect the full county team.

When the new Police Sports Ground was opened at Exeter Torquay kept their promise and sent a strong first eleven for the occasion. Even with such a side the Police managed to hold on for a draw despite the fact their opening batsman was out for a duck and did not take a wicket while conceding 24 runs. Bert Kingdon little realised then just how many years he, and his family, would become such a part of the Torquay cricket scene when he retired from the police force.

The Recreation Ground hosted the Devon v Pakistan Eaglets in July and Devon included S.J.Cray, the Paignton professional and G.R.Byfield their wicket-keeper, both for the first time. A.F.Irish, after just one season for Somerset had requalified for Devon. After two interesting days of cricket the rugby stands were then packed for the annual Police Sports and it was reported four thousand people were in the ground.

Ted Dickinson included the Devon skipper in his side to play Gloucestershire for Emmett's benefit game. Along with H.D.Fairclough was, A.F.Irish, A.H.Holliday and two of the Pakistan Eaglets, Khan Mohammad and Imtiaz Ahmad. With 'Wally' Hammond, the two day guest captain of the visitors, the large crowd were full of expectations. A young Tom Graveney did not disappoint them and what was described as "a spectacular 137" came to a conclusion when he was caught at the wicket. Hammond, batting at number five scored just 32, much to his, and the crowds, disappointment. Gloucestershire were all out for 297 with Torquay's bowlers having figures of Haines 3 for 70 and Pierpoint 3 for 71. Torquay struggled against the bowling of Tom Goddard who took 5 for 43, and were all out for 174. George Coppen 41, and Ahmad 55, almost making the total respectable. Gloucestershire's second innings was something they did not want to remember, all out for 76. George Emmett with 18 and Hammond 17. David Haines had figures of 5 for 12 off six overs. While Gloucester had lost wickets going for quick runs

Torquay lost wickets going for any runs and were all out when Dickinson was caught for seven on a total of 132. Goddard, like Hammond, had gone into the game to attract the people and at fifty plus showed he still had a lot of his skills. One remark quoted was," who minds losing when one sees two days cricket like that".

Khan Mohammad appeared frequently for Torquay throughout the latter part of the season taking wickets and scoring runs much as one would expect from a cricketer of his ability. However, his presence did not in any way account for Torquay actually beating Paignton as he only scored 4 runs and took 1 for 18 with the ball.

Torquay's second X1 got through to the final of the Narracott Cup after beating Barton in the semi. With home advantage, and winning the toss, expectations were high when Paignton were asked to bat. It was not to be, Paignton 106, Torquay 90 and the report said "almost seven hundred people were enthralled by the game".

Two interesting games in the August concerned the derby with Bovey Tracey and the Devon v Oxfordshire match. Bovey had Torquay all out for 100, with Gamble taking 5 for 48. Things did not look good at tea, but Khan Mohammad had a great spell of bowling during which he took 6 for 46, and consequently Bovey were all out, just nine runs short of the required total.

In the Minor Counties match Devon batted first and with Cole 56, and Fairclough 49, those scores gave the county a good start. Irish 106 and Mountford 74 helped to then take the total to 393. Oxfordshire facing the bowling of Cole, Blowey and Haines were soon in trouble, and being all out for 191, were asked to follow on. At 52 for 2 the second day was fully expected to produce a Devon victory but, being the game it is, cricket had another shock in store. Fairclough changed the bowlers and tried every man except the wicket-keeper but Miller, with 122 unbeaten, saw the day out and the game ended as a draw, with Oxfordshire on 265 for 5.

D.F.Ball, H.Dawson, D.H.Cole and Khan Mohammad had scored centuries that season but each one was obtained at the Recreation Ground. From the 45 games scheduled there had been 21 victories, 8 lost, 12 drawn while the four washed out had been at the beginning of the season.

The A.G.M. in March 1953 was marked by Mrs. Gardner, daughter of Charles Dear, presenting a new flag as a memorial to her father who had died during the closed season. Mr. Lee-Barber, after thanking her, then asked the assembly to make her a honorary life member in view of all her father had done for the club. Members were told that a new professional had not yet been appointed and also that a letter had been received from the Devon Women's Cricket Association asking for use of the ground in 1954. They wanted to stage a game between a West of England X1 and the touring New Zealand Women's X1. The President spoke favourably about the request but it was decided to pass it on to the Executive for their consideration.

Within weeks a press release said that Eric Womersley, a 25 year old Yorkshire man had been appointed. He had had trials with Somerset the previous season and had at one time played as a professional in the Bradford League for Saltaire. To those who have never heard of it Saltaire is a fascinating village, founded by Sir Titus Salt who owned the huge mill and had all the houses built for his employees. Being a Quaker he did not allow a public house to be built in his village.

The season opened with Derek Cole captaining the side against Bovey Tracey as Ted Dickinson was on the injured list .Following an opening victory there was much publicity in the press the next weekend as the club were fielding three teams on the Saturday. The second X1, under Harry Snape, were away to Staverton and cars were to leave the Rec. at 1-30p.m. while the Thirds, led by S. Locker, were off to break new ground by playing Manaton. Their coach was to leave the King's Drive at 1-15 and the side included Clive and John Haly, sons of the secretary, who still follow the fortunes of the club today.

With Cole still skippering the side, the first X1 entertained Plymouth Bohemians and this was to be their last season as a "wandering X1" having had a ground opened by the Duke of Edinburgh. Their side included Blowey, the Devon bowler and Toby Irish a county player at both cricket and rugby, but they were well beaten on the day.

During the season Mrs. Stutchbury was noted as the first team scorer while husband Walter, or Bill as he was known when his wife was not about, played in any side from the first to the thirds. Squad players are common in football in the present day but what some of the Torquay members thought of the rotation that went on in those far off days one can only wonder at. To be in the first eleven for several games and then down to the seconds with the arrival of a new player!, J.Bonner, H.Wells, J.White, C.Williams, and the afore-said Stutchbury were among those players who were constantly in and out of favour but remained loyal clubmen.

Early in the June Lancashire, captained by Cyril Washbrook, arrived to play and were a great attraction not only to local followers but the North Country holidaymakers as well. Due to a heavy shower play did not commence on time but when it did Washbrook and Ikin soon made up for the delay. The Torquay pro.was smashed all over the ground and after 33 runs had come from his four overs Womersley was replaced by the Paignton professional Cray. It is totally untrue the Lancashire side had heard the bowler was from Yorkshire and wanted him to suffer! Unfortunately, Gray injured his back and had to leave the field and the 12th man came out. Lancashire eventually declared with 352 for 6 on the score board, Wharton 144 and Edrich 102 not out. Devon's reply was rather disappointing with only Fairclough 45 not out, and Cole 25, showing any sign of form. Malcolm Hilton 5 for 47 and Ken Grieves 4 for 64 showed what class bowlers they could be. The follow on was not enforced and Washbrook was soon out for 2 but when Ikin 40 and Place 54 had quickly added runs the declaration came on 149 for 3. Four hours to score 360 runs, Fairclough 60 and Sullivan 48 were the only batsmen able to cope with Hilton who took a further 6 for 47 leaving Devon all out 162. Somebody said, "great entertainment and to see stars in reality".

Much later in the same month Torquay were again to suffer at the hands of South Devon. A local lad, who was to eventually go on and make a cricketing career for himself, R.J.Coldwell, bowled throughout the Torquay innings. Well, it only lasted a bare ninety minutes!. 13:4overs, 6 maidens, 4 wickets for 10 runs, Torquay all out 63. The normal South Devon "destroyers", Dean and Wildblood had a poor day and even with the bat Cole had both their wickets for 3 and 5 respectively, but that was small consolation on the journey back.

Rumour, rumour, rumour, before the season was actually over "stories" were going around that next year would be something to look forward to. Throughout the winter odd facts were coming to light giving substance to the rumours being true and eventually all was revealed. David Haines and his hard working committee had arranged two, three day games to be played in September, sponsored by the cricket club and guaranteed by the Town Council for £1000. The two games were to be a North v South and an England X1 v A Commonwealth X1. To fully appreciate the work, organisation and planning that had to go into such a venture the reader must realise that these games were to be played at the same time as the annual festivals at Scarborough and Hastings . Those two yearly events, at that time, were in most cricketers diaries with "fingers crossed" that they would get an invitation to participate. Anticipating that numerous players would bring their wives David Haines had, through the good offices of Phillip Osborne, manager of the Victoria Hotel in Belgrave Road, arranged accommodation for players and in some cases families. A local builder had promised to provide a stand to seat 800 and in total the organisers had arranged seating for 3000. With the permission of the rugby club an extra 250 people would be seated in the end section of their grandstand, which would have a good view of the wicket. Harold Gimblett, with his Somerset connections, had arranged for a portable scoreboard to be available so that wherever one was seated the score was clearly visible. Thanks again to the rugby club the long room under the stand was turned in to dining facilities with marquees and tents being erected around the field for the provision of snacks and refreshments. Admission would be two shillings and sixpence but reserved seating could be booked at five shillings a day.

While all this was going on the committee still found time to take all those ladies, who had helped during the season, to see Ben Traver's "Rookery Nook" at the Pavilion after having entertained them to tea. Consideration and thanks was much more evident in those days!

FESTIVAL SEASONS

The opening game was the usual Bovey Tracey encounter and only heavy rain after tea prevented an almost certain victory. Interestingly a young W.J.Traylor had been called into the first team at the last minute for that match, his first team debut, and when he went on to bowl captured six wickets for fourteen runs including clean bowling four with successive balls.

Mention was made earlier of an indoor cricket school and it was eventually opened by Ted Dickinson, who appointed the Paignton professional as coach. Insisting that the Torquay members went there, Dickinson made remarks to the press that, " Cray will sort out their individual weakness and correct it". He certainly did find their weak spots, and especially in the first game between the two clubs that season. Despite Haines taking 5 for 40 and having Paignton all out for just 107 , Cray had Torquay back in the pavilion for 85 and Ted Dickinson's joke did not seem at all funny.! When I reminded Ted about this he laughed and said, "some people learn more slowly than others".

The highlight of June was the Devon game with Pakistan and the 19 year old prodigy, Hanif Mohammad, did not disappoint the large crowd scoring a 63. Waqar Hassan went on to make 137 in a total of 396 for 7 declared. Devon fared badly against the fast bowling of Mahmood Hussain and he had Humphries, Cray and Fairclough all out for just 18. Featherstonhaugh with 52, Bloy and Cooper 47 and 34 respectively, helped Devon's total reach 177 before they were asked to bat again. Eric Cooper was quite an acquisition for Devon when he became the coach at the Royal Naval College at Dartmouth as he had also played for Worcestershire.

During research it was noted that H.G.Uren was home again from Glasgow to assist the club during the summer and a young Sibley was in the second or third team most weeks.

At most games the weather for the cricket festival was frequently discussed amongst the supporter's and there was much speculation as to what September would be like. The first game was between the South and North, batting first the South opened with Torquay's own George Emmett and Jack Robertson of Middlesex. Neither of them were on form and it was thanks to Watkins 81 and Jones 69 that the total reached 347. The North struggled except for the Australian Livingston who had 133 to his credit before being stumped off Mortimore. Frank Tyson, a noted bowler but on this occasion batted well to accumulate 46 runs in a total of 246. George Tribe taking 4 for 22 had the South on 121 for 7 when they declared which left the North to make

223 in some 170 minutes. All out for 161 the South triumphed by 61 runs, Mortimore taking 4 for 45.

The second game had a delayed start due to the heavy overnight rain and when Barnett won the toss for the Commonwealth he asked the England X1 to bat. Kenyon and Emmett opened against the West Indies bowlers of Worrell and Marshall. Dooland with 4 for 80 was the most successful bowler before the England side were all out for 308. Kenyon, Crapp and Spooner all obtained scores in the sixties. The Commonwealth side replied with 311, Livingston 79, Headley 64 and Marshall 59 with Walsh 4 for 74 and Gladwin 3 for 36 the best of the England bowlers. In their second innings England were 41 without loss when heavy rain brought an abrupt end to the proceedings, much to everyone's disappointment.

Apart from the field of play activities, which were judged a success, great credit was given to the organisation regarding the Mayor's cocktail party, held in Torre Abbey on the Saturday evening, the Festival Ball at the Victoria Hotel and the River Dart outings, provided for the wives and children by Mr. Gordon Edmunds of the Toorak Hotel .

During the most successful Devon County season for many years they were left in the position that, should they beat Surrey 2ds in a challenge match at the Oval, they would become champions. After deliberation the Devon Committee decided to accept, rather against the odds. Surrey won the toss and batted, Brazier was top scorer with 95 when they declared on 236 for 8. Exeter's Fairclough was in fine form having taken 4 for 46 before then hitting a superb 117 runs. A lot of time was lost due to the showers and with Devon on 229 for 6 on the second day, tea was taken. Everyone thought the game was over as Devon had to win since a mere draw would leave Surrey champions. The umpires went out to the wicket and Devon got their three points for first innings lead but, a complete waste of time. Surrey were the champions in both the First and Minor Counties, a feat only Lancashire had ever achieved before.

During the 1953/54 era a lot was heard, and read about, of what was known as the Ladmore Scheme. The details of which are far too long to record here and since, thankfully, it never came into being, and the Recreation Ground is still the club's home. At the time however, it did cause concern since had the ground, or even part of it, been taken over for the proposed road scheme one wonders whether Torre Valley would have come into being then and become the third home for the cricket club.! There were enough councillors affiliated to the club then to have overcome the protests of hoteliers in Avenue Road to ensure adequate facilities.

The A.G.M. in 1955 began with the members standing for a minute in a tribute to Tom Kerslake, who had died during the closed season. Mr. Lee-Barber outlined all of Kerslake's activities for the club including the planning of the pavilion.

Following the first Festival games there were some interesting questions asked from the body of the hall and while the big matches had attracted people, the treasurer Mr.J.Kerr, explained the gate receipts, on the whole season, had been down on account of the weather. Considerable expense had been incurred prior to the festival in repairs and renovations of equipment. .He was then asked, "Will the club consider providing insurance for players?" It appeared that this issue had never before been raised, and, after discussion it was agreed the Committee would investigate. David Haines was asked if the touring South Africans were coming to the next festival and he explained just how far in advance one had to plan and what it meant to obtain the finance to cover the guarantees such clubs required. Eventually Reverend Girdlestone paid a glowing tribute to Haines and said, "Only those close to him realise the enormous pressure he is under with all the planning necessary". What happened so frequently in the 1950s happened yet again, another professional was appointed for 1955, Stan Montgomery.

Quickly showing up well with bat and ball the former Glamorgan player appeared to be a real asset to Torquay. 7 for 35 and 59 against United Services, a century in a drawn game against Paignton and 91 not out against South Devon. The first and only time they were found in the record book Anderson's X1, composed of professional footballers, came and defeated Torquay. Jack Rowley, the manager of Plymouth Argyle and a former star of Manchester United, and Eric Webber, the Torquay United manager being the heroes for the side. Webber had three wickets for five runs including the hat-trick.

Prior to the Whitsun weekend it was announced that Khan Mohammad was coming to play for a few weeks. He was to bring the Pakistan Eaglets later in the season but meanwhile wanted practise before the official tour. F.W. Hart, a former tourist with the Ashford (Middlesex) side, had also come to live in the area and had joined the club. For the younger reader to appreciate what Khan Mohammad brought to the club when he played, it should be mentioned that in a Test Match at Lord's he bowled Hutton for a duck and later clean bowled May, Edrich, Evans and Bailey. No mean performer with the bat he had big scores when playing for Torquay in 1952 including a century.

However when he arrived in early July with two other Test players in the squad, Wallis Mathias and Zulfiquar Ahmed, Torquay had brought in Hampshire's Reg Dare to strengthen the team. Played in the right spirit it was great entertainment for the crowd. The Eaglets were all out for 265 and Torquay replied with 266 for 9, batting a second time the visitors had no answer to the bowling of Dare and he had 9 for 32 in their total of 105. Cole thumped a quick 58 and Torquay were 106 for 1.

This season the Second X1 reached the final of the Narracott Cup and since it was to be at the Recreation Ground expectations were high. Barton had already won the Brockman Cup and, having played at the ground in finals on so many occasions, did not feel home was going to be any advantage to Torquay. Barton managed 113 for

7 in their allotted overs with Horswell and Norman scoring 47 and 40 respectively. George Collings with 4 for 49 was the best of the home side's bowlers. The press described Torquay's batting as "Saturday afternoon stuff" and only when skipper Swift came to the wicket did anyone play "cup cricket". Torquay 101 for 7 with Swift on 41 not out. Barton had the rare distinction, at that time, of taking both cups in the same season.

Throughout the season five names were always to the fore with umpire duties either midweek or on a Saturday, they were Aitman, Stuckey, Benson, Kirkham and Windram.

While the domestic season came to a reasonable conclusion all thoughts were turning to the Festival. Since the Saturday First X1 had only lost one match, to Plymouth, and that after declaring on 260 for 4, the season was declared most successful. Stan Montgomery had a wonderful summer, 2,244 runs, 85 wickets, 24 catches. Five centuries and seventeen other scores over fifty made up his massive run total and it was with much disappointment the club learned he would not be available for another season. 21 drawn games were accredited to the weather, and the hard batting wickets, while only 17 victories from the 53 games were recorded. D.H. Cole, both for the club and Devon, had an excellent year as did D.L.Haines who bowled nearly as many overs as Montgomery and also took 76 wickets.

As before, the first game was between the North and the South, representing the sides were, South. J. Robertson, R .Marshall, K. Barrington, W. Jones, J. Crapp, G.Emmett, K Suttle, M.Tremlett, P.Loader, F.Titus and H.Stephenson.
North. D.Brookes, D. Kenyon, L.Livingston, M.Tomkin, A.Wharton, M.Horton, J.Walsh, V. Jackson, K.Andrew, C. Gladwin and R.Tattersall.
The South with scores of 431 and 335 for 9 beat the North 435 and 222 by 109 runs. During the game it was announced that Peter Loader had been chosen for the side to tour Pakistan that winter but he withdrew on his doctor's advice.

While the weather had been superb for the first game the second, between an England XI and a Commonwealth side suffered a brief interruption on the second morning for a heavy shower. Frank Worrell delighted the crowd with a century as did Kenyon with a grand knock of 117. Over the two innings the Commonwealth came out victors by the narrow margin of three runs. Representing the sides were,
England. D. Brookes, G. Emmett, D.Kenyon, M.Tonkin, F.Titus, P.Loader, A.Wharton, K. Andrew, T.Lock, J. Robertson and C.Gladwin.
Commonwealth, B. Barnett, G.Tribe, B. Dooland, B. McCool, J. Livingston, F.Worrell, R. Marshall, S. Ramadhin, V.Jackson, V. Mankad and Phadkar.

During conversation with the press, the Festival secretary, David Haines, estimated that some sixteen thousand people had watched the two games and he felt the weather and the entertaining cricket really had satisfied those who attended. Several hoteliers were convinced the cricket had attracted a considerable number of late visitors.

D.H.Cole, after his fantastic season for Devon in the Minor Counties Championship was the first winner of the Wilfred Rhodes Trophy for the best performance in the Minor Counties.

The annual meeting in 1956 was told there had to be a complete "re-hash" of the pavilion. Throughout the Festival games it was evident that larger dressing accommodation was necessary and better facilities, including showers, which were a definite 'must'. Members were told that the work would "tax the clubs resources" and the committee were considering asking members for donations. H.Stebbings and F.Tappenden both then complained about non members coming in the members entrance from the King's Drive and the number of non members who were sitting in the enclosure. Asking members for more money when such things were going on and while children were using deck chairs for wickets during the tea intervals, did not go down well and eventually the committee agreed to look into the complaints.

Mr. Haly expressed the need for umpires for the third team and especially for their evening fixtures. Reg Dare, who had played occasional games for the club was to be the new professional. Mr. and Mrs.Thompson had run the bar that season while Mrs Snape and other wives had overseen the teas and public refreshments, the profits from both given as, £156 and £180 respectively.

Paignton had requested three fixtures during this season, which was an innovation, and Torquay's first game was to be away at Cockington against the Corinthians. It had been tried the previous season with a match in late April, and having been deemed a success, was to become an annual event for several years.

An interesting game early that season was against United Services at Devonport. Having won the toss Dickinson decided to bat but Torquay lost wickets as though no one wanted to play. 5 for 40 eventually became 126 for 6 but had taken so much time that Dickinson decided to declare. The Services eventually reached the point where they needed 21 to win and still had four wickets in hand. W.J.Traylor had been called into the side, from the second's, as a last minute replacement and was put on to bowl. A run out, and then two wickets with successive balls, saw Torquay scrape home by seven runs. Discussing cricket with Ted Dickinson was more than interesting, it was fascinating. The writer asked him about a Bovey match that season when Torquay had been put in to bat and Ted had declared when he was on 94. The paper reported that when asked why he did not go on for a century he replied, "I needed time to winkle them out, and he did just that". His explanation to this writer when questioned on the incident was, "as a captain you just get those feelings on certain days".

July saw the first of the big games when Torquay, strengthened by the inclusion of Frank Worrell, H.Fairclough and Khan Mohammad, played a full strength Leicestershire side. Batting first Leicester declared on 257 for 8 and in their second innings on 148 for 8. Torquay had 254 for 9 in their first innings but faltered badly in the second and were 83 for 6 when stumps were drawn.

Khan Mohammad stayed on to play against the Reading tourists and also South Devon on the Saturday. The contacts the club had in those days and the ability to attract class players was really amazing.

Reg Dares benefit game was to have been against the usually strong Bourneville touring side that always attracted a good attendance but torrential rain washed out play after only half an hour.

The difficulty of Festival organisation suffered again prior to the 1956 season and from unforeseen circumstances. The Suez Crisis arose and as a result three of the Indians that were due to participate decided to fly home. David Haines had to find, at short notice, three replacements for Manjrekar, Phadkar and Gupte. The number of telephone calls he made are not recorded but he eventually arranged that Bill Alley, an Australian playing Lancashire League cricket would participate, Pettiford, another Australian playing for Kent would stay on after the North v South match and Arnold, a New Zealander with Northants, who was holidaymaking in Barnstaple would come down and play. Derek Cole, after his success for the Devon team was included in the X1 representing the South.

Festival year number three began brightly with the North scoring freely. Cole took Livingston's wicket for 24 and Titmus eventually had Brookes for 72 but at 243 for 3 torrential rains washed out play for the rest of the game. While the weather prevented further action on the field, presentations were made in the pavilion to Fred Titmus and Dennis Brookes of silver tankards, courtesy of William Youngers. Titmus was awarded his for scoring 1000 runs and taking 100 wickets in the season, while Brookes had scored a double century earlier in the season against Somerset.

Due entirely to the weather the game arranged between an England X1 v A Commonwealth X1 never even started .After all the organising and hard work it was disappointing to everyone who had been involved, and to the players and their families who had come for a short break. David Haines was quoted as saying the receipts from the first day would just about cover meals and cricket balls.

Of the club games the first team had actually won 24 of the 45 played, and while Mr. Haly did not provide details for the press he said Reg Dare had a most successful season, scoring the most runs and obtaining far more wickets than any other bowler. The Seconds had won 13 of their 22 matches and had reached the final of the Narracott Cup. In that team he gave mention to the batting of Colin Williams and H.S.Wells while he stressed the prominence of Ken Peppiatt and Bill Traylor in a strong bowling side. Rare press coverage mentioned the revival of the junior side with thanks due to Harry Snape and individuals, Peter Ely, P.Cooke, D.McMorran and L.Matthews.

At both the club's dinner and general meeting members were told that plans were in hand for the pavilion, whereupon the Deputy Mayor, S.H.Peacop, replying to the toasts pointed out that the Torquay Club was actually 41 years older than its landlords!.He wished the club every success with the Cricket Festival and pointed out the great publicity value to the town...

At the A.G.M., following discussion, it was eventually agreed the club needed larger dressing rooms and showers, as had been mentioned before, and this time having set a spending limit of £1500 plans were to be submitted to the Corporation. An upper floor with two large dressing rooms with showers, and a player's balcony plus a scorer's box was planned. It was hoped that the landlords, the Corporation, would approve and then the space on the existing ground floor could be utilised fully for social events. Club chairman, Victor Tucker told the assembly that he knew ex-players who never went into the pavilion now because of the space factor and every member should be able to go into the bar for a drink and not just players. Having approved the outline of the extensions the members then had to pass the proposed increase of subscriptions. Playing members were to be £1 ten shillings, ordinary members £1 one shilling and vice-presidents £2 two shillings. David Haines and Leslie Goodrich made a plea to the committee to keep the five shilling subscription for juveniles up to the age of 14 and after discussion it was agreed. H.H.Thompson took over as the treasurer on the resignation of Councillor Kerr.

Prior to the early trial match a strong side went out to Cockington to play the Corinthians. Seven men had either first class or Minor Counties experience which was a compliment to the junior club. When the actual trial match took place one more ex-Ashford player arrived to join the club. Roy Smith had taken up residence locally and came to join Bill Hart and Richard Barr, old colleagues at Ashford. It was quite a while before it came to light that Ken Peppiatt, who had played for years, mostly in the Second team, was also ex-Ashford.

Hampshire captain, Desmond Eager, had promised to bring a strong side to Torquay for Reg Dares benefit match and he brought the entire county team.Torquay had included Keith Benton, formerly of Paignton and Devon, then on leave from Rhodesia, F.Kingston, South Devon's professional, D.B.Pearson of Worcestershire and Harold Gimblett, England and Somerset. Batting first, Hampshire opened with Marshall the West Indian test player who thrilled the crowd with a century in their 329.Dare himself took 4 for 78 and Haines 4 for 103.Torquay eventually reached 230 for 9 and declared, Dickinson being top scorer with 65. In their second innings Hampshire rattled up 167 for 3 and then whipped out the home side for 74. Burden had 5 for 39 and Wassell 5 for 32.

Great entertainment for the crowd that supported Dare but the whole club were disappointed within a few weeks to learn that the following season he would not be available. He was to take a position with Turner's Sports, a firm in High Wycombe, who always came down to the West Country on a cricket tour. Several companies had a works team, usually with superb facilities, and annually toured. Turner's, once they engaged Reg Dare, invariably defeated Torquay when they paid their regular visit.

While writing about him it should be mentioned that again he had 150 wickets and missed his "double" by a mere twenty runs.

Odd paragraphs tend to catch the eye when on research and the following certainly did for this cynic when a reporter was adding to his analysis at the end of the season.

"The high average age of the team prevents it being described as a great fielding eleven. When he is there Hart is a brilliant cover point, and the side certainly benefit greatly if Ball, Wicks, Dare or Thompson are available to play".

The 1957 Festival began with an England X1 v A Commonwealth side and despite rain during the previous days was able to start on time. Local hero, George Emmett, scored 114 in the England total of 284 and only C.Palmer with 59 was able to really cope with regular visitor, Khan Mohammad, who had 7 for 56. The Commonwealth had no answer to the bowling of Titmus and were all out for a mere 138. Both teams second innings were described as "bright and breezy", Festival cricket, but the Commonwealth, after England's 246, were left hanging on desperately for a draw at 209 for 9.

It was announced that 1800 persons had paid to see the first days play and for the three days the attendances were satisfactory. Overnight rain meant a damp start for the North when they began batting against the South in the second match. Due to the inclement weather fewer seats were occupied. When Titmus and Lock were introduced into the bowling attack they soon utilised the conditions and the North were all out for 225, Titmus 4 for 68 and Lock 4 for 90. Sadly a complete day's play was lost due to heavy rain, and, in an effort to make up for the loss the South declared on 149 for 5. Going for quick runs to also entertain, the North lost wickets in quick succession and were 143 all out, with Tony Lock taking 6 for 35. Although Ray Illingworth took 5 for 84 the South obtained the necessary runs with Marshall, McCool and Emmett all scoring forty runs plus.

The Festival Committee were most concerned over the huge loss on the games arranged and were considering cancelling any further plans. The Mayor persuaded them to wait until the Council held their December meeting and discussed their guarantee to the club. The Finance chairman, Cllr. Adams was against any further backing and insisted the Festival was of no great importance to the town. Councillors Lidstone, March, White, Edwards, Perry and Brockman were all in favour of supporting the Festival for one more year and then if things had not improved Mr. Brockman said, "we stop it all together". It will readily be seen, that in those days the cricket and rugby clubs, in particular, were more than thankful to have Councillors as members on many occasions. In this instance the Council did give its backing for another year with Cllrs. Brockman, Lidstone, Perry, White, March and the Mayor(L.Goodrich !) all speaking on the clubs behalf. At the same meeting the Council also decided to again sponsor the Sea Angling Festival which had also lost money that year, but only £34 !.

An emergency meeting was held prior to the 1958 season since the Committee had been advised by both the architect, Dawes Dingle, and the building contractor, Bryant & Son, that the approved scheme of £1500 would be exceeded by some £400. After much discussion members agreed the extra and were told that over £800 had already been collected from the various events held. £1000 was to be paid on completion of the work and the rest over a two year period. The meeting was also told there would not be an all male club dinner but a cricket ball at the Palace Hotel which, it was anticipated, would bring in more money toward the pavilion fund. Club member, Leslie Goodrich and also the Mayor, said he would see that the event received plenty of publicity.

The A.G.M. at the Queen's Hotel in March members were told the work had gone well on the pavilion and it was expected to be opened for the first match. Reviewing the work Mr. Tucker went on to say "It is often said the pavilion is for the players, and that non playing members are denied the use, whereas actually they are our biggest financial support. Any of our members who want to use the pavilion from now on will be more than welcome". (At times the mind boggles as to what the club was really like years ago.)
R.J. Haly informed members that a new professional had been appointed to replace Dare and he was a left handed all rounder, Ronald Willson, a twenty four year old from Sussex. Mr. Thompson, treasurer, told the meeting the rent of the ground was to double that season but did not state the figure.

Before the first game it was all hands for the paint brush since, with the extension completed, skipper Dickinson decided that the enclosure railings had to be brought up to the mark. Actually the first game was away at Sidmouth and ended in a draw, while the official opening was a week later during the match with the Royal Naval College. The Mayor, A.L. Goodrich did the honours and was entertained to tea by the President, Mr. Lee-Barber.

A brief report explained how the club had lost the services of Eric Cooper, who had been mainly a first team player during the years he had been employed at the Dartmouth Naval College, but he had now taken a position at Bedford School. Derek Cole, such a wonderful all rounder for Torquay, would have more sporting duties at Dartmouth as a result of Cooper's moving, and he was not expected to be able to assist the club as often in the future.

Throughout the season, with all the touring sides to be played, it was interesting to see the number of local players who were called upon to help Torquay fulfil their fixtures. Roy Horswell of Barton and Don Mills of the Cockington Corinthians were two of many. Lloyds Bank on tour actually included Brian Stockman, well known locally since he was employed at their Torre branch, and played for South Devon. Reg Dare was soon back to the Recreation Ground playing for his new employers, Turner's Sports, who were on tour once again. Dare was at his best but this time taking Torquay wickets.

Paignton were badly handicapped in the derby game at the Rec. their professional, Jack Kelly damaging a leg muscle. Ron Willson with 6 for 29 helped to get Paignton all out for 105 before Torquay passed their total with only five wickets down. Late June saw the arrival in Torquay of nine of the Pakistan Eaglets who were staying at the local Y.M.C.A. They wanted the experience of playing on grass wickets prior to their arranged tour of England. Four turned out for Torquay v Weston-super-Mare and five for Paignton v Cauis College Cambridge. In Torquay's victory Amjad took 7 for 50 in 22 overs and Ramzan scored 49 not out. Over at Queen's Park, in another home victory, the Eaglets were also very much to the fore. Anis with 58 and Ijax 31 not out, helped Paignton with the runs while Anis 3 for 55, Iqbal 1 for 13 and Ijaz 1 for 20 did the necessary with the ball.

With Worcestershire promising to send a strong side after their game against Somerset Torquay recruited Hanif Muhammad, Israar Ali and Mohammad Ramzan from the Eaglets, Paignton's Jack Kelly and Harold Stephenson from Somerset for the encounter. To everyone's disappointment rain completely spoiled the first day but there was some great batting and bowling to remember on the second. Worcestershire were all out for 200, with the runs coming mainly from M.J.Horton 113 and R.Booth 55, two superb innings but Israar Ali and Hanif Muhammad had bowling figures of 6 for 54 and 4 for 51 respectively. In reply Torquay managed 171 for 7 when time called a halt to proceedings. Top scorer for the home side was Torquay's professional Willson with 51 not out, while several others had scores of twenty.

Nothing to do with this history but interesting! A Sunday match at Paignton saw the home side play Torquay United and as two United players were injured in training Ted Dickinson played, stressing his ex-Derby County connections! Torquay's pro Willson, was included in the side as an ex-Brighton footballer.

In the return derby game, despite the presence of Paignton's guest player Bob Clarke a former Northants fast bowler, Torquay came out on top. David Haines was in great form and took 7 for 23 in Paignton's all out total of 41. In point of fact Haines performance rather spoiled the day for a lot of the Paignton followers as it was Jack Kelly's benefit game. Both Whitehead and Bill Traylor had been on the injured list for several weeks and while the former went straight into the first team for the Paignton fixture Traylor had a number of second team games before he was considered again.

When Exeter came to the Rec. in August the game started over an hour late due to the state of the ground from the morning rain. That the match got under way lost one individual a small bet, as he thought it would be game number nine spoiled by the weather. A name not seen before on the score-card played that day, Peter Parsons, and a paper report explained he was at Haileybury school. A.E.Hitchman took 5 for 31 in Torquay's total of 117 for 8 while Haines, 4 for 34 and Willson 3 for 12 saw the home side through to victory by bowling Exeter all out for 74.

Two interesting topics cropped up during the August that year. Derek Cole was chosen to play for the Minor Counties against the touring New Zealand Test team. In all the years he became only the third Devonian to receive that honour since the war, Fairclough and Humphries being the others. Wardle had been picked to tour Australia with the Test team during the winter but was, rather abruptly, dismissed by Yorkshire. Speculation as to what might happen was quickly answered by the M.C.C. withdrawing his invitation to tour.

Whereas numerous games had been cancelled throughout the rather wet season the Festival had endless days of wonderful sunshine and all the cricketing stars of the era were on parade. The North v South was the first game and those present enjoyed three perfect days. Both sides completed their two innings and the South ran out the winners by 38 runs. Dews and Horton scored well for the North while Watkins and Ingleby-Mackenzie excelled for the South.

An England X1 v A Commonwealth X1 contained so many great cricketers of the time and most living up to their reputations. Brian Close cracking a century, Ken Barrington 75, Garfield Sobers 74, Frank Worrell 64, Peter Wight 67, Bill Alley 82 and then taking 4 for 40. The Commonwealth were left to get 256 on the last afternoon against the bowling of Tony Lock, Ray Illingworth, Les Jackson, Cliff Gladwin and Brian Close. That they did obtain a two wicket victory, before stumps were drawn, ended another fascinating two days for any cricket lover.

All too sadly the organisers knew this was to be the end of Festival Cricket in Torquay. Within days David Haines was explaining to the press, "that only on one day out of the six had there been enough bums on seats to meet expenses". Over two thousand people had attended that day whereas on the other days the cricket had been poorly supported
He went on to say the players and families had thoroughly enjoyed themselves and he had no difficulty persuading players to come to Torquay for the Festival games. While the decision was up to the Corporation there was no doubt in anyone's mind what the eventual outcome would be, for local cricket lovers it was the end of a wonderful idea.
Later in the year George Emmett was the guest speaker at the Chelston Cricket Club dinner and went on to say, "I have come to the conclusion that not enough people in the Torquay area are really interested in top line cricket. We had the weather this year and, on the day when Frank Worrell and Gary Sobers, two of the finest batsmen in the world were batting, there were not many people in the ground".

In no time at all the Torquay Athletic Rugby Club announced that they would have a Rugby festival in the September to commence their season, and it was hoped this would ensure the continuing publicity for the town. The Council were going to guarantee a sum of £300, since it was felt that the rugby would not be as badly affected by indifferent weather as the cricket club had been.

By the time of the 1959 A.G.M. the club had to accept the resignation of J.E.Dickinson as he had taken over the tenancy of the Mason's Arms public house and he felt he had to give more time to business. After four years as vice-captain to G.S.Butler and then seven years as the man in charge being captain and team secretary, many felt the latter position would be the hardest to fill. Getting mid-week sides together was no easy matter, as has been expressed before, and especially during August. David Haines was appointed captain and Tom Kirkham took over as team secretary. After being re-elected as President, Mr. Lee-Barber said he had been in office for 19 years and would resign next time. He went on to say,"five years ago the powers that be told me I was too old to be the clerk to the magistrates court, and now I am that much older my decision is irrevocable".
Interestingly Mr. Haly told the meeting that through the ladies providing teas they had benefited the club, over a period of seven seasons, to the extent of £1000. He also paid special thanks to the junior members who were responsible for selling ice-creams and the score cards. Mr.Haly confirmed the full £1000 had been paid to the builder but £900 was still outstanding.

What had become a regular pre-season opening match, against Cockington, fell foul of the weather and the first game was against Sidmouth. A new name on view was that of Roger Matthews who had joined the club, originally from Leicester but had taken a position locally as an estate agent. David Post, who had odd games previously, and had assisted Somerset Seconds, was also in the side. Mike Wicks and Bill Traylor were missing because of the injuries they received in their respective winter pastimes, rugby and soccer. Those who did not play saved their reputations, after David Post took four quick wickets and Ron Willson three, Sidmouth were all out for 66 and the game appeared finished. Being the game cricket is the end was near, at least for Torquay. Willson scored 13 runs and he was the only batsman in the team to get double figures, the other ten players making up the side managed a very inadequate 25 between them!

Numerous changes took place during the early games, Ken Peppiatt in and out of the first X1, Peter Goodrich, home from Blundell's and Torquay United's Ray Carter also getting first team places. The professional, Ron Willson, together with Derek Cole, in an unbroken stand of 114, were mainly responsible for a nine wicket victory at Mount Wise. During the Whitsun weekend Bill Hart was noted as having had successive centuries in the two games he played in, which helped the team to victories. Paignton's pro had Torquay all back in the pavilion for 101 and with the team Torquay had put onto the field things did not look healthy, the paper stated! Haines had "one of those days" and, in what was described as a "brilliant spell", he proceeded to take 8 for 41 and led his team, to what had appeared earlier, a very unlikely victory by eleven runs.

Throughout the season new young players were mentioned and Paul Twose was stated by one reporter as "having more patience than his father (Rocker) and was likely to develop into a useful lefthander". J.Kerr quickly established himself while Paul Hawkins came in for more than a little publicity. A 15 year old, Jeff Tolchard, played in the seconds at Plymouth and took 4 for 24 with no one realising what a career he was to have in the game. Rabukawaqa was a Fijian studying at the South Devon Technical College who had several games for the third X1 and from the records available his claim to fame was four cheap wickets against Ipplepen. Gordon Baker appeared regularly for the seconds with odd midweek appearances and is still to be seen umpiring in 2002.

When Torquay played the Pakistan Eaglets and the Australian Collegians they augmented their side with guests of the calibre of Frank Worrell, Bill Alley and Harold Stephenson. Intikhab Alam and Masood Haider, guesting for Torquay played against the touring Old Tiffinians and did immense damage with the ball, ensuring a ten wicket victory, very unfair!

Ted Dickinson did find time for the occasional game, to keep his hand he said, while on the rare visits of Derek Cole he showed his usual form with bat and ball. Late in the season when Cole brought his Western Dolphin X1 side Torquay were hanging on desperately for a draw when stumps were drawn. That was one of the sixteen drawn games of the season when only eighteen of the forty eight played were won. Willson had completed the double, 1000 runs and 100 wickets, but was not available for September as he was contracted to a Western League football club. At that time numerous first team games were played during September, away at clubs who had their own ground.

Late in August the seconds and third team were away to Exeter with traffic reports at their worst. The respective captains, Stuart Swift and Harry Snape led the car convoy via Chudleigh and numerous back lanes to ensure they arrived on time and missed the miles of queues. Local knowledge put to good use.

Early in 1960 the Brockman Cup Committee met and the Narracott club secretary, Reg. Treeby, put forward the suggestion that all games should take place on a Sunday. He was not referring to the Cup competition but all games! His argument was that so many people worked on Saturday morning that it was becoming more and more difficult to be on time when travelling away.

Torquay's first big issue that year was to find a new President as Mr. Lee-Barber stuck to his statement of "20 years being quite sufficient". The A.G.M. confirmed life membership for him and his wife in recognition of all the work they had done on the club's behalf. K.R.Bryant, the ex-Mayor, Councillor and wicket-keeping batsman, was elected to take over as President. H.Thompson, treasurer, reported that the pavilion extension costs had been paid although there was still a £400 loan from the National Playing Fields Association still to be met. A surprise awaited the players. They were told the club had received an invitation to send a side to Taunton on the 28th.April, to give the Somerset first X1 a competitive game as a limbering up exercise for the County rather than another day in the nets.

No details could be found of the venture but in a press statement announcing Ron Willson's impending departure, he was to take up a coaching position in Rhodesia in early June, it said the Taunton trip had been very useful and it was hoped to repeat it again next year. Since the season was about to start and most professionals were under contract the club was fortunate that David Post stepped in as the season's pro. to replace Willson. A regular tourist with the Glamorgan Nomads had come to live locally, Ben Williams was accepted into the club with open arms.

The traditional opener at Cockington took place and a schoolboy starlet, Robert Coombe, took somebody's eye as the following week-end he became a Torquay player and was in the second X1 that played at the Dartmouth Naval College.

In the first derby of the season Paignton were badly depleted, so many of their players had gone over to Sidmouth where one of their members, Brian Lang was getting married. Haines 5 for 45 and Willson 5 for 40 ensured a very easy victory. The City of London Police, on their first visit, inflicted the first defeat of the season and asked for a fixture the following season while still at the bar later in the evening. That season there had been yet another pavilion change, Eddie Parry, a long time member had donated a large plate glass window which enabled drinkers to stand at the bar and watch the game, and yes the bar was in a different position in those days!

Another Cricket Ball was held at the Palace Hotel as well as a couple of club dances at other venues, in order to raise monies to clear the debt to the Playing Fields and re-equip the kitchen. Mrs Tucker, who always did so much behind the catering scene also held canasta drives in the pavilion on days when there was no game. (Canasta, dear reader, was a very popular card game well into the sixties!) The profit from all these functions was just under £500 and rather gratifying to those who organised them.

The Reverend G.H.Nicholson was appointed to a parish in Dartmouth and, having had experience with Devon Dumplings and Tiverton, decided to join Torquay. Either in the seconds or thirds every week he became a reliable club player. This was yet another season when there were frequent moans regarding the difficulty of getting mid-week teams together. Actually when one really investigates there are several tales to be told regarding the make up of midweek teams. John Perry, at the time of the writer's researches the owner of the Livermead Cliff Hotel and a great friend to the club, was during his playing days a medium fast bowler from the time he was at Charterhouse with Peter May. All through his training, at the Palace Hotel, he had to be a midweek player, as did R.Turpin, a very good wicket-keeper. Both were very rarely available on Saturdays because of their professional calling, as the weekends, during the summer, are the hotels busiest period. Bill Traylor tells the story, confirmed in discussion with Ted Dickinson, that when he was an apprentice with Vanstone Ted would phone the foreman when he was short of a player and would ask if Bill was available for the afternoon. He was always told "Yes, but Bill would not be paid"! Bill knew Ted would pay him either five or ten shillings depending how well he performed.

An example of the attitude towards cricket in those happy days was when the Plymouth Seconds arrived on Saturday afternoon. Heavy rain had made the square unplayable but as the ground dried out the players took an early tea. Members rolled and marked a wicket at the sea-end, not ideal but as the report said, " it was not a wasted journey". To all concerned it was disappointing that the same was not possible when the Australian Old Collegians arrived, members loved their visits and they were popular in the bar.

Malcolm Kerr, Torquay's opening bat had a great season for the club and was chosen for Devon after a 93 against South Devon. Along with wicket-keeper John Bonner he played against Berkshire at the Recreation Ground and although the first day was washed out it was thanks to Jack Kelly, the Paignton pro, that Devon won by 89 runs. Poor Kerr, despite his excellent club form he had five innings for Devon and his total of runs was only a mere 44.

Torquay's return game with Paignton in Queen's Park occurred when Kerr and Bonner were away playing for Devon, with Bryan Lang and the then promising Roy Kerslake back in the home side, supporters wondered what might happen. As it transpired everyone performed to their full capabilities and followers came back happy with another win over the "old enemy". Interesting to note that the club umpires that day were Jack Padfield and Bert Whitehead, stalwarts of their respective clubs and still helping out at an age when others tended to put their feet up.

Sadly the rain, which affected so many of the August fixtures, struck when George Emmett brought down the Gloucestershire seconds. No play was possible during the morning and after an early lunch, and before a small Bank Holiday crowd, Emmett and A'Court went out to bat. Trying to make up for lost time the two openers gave the County a great start with 55 and 46 respectively before a declaration was made at 164 for 5. Torquay lost opener Colin Williams for 13 and at 16 for 1 the heavy rain washed out any chance of further play.

That season a special game was arranged between the Brockman Cup winners and a representative side which included a Torquay third team lad of great promise,

"Bobby" Combe. He certainly showed his promise that day and took all ten wickets for just seventeen runs, and at the Brockman Dinner later he was presented with the ball, mounted and inscribed.

A reporter summarised the cricket season as,"rather like the weather, some bright days but generally very disappointing". Soft wickets and negative bowling were given as the reasons that only 13 wins were recorded out of the 48 games played.True only 12 were lost but half the games having no result did not appear to please the members. One man, who despite the weather, enjoyed his first season as the professional was David Post who took 89 wickets, supported by Haines and Irving who had 62 and 51 respectively. For the first time in several summers there was no record of a batsman obtaining a century.

Everyone at the club and in cricketing circles generally, were devastated by the sudden death of David Haines in the December of 1960.at 46 years of age. He came to Devon after the war and was living at Yealmpton, near Plymouth. He was introduced into the Torquay club by his brother which was a most fortunate happening , not only for his playing qualities but he will always be remembered as the organiser of those Cricketing Festivals which brought so many world famous players to the Recreation Ground. Well known as a B.B.C. sports commentator he was closely associated with Ted Dickinson, joining him in the sports outfitters in Torwood Street before taking over completely in 1957. Haines became vice-captain to Dickinson for some years before taking over when Ted relinquished the captaincy. A huge attendance at the church heard the Rev. W.J.Troop sum up David Haines's life in cricketing terms. "In the old days of cricket there were 'gentlemen' and 'players' but David Haines, in his life and his character, combined these two headings to a greater extent than anyone I have ever known".

At the March A.G.M. the President requested all members to stand as a mark of respect after he had opened with a tribute to the memory of Mr. Haines.V.G.Tucker announced that after much discussion the committee had decided to ask Ted Dickinson to resume the captaincy again and he had eventually agreed, choosing as his understudy George Irving. The new professional was to be Jack Kelly, who had been such a success at Paignton. David Post had obtained permanent employment but would still be available to play for the club at weekends. H .H. Thompson then spoke about the falling membership, the elders dying off and young new members not being recruited. He went on to say that had it not been for the £50 payment made to the club for parking, during the visit of the circus, expenditure would have exceeded income.

Alan Hitchman, who had played on occasions in previous seasons, was announced as a new member as was Ghan Patel.With the wet weather causing cancellations the first game was not played until the 14th.May, when the Dartmouth Naval College were beaten. Hitchman started with 3 for 16 and in the following games took 5 for

27, and 3 for 30. While Jack Kelly took a little longer to find his form he was in his element against Glamorgan Nomads, 7 for 21 and helped in another victory over Taunton, 3 for 20. As the season progressed Kelly was consistent with bat and ball while Paul Twose, Roger Matthews, Malcolm Kerr and George Irving were all chipping in with better than average performances.

A sign of the times, nothing to do with Torquay but with cricket. In late June it was announced that portable radios were to be banned from Lord's cricket ground, as in the writer's opinion they should be from every cricket field.

Little did anyone realise that when Devon took on Berkshire in a Minor Counties match at the Recreation Ground in August that they were about to see a bit of history made. Batting first Devon ran up a total of 249 with Yeabsley contributing 41 not out and Fairclough 41. Berkshire had a father and son combination playing and the lad was just 17. The young Joe Mence, in his debut for the county bowled 32 overs, eleven being maidens, and had figures of 5 for 81, quite a performance for a 17 year old. When Berkshire began their reply Mence senior soon had 56 to his name before getting caught from the bowling of Jack Kelly, and at the close of play on the first day his son was out for 4, with the total at 149 for 7. Kelly had taken all seven wickets for just 59 runs and discussions were all about the chance of "all ten" the following morning. He did just that and had bowling figures of, 20:1 overs, 5 maidens, 50 runs and 10 wickets. I could find no record of the ball being mounted and given to Jack Kelly but surely it must have been! Devon declared at 143 for 7 and Berkshire were 122 for 3 when stumps were drawn. A tame result but long remembered by Devon supporters for Jack Kelly's bowling.

August saw several strong touring sides suffer defeat by the various sides Torquay were able to put into the field midweek. Against the Staffordshire Pirates, still coming on tour in 2004, Kelly had a great day, scoring 71 with the bat and then taking 7 for 6, a very popular man in the bar with the home team! John Bonner and David Post were both absent with Devon, when Plymouth came at the end of the season and took away Torquay's unbeaten Saturday record. Kerr, Kelly and Roger Matthews were all out for very little and only Paul Twose, in partnership with Colin Williams and Peter Goodrich gave the home side a respectable 163 for 7, Twose being responsible for 68.

The September games in those far off days were not second class fixtures and with holidays finished, the end of school and college vacations, plus rugby and soccer taking its toll many lesser players enjoyed first team places. Jack Kelly passed his 2000 runs for the season at Tiverton Heathcoat. Tom Tolchard was noted as umpiring at Tavistock in September while Peter Hobbs had umpired a number of first team matches during the season.

When Ralph Haly summed up the season he said, "After losing David Haines few people would have believed the club would have such a successful season.

Persuading Ted Dickinson to take up the mantle again, with his great fortune with the toss, his leadership and the ability to get players, were all big factors in the team's success". In the first team games the toss was won on 35 occasions out of the 55. (the author would suggest Ted's "great fortune with the toss" was his opposite number calling wrongly!). The record of 35 victories was the most in any season since 1934. Torquay had declared on 29 occasions and only once had been bowled out for less than a hundred. Jack Kelly had scored three centuries and had been out in the nineties on three occasions. Following his excellent performances for Devon he had been selected to play for the Minor Counties against the Australian tourists, joining Butler and Cole who had been thus honoured from the Torquay Club. Mr Haly also paid tribute to J. Swift, Ken Gale and Harry Snape for all the work they did with the second and third team players, "always there to help and guide he said".

1962 began with the amazing news that the Brockman Committee had decided, that with a diminishing bank balance, the admission to their Cup Final would be increased to one shilling, (5p) but earlier rounds would still be six pence. To the present day reader it is probably hard to imagine that as many as five hundred people would attend a final and, on certain teams appearances, more than that.

Torquay Cricket Club's A.G.M. was unusual in that there were three nominations for the position of first team captain. J.E. Dickinson felt it was time for a younger man to take the reins, plus the fact that he would have certain business duties that summer. The committee then showed members they were not in unison on the matter when team secretary, Tom Kirkham, said only players should vote for a captain. V. G. Tucker (Chairman) was against that as he felt that the committee gave more thought to the suitability of individuals and continued, "The captain has to have time for mid-week games, a certain amount of ability, and the necessary qualities to entertain guest sides of many seasons". Peter Ely then suggested that the players and committee should be the ones to decide and members should have no say in the matter. After discussion the previous vice-captain, George Irving was chosen to take over from Dickinson. No sooner had the captaincy question been settled than Mr Tucker dropped another bombshell by telling the meeting the committee had approached the Corporation for a new lease which had to exclude the ban on Sunday cricket! The President, Ken Bryant, explained that junior clubs on Corporation grounds had Sunday cricket and Torquay wanted to be in the same position if the players wanted it. Ralph Haly then pointed out if it was agreed, no play would start until 2p.m, and there would be a no gate money ruling. The Lord's Day Observance Society, already mentioned, would not allow monies to be taken. (the writer's personal feeling is that the Society was a menace to all sorts of sporting functions, irrespective of the cause they were held for).

The preliminary games that season, at Taunton and Cockington were worth noting. For the trip to play Somerset Torquay took along the Devon bowler Gerald Trump and with P.B. Wight retiring on 56, Bill Alley 46 and Ian Lomax 65 Somerset declared on 230 for 8. Trump was the most successful bowler with 3 for 43 while Post and Cole only managed a wicket each. Torquay found it hard batting against some class bowling and only Malcolm Kerr with 52 in Torquay's 112 for 7 showed early season form.

Although the club won by eighty runs in their Cockington Corinthians match some of the batsmen had quite a fright when they encountered the new bowler that Cockington had acquired. From 81 for 1 Torquay suddenly found themselves 93 for 6. Ken Steer, a Westminster Bank employee who was always in their touring sides, had been transferred to the West Country and he took 5 for 72, including three wickets in a single over. Don Mills who had occasional midweek games for Torquay also did well taking 3 for 6. Paul Twose with 55 and Jack Kelly 54, after his 6 for 22, sealed the victory in an interesting game against a so called junior side.

After three consecutive wet weekends Tiverton Heathcoat were the first to face and fall to the Torquay club. Torquay struggled to 139 for 7 with Paul Twose making 57 of that total. When the visitors were 123 for 4 most spectators were anticipating defeat but Jack Kelly 6 for 31 soon wrapped up the tail and the visitors were a few runs short when the game finished. As far as the writer is able to tell this was the first, first team game for Barrie Matthews who played for St. Marychurch midweek and a Torquay team on a Saturday.

During research a number of names were continually missing from team sheet records and included, Alan Sibley, Alan Hitchman and Nic Chamberlin. These three were, it was discovered, frequently off for athletic meetings or Territorial Army training.

June was quite a month, not only for club victories but for Ted Dickinson in particular. Having played in a couple of games, and with Trowbridge turning up short of players, he and Braham Fredman decided to play for the visitors. The scorebook reveals the visitors were all out for 66 with Hitchman taking 6 for 10. More revealing is the detail, Dickinson 26 and Fredman 31, what the score might have been without Ted and Braham's contributions one shudders to think. However the last match of the month, against a team of accountants from Bristol, the "Adders", saw Torquay's first defeat. Having scored 189, supporters felt it was a big enough total but with the last pair at the wicket in the last over the visitors won off the penultimate ball, great entertainment on a lovely afternoon!

July saw the first of two centuries by Jack Kelly, 123 against Exmouth who quickly settled for a draw after Torquay had declared at 231 for 3. His 165 against Barnes ensured another comfortable victory, but he only got fifty against the Imperial College as the damage had been done by Ben Williams, who had seven Imperial wickets for twenty nine runs and another century was not required!

The month also saw the first Saturday defeat and as such really did receive press attention. Hounslow were the victors and the young Barrie Matthews, with 50, was the highest scorer, thirty runs more than the next best, Alan Sibley. Torquay's 137 for 7 did not look too bad when Hounslow were 99 for 7 but, even with Kelly's 4 for 44 their total became 138 for 8 and that was that.

During the August Torquay had a home and away fixture with Paignton plus a Wednesday game at the Recreation Ground. For the midweek game Paignton arrived with only ten players so Ted Dickinson put aside his umpires coat and played for the opposition. Torquay declared on 189 for 8 but with Paignton on 133 and Dickinson, still at the wicket with 44 to his credit, the game ended in a draw.

For several years, during the holiday period, the club's schoolboys had a midweek game against the Old Grammarians. In this year it was decided to make it a 12 aside game with Torquay's boys captained by Harry Snape, the Thirds skipper. His team read, B.Bettesworth (Oratory), A.Bradburn (Highgate), G.Gregory (Taunton), R.Lear (Crediton), M.Williams (T.G.S.), M.Goodrich (Blundell's), S.Sullivan (Malvern), T.Sanbrook, P.Whatton (both T.G.S.), R.Coombe (S.D.C) and J.Arlott (Highgate).The last named being the son of the famous commentator John Arlott.
Old Grammarians were represented by, W.Webster, R.Gerard, H.Lowe, C.Beer, C.Nex, T.Knowles, O.Christie, R.Linnett, A.Libby, R.Brooks, J.Westlake and K.Crabtree.Under Harry Snape's leadership the club's boys declared at 193 for 5 with Bettesworth contributing 86 not out. Gerard had bowling figures of 3 for 37 and then he scored 46 of the 97 runs the Old Grammarians were able to manage. Lear had seven wickets for just twenty six runs and eventually became a very useful member of the club, both on and off the field. Many of the other players, in both teams, became club members in the ensuing years as will be seen as this history unrolls.

One of the games in late August saw a happening that occurs occasionally but not very frequently. The touring side Old Olavians were beaten at the Rec. by a team containing two fathers and their two respective sons.Tom Tolchard, who had been umpiring more regularly than playing, opened the innings with Leslie Goodrich and were later followed by Roger and Jeffery Tolchard and Michael and Peter Goodrich. While Jack Kelly and Alan Hitchman had already set the scene for a victory by each taking 3 for 14, the senior Tolchard top scored with 20 and the young Peter Goodrich 15.

George Irving was not available to take the team to Sidmouth near the end of the season so David Post was to captain the side. Bert Whitehead travelled to umpire but there was no explanation as to why A.Pegg was not available to take his usual position in the white coat.That same week there was a short article in the Torquay Times to the effect that the club would not be renewing the professional's contract. Later Victor Tucker the chairman refused to answer any questions despite great pressure, it was pointed out Jack Kelly had again done the 'double' and had scored four hundred runs in his last seven innings!

Mr. Haly, in his summing up of the season admitted Kelly had a batting average of almost fifty but would not enlighten the press as to why J.K. was not retained. He felt the club could look forward with confidence with the younger players making their mark. During the season Alan Sibley had established his place in the first team, Barrie Matthews had a few matches in the firsts and was a definite for that side in the future. Commenting on how much John Bonner had been missed behind the stumps, the secretary went on to say, "16 year old Roger Tolchard was probably the youngest ever Devon keeper when he played against Somerset 2nds and certainly has the makings of a good un".

During the research for this book there were times when the writer wished he had been at a "particular match or one of those meetings" and the A.G.M. of 1963 at the Queen's Hotel was one of those occasions. Prompted by the retiring captain, George Irving, members were urged to vote and accept a proposal for six Sunday matches a season. He explained that many of the players were in favour since so many of them could not play midweek due to business committments, and there was the possibility of players going to clubs where Sunday cricket took place. Cynic that the writer is, he laughed when he read that Ted Dickinson was against the proposal. Ted was reported as saying, "Sunday cricket interferes with the midweek", "restrict it to six and I will accept it". This from an individual who had been going all over the County on Sundays for years with his Dickinson X1.or going across to Paignton for a game! (Ted laughed when I reminded him of that and promised him it would be in the 'history'). Ralph Haly was against any Sunday play whereas Tom Kirkham pointed out that other clubs played and had overcome the snags that were being discussed, before going on to say, "Give the lads a chance". An unnamed lady said she was not prepared to do teas on a Sunday, whereupon another jumped up and said she would! David Post told the meeting several first team players were all in favour and felt they could muster sufficient females to provide the teas. Ken Bryant pointed out that under the terms of the lease it would mean another £30 rental charge and the Corporation would not provide the labour to mark out the wicket on a Sunday. Since play could not start until after two o'clock and no money could be taken at the gate the proposal needed careful consideration. However when a vote was taken the proposal was passed by 32 to 13. Alderman Leslie Goodrich then asked the meeting to consider "an entertainment allowance for the captain of the first team". He pointed out it was an unnecessary financial burden for the captain to be paying for drinks to entertain the visiting players. After a certain amount of discussion the idea was approved and it was left for the committee to work out the details. A.L.Goodrich then informed the meeting that Mrs. Ann Haines, in memory of her late husband David, was donating a wrought-iron railing enclosure to replace the existing wooden one, there would be double gates incorporating D.L.H. at the entrance to the pavilion. The gift was "accepted with deep gratitude" and the meeting elected Mrs. Haines a life member.

Joint first team captains were elected, J.E.Dickinson and David Post with R.W.Matthews their vice-captain. J.Swift was to take charge of the second X1 with K.E.Gale his understudy and H.Snape had yet another year with the thirds with Leo Matthews his second in command.

Before play commenced it was announced that the new professional would be D.J.Semmence and, like Kelly, he had built up quite a reputation locally, with Paignton. He was introduced to all the players when Dickinson and Post held a cheese and pickled onion evening in the pavilion. One other new face for the team to meet was that of Brian Stockhill, a Yorkshireman who had played in the Bradford League. On moving down to Kingsbridge he had written to the Devon County C.C.asking for a club to join and they had, fortunately, recommended he joined Torquay. A wicket-keeper batsman he soon proved his worth in the first eleven. Wet weather again prevented the nets from being erected but the mid-week Taunton exercise went ahead against Somerset. They had a slow bowler on trial, David Doughty, who assisted Torquay and he took 4 for 63 in the Somerset total of 227. Malcolm Kerr opened and scored 53 runs followed by Semmence with 43 and Peter Goodrich 40, but the rest fell cheaply and Torquay were 57 runs adrift at the end.

Former Torquay favourite Bob Stainton shook more than one of his ex-colleagues in the traditional opening Saturday game at Cockington by taking 5 for 54 in a total of 127 for 9.However, the soft wicket had made scoring difficult and this was endorsed when the Cockington lads were only able to post 52 for 6 at the end of play, with C.Heath on 30. After his spell in Rugby League, with Huddersfield, Mike Wicks had returned to the town and was ready to play cricket again.

The official inauguration of the Haines railings was before the St. Luke's game on May 18th. Mrs Haines was unable to attend so her daughter, Mrs. Sneyd, deputised for her. The President, Ken Bryant,said, "It was appropriate that the railings should put the finishing touch to a pavilion in whose re-building David Haines had been such a prime mover". It is probably hard to imagine how neat the enclosure looked when those new railings replaced the old wooden ones that were there and dozens of small folding chairs filled the member's only enclosure.

   During the game the St.Luke's skipper had Torquay in all kinds of trouble, especially with his bowling but the last pair managed to bat out time. Luke's had only managed 121, with captain Cope top scorer with 34. Kerr with 37 and Twose 34 gave Torquay a good start but then Cope took 4 for 9 in eight overs and the struggle began. Interesting to those who knew them, David Post took 6 for 27 but was bowled for a duck by the future Devon bowler Yeabsley, after David had Yeabsley for the same score!

Headlines during the month of May made much of the fact that Barrie Matthews had a ticket for the Cup Final. He was off to Wembley and would not be in the team to play Tiverton Heathcoat. Soon afterwards Peter Goodrich left the town to further his career in Godalming, Surrey.

Batting for over two and a half hours for 136 for 5, Torquay's performance was not at all impressive against Paignton. However their bowling certainly made an impression, Paignton's innings lasting just seventy minutes for 32 runs. Post had 7 for 8 in 10:2 overs and Irving 3 for 11 in 10 overs, which made everyone realise just how difficult batting had been in the conditions.

Whitsun was not a happy weekend, Monday and Tuesday's games were lost to the weather and on the Wednesday Torquay lost to the Glamorgan Nomads, by five runs, when neither side managed a three figure total.

During the June a newspaper headline announced the fact that Torquay would have to put up with only one captain for a while as David Post was getting married and would be away on his honeymoon. With reports of Ben Williams taking 4 for 9, Alan Hitchman 6 for 70 and Robert Coombe 4 for 19 as well as the batsmen getting runs it did not appear that D.P. was too badly missed.

Alan Sibley who had joined the club while at the Grammar School, had worked his way through to the first X1 but was one of those players frequently "missing" from the team sheet. Research revealed he was also quite an athlete, his absence from the cricket field during the time he was at St.Luke's was because he was running for the University .One report found, quoted him as missing from the Torquay X1 to run for Devon in the A.A.A. Championship at Devonport where he won both the 100 and 400 yards and in the latter, to everyone's astonishment, set a new record time of 50:2 second. The sensation was due to the fact he was running entirely alone, there being no other entrants.

Somerset brought a strong team down for a match arranged as a benefit for one of their players, Peter Wight. Guesting for Torquay was Cecil Pepper from Lancashire League and in the one day game there was some very entertaining cricket. Somerset declared on 264 for 9 after Graham Atkinson had hit 97 in 55 minutes. Pepper had 5 for 96 and Alan Hitchman 3 for 67. When Torquay batted Paul Twose gave the home side a good start with 41, but as the drizzle became rain, and with Derek Semmence 53 not out the game was abandoned as a draw.

Both Paignton, for their professional's benefit, and Torquay, played Torquay United in the same week. Whereas Paignton managed to beat the footballers Torquay did not as the Paignton pro played for the Torquay United team against Torquay and took 6 for 33, as well as scoring 63 runs. Sibley 47 and Fredman 26 were the only batsmen who seemed able to cope with his bowling. Hitchman actually took 8 for 69 and hardly deserved to be on the losing side. Torquay's home game with Paignton was washed out by torrential rain when the home side were 103 for 4.

In reviewing the season the secretary said, "Although more defeats were sustained there had been two more victories than the previous season and two less drawn! The honours, as regards the batting, had gone to Derek Semmence who had scored 1874 runs at an average of just over 50 and was definitely being re-engaged as the professional for the next season. Jeff Tolchard and Brian Stockhill had been regularly available for the mid-week team and had strengthened it accordingly. Stockhill had proved a first class wicket-keeper, taking over forty victims behind the stumps, and had scored well over 700 runs. Alan Hitchman, with 112 wickets, had managed a feat no amateur had done for the club for more than twenty five years, had he been available on more Saturdays the total would of course been higher still. Roger Matthews, Malcolm Kerr, Alan Hitchman, Roger and Jeff Tolchard had all played for Devon during the season".

Reviewing the previous season at the A.G.M. in 1964 caused a lot of discussion, and when it was announced that the Committee were putting up the subscriptions, that did bring members to their feet! A Mr. Wildblood said refreshments had gone up the previous season by 50% and he wanted that discussed. The President's wife, Mrs. Bryant, at that time very much part of the ladies committee, replied ,"sixpence is not excessive for a fresh cup of tea with as much milk and sugar as you like, the ladies work hard and have supplied over 1800 meals". Leslie Goodrich, a vice-president, told the meeting there were many vice-presidents that never came near the ground and might, with an increase, cancel their existing payment. Eventually it was agreed that the subs for vice-presidents would remain at £2 and two shillings, but all other subscriptions would increase. Harry Snape who had completed thirty years with the club, playing in every team and at that time "fathering the thirds" was made a life member on the motion of J.E. Dickinson.

The early season games arranged for Taunton and Cockington were washed out by the weather as was the first Saturday fixture at Chudleigh. Initial results were poor but how the bowlers must have felt after returning figures of, Post 3 for 14, Roger Matthews 3 for 16, Derek Semmence 6 for 16 and each time on the losing side! (The author can only conjecture.) Whit Monday saw the first victory when Bridgewater were beaten, Stockhill and Sibley getting the runs and David Post taking 7 for 21.

Jim Parks of Sussex, in his benefit year arranged a game at the Recreation ground and the club, through the courtesy of Mrs. Haines, invited Sir Frank Worrell to play. He had another engagement but promised to come and play against the Australian Old Collegians in late July. However, on the day of that fixture both Parks and his county captain, Ted Dexter, were in the M.C.C. team playing the Australians at Lord's, but otherwise the full county team came for the game. Actually it was "games", the reason being that over the two days Torquay were to have different guest players, including, Brian Handley (Paignton professional), Terry Barwell (St. Luke's captain) and David Shepherd. The latter a North Devon player, who went on to become one of the elite International umpires, but can still be seen at the Instow ground when he is home. Sadly both days were a complete wash-out and while

Sussex paid their own travelling expenses Torquay were left to pick up the hotel bills which were estimated at over £100.

When the Old Collegians arrived Sir Frank was unable to keep his promise having broken a finger. Both sides had twelve men but only eleven were allowed to field at any given time. The visitors batted first and made a poor start losing six wickets for 49 runs but, recognised batsmen, going in much lower than usual, took the score to 179 for 10. Semmence had 4 for 42 and Hitchman 4 for 59. Torquay fared little better and lost wickets cheaply being seven wickets down for only eighty runs. Ben Williams joined Brian Stockhill and they put on some twenty runs before the former Torquay captain, George Irving, replaced Williams and began the run chase. He and Ted Dickinson were still there when stumps were drawn but the score was only 154 for 9, and Irving had 31 not out.

During July both the cricket and rugby authorities had cause for worry, at a Council meeting numerous councillors were advocating the need for more amenities for children and putting forward suggestions for the use of the Recreation Ground! The President of the Trades Council, W.V.Cooper J.P., pointed out that £75,000 had been spent on Torre Valley and the ground was little used, whereas in his opinion it could be the base for both the cricket and rugby clubs. A comprehensive sea-front scheme, including the Recreation Ground with children's amenities, would be revenue producing and beneficial to the town. (Now, as the writer records this, yet again the revenue problem crops up!)

The Rec. was host to thousands of people during that summer. In addition to the cricket spectators the Police held their sports day and the locals, as well as holidaymakers, poured in to see Lynn Davies, Bruce Tulloh and Janet Simpson etc. participating.

A strong, but not full strength, Somerset side came for a Sunday fixture which ended in a drawn game. With Bill Alley 52, Williams 44 and Greetham 32 not out, Somerset declared at 195 for 6. Hitchman had taken four of the six wickets for 108 runs. Torquay did not sit on the splice and in the two hours left for play made 158 for 8, Semmence 52, Patel 25 and Roger Matthews 29 not out.

Before August Ghan Patel was off back to his native Kenya. Mainly a second team player on Saturdays, he had a number of midweek games and was a member of the team that won the Len Coldwell Cup at South Devon. For history, the other members were R.Williams, B.Bettesworth, H.G.Baker, A. Rich and A. Holloway. Mention of cups, an innovation during the latter part of the season was the introduction of a Single Wicket competition, which was won by Michael Goodrich who defeated Robert Coombe in the final, after each had eliminated more fancied opponents.

Team sheets show Jack Blood, a former South Devon player, frequently playing throughout the season. One week in July Derek Semmence really entertained the crowd on successive days, against Reading he had 5 for 62 and then 103 not out, the next, against Cirencester another 104.

Near the end of the season a new electric clock had been placed in the pavilion with an inscribed plaque stating, "Presented by Miss Edna Douglas in memory of her brother J.W.H.T.Douglas". Numerous supporters asked "who was J.W.H.T.?" a question cricket lovers should be able to answer! However the writer was unable to find out details of Miss Douglas. Why did she wait some twenty odd years before presenting the clock and had she been a regular supporter? For the younger reader Johnny-Won't-Hit-Today-Douglas was so nick-named by the Australians from whom he recaptured the Ashes in 1912 when he captained the Test team, as he did in some 18 games. Following the 1914-18 war, during which he attained the rank of Lt. Colonel, he again took an M.C.C. side to Australia and in 1924-5 toured again in Gilligan's side. He captained the England team in the first two tests when the Australians came here in 1921 but was deposed in favour of Tennyson, although still retaining his place in the team. Douglas won an Olympic boxing medal in 1908 when he defeated Tom Richards in the middle weight final. (Tom Richards is the only Australian rugby player who has also played for the British Lions) Douglas died in 1930 when the ship in which he was travelling with his father was in a collision in the Baltic Sea. Questions were being asked again in 2002 when several bench seats in the enclosure were being given a long overdue overhaul. Roger Biddick took off a brass plate and cleaned same to read the inscription. So, as yet, there is another mystery, what happened to the clock? who put the plate on the seat?. As this is being written in 2003, the plate has yet to be displayed again in the pavilion and it is a piece of "club memorabilia" that should be treasured.

J. E. Dickinson was elected captain for the fourteenth time in 1965 but he told members they must start looking for a younger man. The treasurer told the assembly that the £30 extra rent had been well and truly covered by the Sunday monies for tea and the bar takings. Good wishes were sent to Roger Tolchard who had been signed by Leicestershire to start his cricketing career. Ralph Haly thanked the vice-captain of the seconds for the work he had done during the winter, which included making a complete new sight screen, before introducing a new member, Ian Scofield, a former captain of Nottingham University cricket.

What had become the Taunton Day did not take place but the trip out to Cockington did. Sadly play ended at tea time with the heavy rain making matters impossible. The first Saturday match was a drawn game with Chudleigh, Semmence getting the first century of the new season and Jeff Tolchard 60. While David Post took 4 for 23 and Roger Matthews 3 for 15, 'Doc' Emmett, the Devon rugby player, held Chudleigh together until stumps.

The fascination of research, well it has been for the writer. Ghan Patel, back from Kenya, was noticed playing for the Seconds on a Saturday and then playing for the Corinthians on a Sunday with Barney Bettesworth doing exactly the same. In a different way the reports of the club's games against H.M.S.Thunderer, over several years, are just as interesting. How one man could make a team is a mystery but, if Roger Moylan-Jones was in the naval side Torquay rarely won, when he was absent playing for the Free Foresters it was an entirely different story. This season Barrie Matthews, Gerald Birt and Jeff Tolchard had made most of the runs in Torquay's 159 for 7 and Roger Matthews, 6 for 16 had the barracks all out for 67, with no R.M-J in sight! Similarly his presence in his home team of Paignton appeared to give them more victories when he was playing.

Alderman Arthur Elson, President of the Chelston cricket club and Mayor-elect, was invited to bring his team to the Recreation Ground for a Sunday fixture in honour of his forthcoming civic position. In those days the club had so many councillor members and the committee were "alive" to every opportunity to build friends. Bill Traylor, who has already been mentioned with his bowling exploits for Torquay, went back to Chelston, for personal reasons, and with his experience had guided that club to better things. He enhanced their fixture list, had taken them on various tours and, as will be explained later, really was a man in advance of time. This was to be Chelston's first game against Torquay although they had played at the Rec. in Brockman and Narracott cup finals. Batting first Torquay scored 187 for 7 with Handley 51, Sibley 34 and Clarkson 31. Bill Traylor captured 3 for 11 and his brother David 3 for 57. Apart from David Traylor with 48 runs, none of the others were able to cope with Torquay's bowling and were all out for 73. Interestingly David Traylor played for Devon while still at that junior club but later came to Torquay along with his brother Bill who eventually returned to the fold.

Umpire A.R.Pegg and his co-federate, scorer C.W.Wootton, had worked in tandem for some time but with a heart problem the latter was forced to take it easy from the June of that season.

Another season and Torquay were again second best to St. Luke's College, having declared at 154 for 8 and left Torquay over two hours batting supporters were sure "our batting will do that". Moffatt, a fast bowling rugby player from Oxfordshire had other ideas and took 7 for 24, including clean bowling David Post in the last over, which ensured his teams victory.

The new professional at Paignton that year was the man to become a famous umpire in his white cap, none other than Dickie Bird. However, it was that man again Moylan-Jones, well supported by Brian Sambrook, who saw Paignton earn a draw when it appeared Torquay would win. In the June Ted Dickinson led a Torbay X1 in Queen's Park against Turner's Sports taking with him from Torquay, Semmence, Roger Matthews, Handley and Birt. Semmence had 80 not out which was the basis of Torbay's 143 for 8. Hadley took 6 for 53, Matthews 3 for 44 and Semmence took the last wicket a few minute before stumps were due to be drawn.

Derek Semmence had his benefit match against a "Show-Biz X1" which was described as "most successful". Mike Sangster of tennis fame, played for Torquay as he had done in the midweek team on odd occasions. Comedian Dickie Henderson, actor John Slater, and his son Robert, were among the representatives of the local summer shows who had replied with 106 for 6, to Torquay's 166, when the rains came and spoiled the afternoon. A report said there were over 2000 people in the ground and the pro was expected to pocket some £150.

One of the first noticed bowling performances of Barrie Matthews was against South Devon. After more than two hours at the crease they had totalled 69, Barrie Matthews 5 for 30, Derek Semmence 4 for 29 and Roger Matthews 1 for 0. Only Handley and Clarkson had to bat for Torquay.

During the August there were drawn games with Exeter, when Semmence had another century, at Plymouth where Harold Uren got a half century against a team captained by his uncle and Paignton where Bird was the hero for his team. David Post skippered the side to victory at Sidmouth where Clarkson 68 and Semmence 48 made the most of batting opportunities. Barrie Matthews 3 for 30, Clarkson 3 for 10 and Post 2 for 20 then did all that was necessary with the ball. The last two matches of the season were completely washed out.

At the end of the season D.J.Semmence had not achieved his double but had scored over 1800 runs and taken 69 wickets. After three very successful seasons the club were disappointed to learn he was not asking for a renewal of his contract and intended returning to his beloved Sussex and go into the family business. He, along with J.Kerr, B.Handley, B.Stockhill, A.Sibley and B.Matthews had all been called upon by Devon while T.Clarkson had played for Somerset 2nds.
Once again the first team results were published as,

Saturday X1   Played 21   Won 4   Drawn 13   Lost 1   Abandoned 3.
Mid-week   === 39   === 7   ==== 21   === 5   ==== 5   1 cancelled.

Victor Tucker, chairman, told the 1966 meeting that while the committee had interviewed a number of individuals to fill the position of club professional, "no suitable person, at the price we can afford, has been found". He went on to say "men of such standing as David Halfyard of Kent had been interviewed, although the tenancy agreement condition said we should employ a professional coach it had been impossible to find one. Applications had come from as far away as India and Ceylon". As a result the committee had decided that Bert Whitehead, the former pro, would act as coach to the younger players and assist in ground duties. Actually Bert Whitehead was a wise choice as he had been the club pro for three seasons, and had experience at Yorkshire, Durham and Oldham prior to coming to Torquay, all who knew him realised how much he loved his cricket.

Ted Dickinson resigned the first X1 captaincy and proposed Paul Twose as his successor, this was endorsed and Dickinson himself was appointed social secretary. Ian Scofield wanted to know why so few Sunday games had been arranged when there was any amount of members who could not find the time to play midweek. President Bryant quickly told him the ground had to be "rested" sometime for the groundsman to do his work, apparently forgetting the talk was about Sundays. However, Bob Haly told the meeting more Sunday away fixtures were being arranged even though, as Corporation tenants, we had an obligation to provide a seasonal amenity . Before the meeting closed Roger Matthews was chosen as vice-captain for the first X1, John Haly for the seconds and Leo Matthews for the thirds, while R.A.Lear was elected onto the committee. A new cup competition, The Rothman Devon Knock-Out Cup, had been sponsored and the club had entered, as well as including the 2cd and 3rd teams for the Narracott and Brockman cups.

Prior to the season commencing, there were newspaper reports of a Parks Committee meeting of the Corporation that made interesting reading. Alderman F.Felce commented on the cars he had counted on the hard standing at the Recreation Ground, and the number of occupants he had watched go straight onto the beach, not into the cricket or bowling as was intended. When he suggested an official car park there the solicitor, J.Bradley said, "while the Corporation might get away with providing a public car park the leasing cricket club would have to be consulted, and the covenant stated the ground had to be used for sports, agricultural shows, circuses and public gatherings." Alderman Ken Bryant, (the cricket club president) pointed out that the Corporation car park in Walnut Road was never full at the present time, while H.S.Hore, also a member refuted the suggestion that the ground was not being used as it should be.

With the season commencing with a wash out at Cockington, the first game at Chudleigh showed how the bad weather had highlighted the lack of net practice. After batting for over two hours it was thanks to a 17 year old newcomer, Barton J. Sewell with 39, Paul Twose 16 and 14 each by David Post and Peter Goodrich that Torquay eventually reached 91. Fortunately Chudleigh also struggled and David Post and Ben Williams each took 5 for 12 and had the home side all out in less than an hour for 27.

B.J.Sewell was a Warwickshire colt who had arrived in the area and was to eventually play for most of the clubs, at one time or another. Ron Williams, the club's former professional, home on leave from Rhodesia was a welcome addition since early in the season Handley, Semmence, Clarkson and Roebuck were all absentees for a time. Another new name appearing on the team sheet was that of C.Sloan, a local government employee, who had experience in the Lancashire Ribblesdale league.

During May the first rounds of the new Rothman Cup took place and it was eighteen overs a side and no bowler allowed more than four. The first opponents were Barton and Torquay were quickly into the second round with a 102 to a 50 run victory, Kempton taking 6 for 4 in his allotted overs.

With Roger Matthews having to undergo knee surgery, and expected to be out of action for the rest of the season, David Post took over as vice-captain. The first game at the Recreation Ground saw St. Luke's provide the usual struggle with Twose and Scofield hanging on grimly to earn Torquay's draw.

Torquay suffered a couple of shocks during June despite the strong sides they were able to field. Anticipating another victory, or so the papers reported, they were well beaten at South Devon when Alan Sibley, Barrie Matthews and Jeff Tolchard were all out without scoring. Then in the next round of the Rothman against a junior side, Chelston, found themselves 130 for 8. Fortunately the bowlers were at their best and in the eighteen overs Chelston were reduced to 82 for 8. In the next round Torquay again progressed but it was only a five run victory over Exeter St.Thomas.

Early in July all the Torquay members were delighted to hear of Roger Tolchard being awarded his county cap at Leicestershire. South Devon's annual Len Coldwell cup competition was won for the third consecutive year by Torquay's six a side under the leadership of Barney Bettesworth with victories over Paignton, Tavistock and Exeter St. James.

The much publicised attraction of the New Zealand Women's Touring X1 v the South West Ladies was eventually spoiled by rain. Batting nearly all the first day for a mere 166 the tourists almost ensured there was little chance of either side getting a result. After a run chase on the second morning the South West captain declared at lunch on 110 for 5 but the rains came and washed out any further play.

Both the Goodrich's were missing when the Exeter team were the opponents, Peter was off to Guildford to get married and Michael was to be his best man. On such occasions the researcher found it interesting to see who was promoted and would have loved to have been around at the time to understand the reasoning behind certain selections. New arrivals with a reputation invariably found their way into the first team and then descended into the seconds or even thirds, rather than work upwards. Individuals like, J.Swift, K.Gale, K.Peppiatt, R.Pamplin, R.Williams and A. Rich appeared the backbone of the seconds for years from scorebooks, with only the odd first team appearance in midweek matches. In many instances it must have been embarrassing for the new comers, as records show that later in the same season, they were more often in the seconds or even the third X1.

During the August Ghan Patel was back playing again and skippering the odd mid-week side. B.J.Sewell had returned from a month away with the Warwickshire Colts and Paul Dunkels was often quoted in the side. Having beaten Exmouth in the Rothman Cup Torquay were due to meet Plymouth in the final at Exeter during September. Plymouth, having thrashed Tiverton Heathcoat in the semi-final, and, only having lost to Torquay by eighteen runs in a normal game, were confidently tipped to provide an exciting final.

Sad to relate the final at Exeter St. Thomas ground did not go as anticipated. Torquay won the toss and decided to bat, but both openers were out quickly. Sibley and Birt, five and seven respectively were good wickets for Plymouth to get so cheaply and only 38 runs were scored off the first 20 overs. Fox made a useful 20 but it was left to Patel with 30 to make the score even remotely respectable at 123 all out. Plymouth had a great start from Waldock and Baker with 64 runs on the board before a wicket fell. Torquay helped with bad fielding, including three dropped catches and with such a small total to chase, Plymouth were 124, with wickets and overs in hand long before the expected time closing schedule.

Blunt speaking Ralph Haly reviewed the season making several points quite forcibly. He felt Paul Twose should have batted himself higher in the order on many occasions, that Roger Matthews was sadly missed through being on crutches almost all the summer, Alan Hitchman's all too few appearances did not help and the lack of a "pro" midweek was most evident. He went on to say Jeff Tolchard, when he did play midweek, was a steadying influence and a great leader, but badly missed when he was absent. Commenting on the "tidy wicket-keeping of Jack Fox" he was scathing regarding sloppy mid-week fielding and said it must be improved. Barrie Matthews came in for praise regarding his consistency throughout the season but Mr. Haly was not amused that a pre-season football training injury had kept him out of the last few cricket matches. As usual the details were given regarding Saturday and Midweek matches.

Saturday X1   played 22   won 10   drawn 9   abandoned 3.
Mid week   === 36 === 11. === 9   Lost 15   abandoned 1
In 35 innings Jeff Tolchard had scored 1056 runs while Barrie Matthews had 910 from 30 visits to the wicket.

During the "closed season" the club suffered the loss of its chairman by the sudden death of Victor Tucker. Elected to the committee in 1946 he had been the chairman for six years and following his death the members voted his wife a life member at the '67 A.G.M. in recognition of all the work they had both done for the club. She later presented a silver salver to be given annually for the member, adjudged by the committee, to have done the most for the club during the cricket season by work or organisation and not necessarily playing.

Reading the minutes of the 1967 A.G.M. one tends to wonder what had gone on in the previous season! Space was given to thank all those involved behind the scenes providing teas, refreshments and operating the bar but the treasurer, H. Thompson, then stated, but did not explain, "Less profit was made from teas because of the extra expense of more help in the kitchen". He went on to announce that the club had to find more income as there would be a new professional. Chris Greetham, an ex-Somerset all rounder, was the man who had been selected by the committee. After the election of officers the first team captain, Paul Twose, told members the club needed to attract more "under 16 year olds" and put it to the meeting that subscriptions for them should be reduced to five shillings. Once more, even the captain, was quickly put in his place and told suggestions had to be in writing for members to consider changes! Eventually it was decided that a sub-committee would look into the matter.

Several Council meetings had discussed the Ladmore Scheme and the club were still waiting to hear what was to happen. A long lease had been approved for Torquay United at Plainmoor but, even with the backing of the Devon Playing Fields Association for a 21 lease on the Recreation Ground, the Corporation refused to discuss the matter.

The one new player joining the club was mentioned as M.J.Osborne who had experience with Surrey 2cds, in his first game he was reported as, "scoring an excellent 46 before being run out". Another very wet May saw both of the scheduled Saturday games washed out and when cricket did commence the reporter noted a "dull draw against St. Luke's".

Following the formation of the Torbay Regional Committee, a part of the Devon County Cricket Club, two teams were chosen for a game to be played at Queen's Park, Paignton on a Sunday in late May. A further selection would be made to play the Plymouth area, at Plymstock, during June. It was to be yet another attempt to find young cricketers for the County side and for older readers the names were,
"A" team. Richardson, captain(S.Devon) Oliver(S.Devon) D.Traylor (Chelston) Friend(Paignton) Blackmore(Paignton) Pugh(Barton) Dunkels(Torquay) Cassells(Barton) Gibbs(Bovey Tracey) Burgess(Corinthians) M.Goodrich(Torquay)

"B" team. Sambrook(Paignton) Pinney(Paignton) Hunt(S.Devon) Scott(S.Devon) Markham(Dartington) Jenkins(Kingskerswell) Blackler(Brixham) B.Matthews(Torquay) Calland(Barton) Abbott(Buckfastleigh) Satterly(Corinthians).

When the final eleven were chosen to go to Plymstock, Jeff Tolchard, a regular Devon player was included as was Torquay's Ian Scofield. The team, captained by Tony Richardson(S.Devon) was completed with C.Hunt, B.Matthews, W.Jordan, P.Dunkells, D. Traylor, M. Pinney, P. Cassells and B. Sambrook.

It is hard to believe in this day and age that the pro was not selected for some of the early matches, but the captain and committee wanted to give all the first team contenders a chance to stake their claim. Ray Haydock, previously with Babbacombe, became a very useful club player and about this time it was noted that stalwart Ken Peppiatt's son was following in the family tradition in the thirds.

June saw the first eleven obtaining Saturday victories over Paignton, Exmouth and South Devon with the fixture at Sidmouth rained off. A mid-week match against the Glamorgan Nomads was typical of touring cricket teams and their players. Having had no game at Exeter on the Monday, neither at Mount Wise on the Tuesday, both because of the weather, the tourists found the square at the Rec. too wet. Desperate to play, they accepted a wicket at the sea end and supplied a player to Torquay who were short. The "loaned" player, Bryn Thomas was the reason Torquay won!, taking five of his club mates wickets for 13 runs and the cricket starved visitors were all out for 89. Ian Scofield top scored with 28 but there were wickets in hand when the winning runs were obtained.

Ken Gale led the Seconds to a Narracott cup final at Queen's Park against Chelston. Torquay had never reached the final before whereas Chelston had twice been the winners, and were again, albeit by one run and off the last ball.

Torquay went through to the semi-final of the Rothman competition and were drawn to play North Devon at Instow. Hopes were high that the final would be reached and the Plymouth defeat of the previous season laid to rest. North Devon batsmen gave several catching chances that were not held leaving Torquay supporters wondering if the penalty would be paid later. Chris Greetham only conceded nine runs in nine overs and the home side were restricted to 149. Alan Sibley and Barrie Matthews gave Torquay a great start with 55 and 45 respectively and later Roger Matthews and Barton Sewell reached the target with still six wickets in hand.

The final at Queen's Park was, as hoped, against Plymouth, but neither team was at full strength. Plymouth were missing their Devon bowler, John Swinburne, who earlier that week had helped Devon to victory against Oxfordshire with, 9 for 48 and 5 for 37. Torquay were without B.J.Sewell, who was having his tonsils removed, and captain Paul Twose plus Ian Scofield who had both gone on their respective holidays would you believe!

Peter Goodrich skippered the side which included A.Sibley, J.Tolchard, B.Matthews, M.Osborne, D.Post, B.Williams, R.Matthews, J.Fox, G.Patel and C. Greetham. That particular score book could not be found but the local paper reported,

"A fine innings by Alan Sibley of 54 helped Torquay to victory
in the Rothman Cup final against Plymouth. The holders paid
the price for dropped catches. Sibley was supported by Fox 18,
and Osborne 23 which enabled Torquay to reach 134 after Greetham
and B. Matthews were lost for five runs. Plymouth ended the game
eleven runs short of the required total and the cup was Torquay's".

Out of the sixty one games the first X1 had played Chris Greetham had participated in 42 and had scored 1491 runs besides taking 39 wickets in 390 overs. Alan Sibley and Barrie Matthews had each attained their 1000 runs during the season, playing in the same number of games and each registering a century. Roger Matthews was the most successful bowler with 75 wickets from 300 overs while David Post's 150 overs had produced 43 wickets at an average of 12. As was normal at that time when producing the details of the season great play was made of the Saturday team being unbeaten even though they had to settle for drawn games on nine occasions.

After 16 years as secretary Ralph Haly announced his resignation at the A.G.M. of 1968. Speeches were made in appreciation of work on the club's behalf and, after presentation of a 23in. television, he was made a life member. Mr. Haly announced he would be down to the Rec. as often as he could but, "as an arm chair critic". H.S.Wells was elected to take over the onerous position. The treasurer, H. Thompson, told the meeting that Chris Greetham had been engaged for another season and while the increase in subs and extra profit on teas had helped the finances, the club had also been badly hit. The worst break in the club had ever experienced took place during the end of the season and a large amount of drink had been stolen. Monies had been spent on new covers and players should see that they are used sensibly. A big game for the season would be the Minor Counties against The Australian Touring team.

Torquay had one early match at Taunton against a Somerset X1. Led by Roger Matthews, Torquay had the home side 107 for 8 at one stage, when in came a certain Australian, Greg Chappell, and the total went to 240 before the last wicket was taken. Torquay's reply was 168 for 8 at the close of play, Greetham 58 and B.Matthews 44.

The bugbear of cricket, rain, saw the cancellation of three early fixtures and then on the last Saturday in May it happened again! St. Luke's College came and took away the Saturday record. Some of the supporters were not unduly surprised and felt the "writing had been on the wall" midweek when Chelston were played in the Rothman Cup. Torquay had managed only 94 when Chris Greetham went to the wicket with two overs left. Opening his shoulders the fours and sixes rolled off his bat and Chelston had to chase 140. David Traylor hit what was described as "a brilliant 87" and set Chelston on their way. In the last over Chelston needed 16 to win, which against a bowler of Ghan Patel's ability appeared a "tall order", it was, and they lost by just three runs.

In the days of friendly fixtures there were always two ways of looking at games and one of the Paignton fixtures that season was a case in point. After a considerable time at the wicket Torquay declared at 220 for 3, Barrie Matthews 95 and Ian Scofield 100. Torquay supporters felt Paignton made no effort to go for the runs while the Paigntonians felt it was an unrealistic total to chase in the time left, Dickie Bird managing 91 not out in the total of 140 for 3.

This was the 21st. year of the popular Heffle Cuckoos touring the Westcountry, and as this draft is being prepared 2002, they are still touring. Initially they had players from Kent and Sussex whereas in recent times more come from the Tunbridge Wells area of Kent. The odd outsider was included in the party and Bob Gale the

Middlesex and M.C.C. opening batsman had toured with them. Their tour headquarters had been the Rosetor Hotel in Chestnut Avenue and the owner arranged a dinner and dance to celebrate 'a long and happy relationship'. When the hotel was passed to the Corporation for the Riveria Centre to be built the Cuckoos transferred their H.Q. to the Livermead Cliff Hotel. The writer was privileged to be entertained there, with members of other clubs the Heffles visit, on the occasion of their 50th.tour. What was so kind and thoughtful was that the organiser of the dinner, Freddie Morris, remembered the original hall porter who had taken care of their luggage fifty years earlier and he and his wife were also guests. Many players of years ago still tour with their teams to meet old friends and spend hours on the various golf courses rather than cricket squares.

During the June Torquay acquired a new player who proved to be a very useful addition, Peter Anderson, a police officer who was transferred from Plymstock .Yes, the same Anderson who now has so much to say for Somerset County Cricket Club.

Peter Goodrich who had broken his shoulder during the football season was gradually getting his fitness back with games in the second X1, and was eventually a member of the side that once more won the Len Coldwell Cup at South Devon.

Joey Oliver, who had often been noted playing midweek for Torquay, was the mainstay of South Devon's batting against Torquay that season. Roger Matthews 4 for 9, David Post 3 for 33 and Barrie Matthews 3 for 12 had bowled them out for 95 but Oliver had made 63 of that total. While that was an easy victory the return in August was actually an exciting draw. Having declared on 158 for 7 South Devon appeared to be facing defeat with Torquay on 157 for 5 in the last over. A lofted shot from Peter Goodrich seemed to have won the game but he was caught by Mervyn Scott and as Jeff Tolchard could not score off the remaining balls, that was that.

August saw the Devon v Cornwall match and the long awaited visit of the Australian Test party. In their first innings Devon had obtained a useful lead over the Duchy team, the scores being, 217 and 176. Jackie Fox and Barrie Matthews 45 and 40, had been the top scorers while in the second innings Fox did not get to the wicket and Matthews's contribution was a duck. Skipper Cole and Solanky held the batting together and Cole was able to declare on 153 for 7, Solanky not out with 60. With all Devon's bowlers on form the Cornish side were bowled out for 87 with Ben Williams 5 for 22, the hero. The Devon party then began a three match tour of Oxford, Berkshire and Wiltshire taking Greetham, Sibley, Newman and Jeff Tolchard from the Torquay club, under the captaincy of Gerald Trump.

Representing the Minor Counties under the captaincy of Derek Cole were, C.J.Saville(Norfolk), J.Sutton(Cheshire), M.Maslin(Lincoln), J.Bailey(Durham), I.D.Prior(Suffolk),C.M.Old(Yorks.),A.G.Marshall(Wilts.),N.McVicker(Lincoln),D.H. Fairey(Cambridge), F.W.Millett(Cheshire) 12th man M.Osborne(Devon).

AUSTRALIA. W.M.Lawry, R.J.Inverarity, N.J.N.Hawke, A.Mallett, H.B.Taber, L.Joslin, G.D.McKenzie, K.D.Walters, R.M.Cowper, I.M.Chappell, A.P.Sheahan and 12th man, A.N.Connolly.

As expected a very large crowd saw the first morning's play and yet the paper gave more space to the entertaining of the two teams to lunch at Torre Abbey by the Mayor, our own Ald.A.L.Goodrich. Resumption after lunch was delayed because of rain and the Minor Counties eventually declared on 176 for 4 with Sutton 76 and Millett36.Australia, in their turn, declared at 178 having lost nine wickets, with the most successful bowler being Marshall 5 for 63 off 14 overs. In the second innings Sutton had another knock of 75 before being bowled by Ashley Mallett while Maslin's 48 enabled Derek Cole to declare at 189 for 7.Bill Lawry had tried seven bowlers, including himself, while it was reported the runs had been made in "just over two hours".

Later opinions were divided whether Australia lost wickets going for quick runs but with McVicker quickly taking 3 for 30 Lawry and Inverarity 'putting up the shutters' at 66 for 5, the fall of wickets did make interesting reading. 1 for 12, 2 for 24, 3 for 28, 4 for 38, 5 for 66 and then the two batsmen only increasing the total to 101 in the final hour there certainly was a talking point.

Reviewing the season for the local reporter, secretary Mr. Wells mentioned Chris Greetham and Barrie Matthews for having again completing their thousand runs. Eight club members had assisted Devon who finished second in the Minor Counties League to champions Yorkshire. For the record these were J.Fox, C.Greetham, A.Sibley, B.Matthews, M.J.Osborne, J.Tolchard, B.Williams and Derek Cole the Devon captain. He went on to make great play that the M.C.C. had sent a side for the first time in thirty odd years, and would be coming again but little of the fact that the Rothman Cup had been lost.

By the time the 1969 A.G.M. was held the professional, Chris Greetham, had informed the club that, having completed two seasons he would no longer be available for the club in that position. He had taken employment as a company representative and would be travelling most of the week, however he still intended playing weekends and would not be severing his connections with the club.At the meeting Barney Bettesworth raised the point that the quality of players in the mid-week side was so often below first team standard, were frequently beaten, that it was bad for the club's reputation and it should only be quoted to the paper as a mid-week X1, not Torquay firsts. Barrie Matthews became captain of the first X1 while Ted Dickinson was elected club captain and Paul Twose social secretary.

The cancellation of the first game, against Chudleigh, was disastrous for Devon.An early round of the Gillette Cup for the County was against Hertfordshire at Stevenage and the county called on four Torquay players. With no match practice whatsoever Devon were out at the first hurdle. Herts.173 all out, but Devon could only muster 75, Greetham 32, Matthews 15 and Tolchard 10 were the only batsmen to get double figures. Although on the losing side Bob Healey won the Man of the Match award for his having taken six wickets for just fourteen runs.

An early season shock for the club was on a Monday evening in May, when Chelston knocked Torquay out of the Rothman competition, by three runs. As already recorded the previous season the result was in reverse. Bill Traylor won the toss for Chelston and decided to open the batting with his brother Dave who was just back from the Devon v Hertfordshire game. He was the top scorer with 22 in the Chelston total of 79. Chris Greetham was out to a smart catch by D.Traylor off W.Traylor's bowling and Barrie Matthews was soon dismissed .Torquay were half way to the total needed with five wickets in hand, but the lack of practice and the pressure applied by Chelston got the junior side the victory, ironically by just three runs. All the Chelston bowlers did well that night and Torquay's total of 76 was "echoed" around the area. Bill Traylor 3 for 17, Peter Madge 2 for 10, Dave Chick 2 for 4, and John Bradley 2 for 13 did not forget that game for a very long time!

After lengthy absences B.J Sewell's name was cropping up on team sheets along with G.Jennings and D.Merrikin. The latter held his place in the second eleven while after several games Jennings was then more frequently in the thirds. When G.Baker was behind the stumps the reporter would explain the absence of Fox or Sibley, but other team changes were only noted when players were holidaying or on county duty.

Umpiring duties were shared during the season by Dickinson, C.Cockrane and A.Pegg for the first team while H.Chavasse was a fixture with the seconds. Ken Peppiatt if not playing would don the white coat for the thirds when Harry Snape was not available. Great club stalwarts every one but almost forgotten in the passage of time.

The game against Paignton at the Recreation Ground, although ending in a draw, was one that could have gone either way and held the supporters interest throughout. Barrie Matthews and Trevor Ward, the respective captains were both very competitive and played for victories, on winning the toss Ward told Torquay to bat. Matthews made a quick 53 and was followed by Greetham 16, Anderson 15, Sewell 19 and Roger Matthews 27. Declaring at 165 for 7, Torquay had Paignton reeling when Patel had Dickie Bird caught and bowled for 6. Worse was to follow and at 38 for 4 the home supporters were looking forward to an early night. Malcolm Pinney made a half century for the visitors and their followers' hopes rose. In the entertaining battle Daniel and Scott lasted out the last three overs to ensure a draw at 142 for 9.

Several Devon Club and Ground X1's were selected to play against area sides throughout the county. Local players like Dave Traylor (Chelston) and Arnold

Calland (Barton) Jack Fox, Paul Dunkells, Peter Anderson and Roger Matthews all of Torquay were called upon. The Torbay Area side also included J.Oliver (S.Devon) and T.Friend (Paignton) but it was Torquay's Chris Greetham and Plymstocks Brian Lambert who were mainly responsible for the Locals defeat. Greetham made 84 of the 179 scored by the Club and Ground while Lambert took most of the wickets of Torbay in their 160 total. The mainstays of the locals were Calland 35, B.Matthews 31, Friend 28, and Oliver with 26.

By the beginning of August Michael Goodrich had taken 76 wickets but then he announced that he was off to a Law School at Guildford and was unlikely to play again that season. With Sibley, Tolchard and Anderson playing for Devon against Dorset at Dorchester, it was a very different looking side that went down to face Plymouth. Yet another of the dour draws was the result and more ammunition for the captain's complaint that cricket was being stifled, and a lot of fun was going out of the game. In his first season as skipper Barrie Matthews had rather a torrid time what with the diabolical weather at the beginning and several players going through rather lean spells with lack of form. Matthews himself did not obtain his usual thousand runs plus, albeit by just fifty, in his 39 matches. Chris Greetham had only played in nine of the Saturday fixtures but had been chosen for the Devon games. While Paul Dunkels headed the bowling averages, his 66 wickets were second in total to Michael Goodrich. David Post, only available on a Saturday this season was not at his best and had numerous games in the seconds as a result. The all important results read,

Saturday X1.   Won 5   Lost 2   Drew 8   Abandoned   6.
Mid-week   == 12   == 9   === 10   =====   4.
Sunday   X1.   =====   == 2   == 3.

Ken Peppiatt's treasurer's report at the 1970 A.G.M. revealed just how much the weather had affected the club's cash flow besides causing problems for the actual cricket. He pointed out that while admission charges had gone up the committee were going to have a serious review of the catering and bar prices, since the income had not matched the outgoings. He told the meeting the one arm bandit had even failed to make enough money to cover its hire charge. Sunday games again came in for discussion as the lack of interest by both players and supporters was quite evident according to one speaker. A.E.Whitehead, Bert to all and sundry, was made a life member in recognition of his services to the club. After his return from Paignton he was a normal member, rather than the club employee he had previously been. A well deserved tribute for years of service.

Prior to the start of the season local cricket lovers were delighted to hear that Somerset County intended to play one of their John Player Sunday League games at Torquay. However, a later announcement that Somerset had changed their minds and were taking the game to Weston-super-Mare instead, was quickly forgotten when Torquay announced that Ted Dexter's International Cavaliers would play at the Recreation Ground on August Bank Holiday.

Once more May proved to be a bad month for cricket and after cancellations at Plymouth, Manadon and Peverall Torquay eventually had a winning start at Chudleigh. Matthews had persuaded Vaughan Hosking to join the club from the Teignmouth team and another newcomer was Andrew Scott from Paignton. During May the thirds had been unable to raise a side to go to Exwick, almost at the same time Yelverton cancelled their game against the seconds. Off went the seconds to Exwick to fulfil the fixture and enjoy a game of cricket. Put into bat they made 161 for 6 with Ray Haydock scoring 79. Exwick had no answer to the bowling of Derek Merrikin who had 6 for 12 and ensured an easy victory. Merrikin found himself in and out of the first eleven on numerous occasions during the season with his bowling.

After hanging on for a draw against Tiverton Heathcoat but then losing to St.Luke's College again, Torquay did manage to defeat Paignton and go through to the next round of the Rothmann Cup. Alan Sibley made 54 out of the 124 for 5, supported by Peter Anderson with 21. Paignton were all out for 100 with Patel, Matthews, Merrikin and Goodrich each taking two wickets. The next round was referred to in the press as "Father versus Son" fixture as ex-Devon captain, Derek Cole, had teamed up to play for Dartmouth, against his old Torquay colleagues who had his son Clive in the team. Although father took 2 for 8 in his allotted four overs, son Clive had an undefeated 56 to his credit which easily won the game.

Rumours had been rife for sometime and at the end of June it was formally announced that in the 1971 season a new South Devon Cricket League would commence. The Torbay Regional Committee of the Devon County Cricket Club gave the names of the eight clubs who would play on a home and away basis for a trophy to be known as the Shiphay Manor Cup. Games would take place on Saturdays and Sundays and in many cases friendly fixtures would be converted to league games. The teams that had been approached and confirmed their participation were Barton, Chelston, Chudleigh, South Devon, Bovey Tracey, Buckfastleigh and Torquay. Paignton had declined their invitation and the Cockington Corinthians had accepted the vacancy. More details were to be announced later but at the time this was a talking bombshell for local cricket lovers.

During July Torquay went off to play Exeter and with Paul Dunkels not available David Post was drafted in from the seconds. Post had a poor start to the season but he made no mistake with this opportunity in the first team, in fifteen overs he took seven wickets for thirty four runs. Michael Goodrich had the other three wickets for twenty two. In little over an hour Torquay had knocked off the necessary runs with Barrie Matthews 54 and Clive Cole 20 both not out. The result was real surprise, an eight wicket victory at the County Ground.

In the same month the S.W.Counties were due to play Jamaica at the Recreation Ground and, when in the early hours of the morning a thunderstorm broke, only the quick action of Bert Whitehead saved the day. Leaving his Paignton home at 4 a.m. he drove into Torquay, climbed the locked gates and got the covers onto the wicket. Yes, in those days there were gates and they were locked. In the 40 over match Jamaica bettered the South West's score of 140 for 7 with 142 for 8 in the penultimate over, quite exciting, but that the match took place at all was due entirely to a dedicated clubman.

Torquay avenged the previous seasons defeat by Chelston in the Rothman Cup and went on to dispose of the challenge from South Devon, thereby setting up a semi-final with Plymouth. On the Saturday, in a normal fixture, Plymouth struggled to 108 against the bowling of Michael Goodrich 4 for 23 and Clive Cole 3 for 17. When Torquay batted Matthews 30, Anderson and Cole, with 34 and 23 both not out, helped to take away Plymouth's unbeaten record. So for the Sunday cup game hopes were high amongst the Torquay supporters. The song says, "What a difference a day makes", and it certainly did in this case. Torquay were all out for 109 with Bob Luffman taking 5 for 23. Paul Dunkels and David Post bowled well to record figures of 3 for 17 and 2 for 31 respectively but the batsmen had not set a high enough target to give the bowlers a real chance and they were unable to prevent a very comprehensive five wicket victory for Plymouth.

Having gone out of the Rothman Cup competition the reporter then went back to the "Saturday Record" headlines again. On successive Saturdays Torquay were to play at South Devon and then home against Exeter. All the reporters' speculation about the game at Newton gave the supporters a shock when three wickets were down for just twenty eight runs but Peter Anderson 71 and Barton Sewell 47 saw the total to 163 for 5. Roger Matthews 5 for 19 and Michael Goodrich 4 for 50 did the necessary to ensure another Saturday victory. Torquay became the first Devon side to obtain the double over Exeter, Barrie Matthews 74 and B.J.Sewell 54 were the batsmen in form and Roger Matthews 5 for 35 and Michael Goodrich 4 for 20 gave the supporters an early night..

There was a certain amount of disappointment over the Bank Holiday when Somerset entertained the International Cavaliers at the Recreation Ground. The advertised stars of Ted Dexter, Godfrey Evans, Trevor Bailey and Freddie Trueman did not appear. The manager, Colin Milburn explained that Dexter had been called to London to do a TV. commentary of the Surrey v Worcester match and all the other players were injured. Since it was the Bank Holiday and all the other counties, with the exception of Somerset, were playing that weekend the Cavaliers had found it difficult to replace the stars. Some two thousand people were reputed to have been at the game and Somerset's spokesman said later, "the day had been a financial success and they were well pleased with the gate receipts of £455".

Torquay wound up their season with a successful weekend that included away victories over both Tavistock and North Devon. Paul Dunkels was in great form taking 6 for 21 at the Tavistock Ring and 6 for 10 at Instow. Having finished second in the Devon Minor Counties League averages with his 29 wickets he had had a season to remember.

Records found for the 1970 season showed that Barrie Matthews in his 36 innings had scored 1137 runs and Barton Sewell in 11 trips to the wicket had 344 runs to his credit. Paul Dunkels with 58 wickets at an average of 10:3 was just ahead of David Post, 23 wickets at an average of 11:6, whereas Roger Matthews who had bowled more overs than anyone else was third with his 43 wickets at 12 apiece. Useless statistics! But all part of the records.

THE SHIPHAY MANOR LEAGUE

An interesting article in the Torquay Times of March 1971 illustrates how the club missed out on what would have been a very precious piece of cricket memorabilia. The former club secretary, Ralph Haly, wrote to the Devon Club Cricket Association, Francis Doidge, suggesting a letter was sent to Lady Mallowan, or Agatha Christie as she was better known, to congratulate her on becoming a Dame of the British Empire in the Honours List. The article relates how Mr. Doidge received a reply in which Dame Agatha confirmed her interest in cricket as a child and helping her father score on occasions. She also wrote that when she was in Devon she often had the chauffer drive past the old cricket ground, just for the sake of memories long ago and Chapel Hill, where she used to walk with her nurse. Despite research and numerous telephone calls the actual letter appears lost in the passage of time.

During the closed season various alterations had been carried out on the pavilion costing nearly £900. A side entrance had been formed for the players to go to and from the wicket rather than through the bar area, while a new tea room had been created at the opposite side of the pavilion. Numerous events had been organised to raise funds and early in April a sponsored Sunday walk of some 15 miles took place, starting from the old Shiphay Manor, to the younger reader that is where the Boys Grammar School is now.

With the new Shiphay Manor League commencing it was decided that Barrie Matthews would be the captain and Ian Scofield would be in charge of the Sunday team

A brief interview with Barrie Matthews regarding the formation of the league reported that, "Matthews was convinced that in time the league would include teams from all over the county"! Was that only thirty odd years ago?

As soon as the league season began it created so much interest that attendances increased, but the almost forgotten snags began to appear for Torquay. The first match was away against Chudleigh and after winning the toss Matthews elected to bat. He and Peter Anderson put on 58 before the first wicket fell and a later 42 from Peter Goodrich took the total to 150 for 9 at the end of the allotted overs. Roger Matthews then took 5 for 27 in Chudleigh's total of 79 and the first five league points were achieved.

Having such a strong Saturday fixture card, which had been in existence for many years, meant that some of the league encounters had to be played on the Sunday, and that side included anyone available. Against Barton, on a Sunday, the next league game resulted in a draw. Replying to Barton's 181 Torquay managed only 110 for 7 and got one point against the visitors three. A good thing, however, did emerge after this match as Braham Fredman, who had previously played for the club, decided to come back from retirement and assist the Sunday X1.

Torquay went off to Sidmouth on the Saturday and secured a five wicket victory but on the Sunday, in a league game against Chelston, they were soundly beaten at Cockington. Barrie Matthews, in a rare Sunday appearance, and Ken Creber, who had been in the third X1 the previous day, were the mainstays of Torquay, but none of the bowlers were able to restrain the home batsmen and Dave Traylor undefeated with 52 runs, saw his team pocket the points.

By early July it was felt that the league title would eventually be won by the team that had the most luck with the weather. Numerous games were being affected by rain and resulting in the two sides sharing the points. One week-end however Torquay had that little bit of luck. All the Saturday league games had been rain affected but on the Sunday, at Bovey Tracey, the weather stayed fine. Bovey were bowled out for 114 with Vaughan Hosking taking 5 for 23. Matthews and Hosking had both been bowled without scoring and things looked rather bleak until Ian Scofield and Bob Stainton put on 108 in a fifth wicket stand to ensure the victory.

When Barrie Matthews took the team to play Plymouth in the annual fixture he suggested to their captain, Chris Uren, they play 45 overs each. After consultation with his team Uren agreed and an exciting game ensued. Torquay were 183 for 7, Peter Goodrich the top scorer with 80 runs. Plymouth were all out in the last over, just fifteen runs short of the necessary runs, with Clive Cole 4 for 41 and M.Mitchell 3 for 30 being the successful bowlers.

Late July saw Torquay with two league games to play and ten points at stake, it was the second X1 who went to Buckfastleigh to play the League game on the Saturday, and lost. They were bundled out for a mere 98 runs by Buckfastleigh, with only Dick Turpin 29 and Derek Merrikin 18 managing double figures. The first X1 fulfilled a normal fixture and won. For the Sunday league game against the Cockington Corinthians a stronger side was selected and Vaughan Hosking with 76 helped Torquay to 170 for 8. However they were unable to bowl out the Corinthians and a young Hiley Edwards, later to join Torquay, with a not out half century ensured a drawn game. A bad weekend for the club since only three points had been obtained.

During July local cricket lovers did have a treat when Somerset played one of their John Player games at the Recreation Ground. Some 4000 people were attracted to the game against Surrey and, with gate receipts of over £1200, set a record for a

Somerset Sunday match. Roy Virgin made 91 not out in Somerset's total of 219 for 5 and the Surrey reply of 215 for 8 in their forty overs made for a very exciting finish. Brian Close was taken to hospital for dental treatment after a ball damaged two teeth, and a woman spectator also had hospital treatment when a Micky Stewart hit six landed on her knee.

Described as a promising young player a bowler joined the club from Babbacombe and after taking 3 for 17 in his first match in the second X1 Martyn Goulding was a marked man. Within two weeks he was selected for the Sunday side that had a return League match with Buckfastleigh. Taking 3 for 11 along with Michael Goodrich's 3 for 27 he put Torquay well on the way to a victory. While that actual win did take Torquay to the top of the League subsequent defeats, including one by Chelston, saw South Devon become the first winners of the Shiphay Manor League.

With Barrie Matthews injured Peter Anderson took over the captaincy and the season ended with a 14 run victory over the Devon Cup winners, Tavistock, and a more comfortable win against North Devon. At Tavistock Roger Matthews 5 for 58 had seen their total restricted to 142 and Jeff Tolchard, guesting for his old team, had scored 87 in the winning total of 143 for 6. In the game at Instow it was Clive Cole and Vaughan Hosking who scored undefeated 83 and 47 respectively, in a total of 205 for 3, to set the team on its winning trail. North Devon were all out for 191 with Braham Fredman taking a catch to finish the innings, Cole had 3 for 22 and Goulding 3 for 37. The promising youngster had certainly proved his worth in a couple of months and was to go on to prove a real bonus for the club, and Devon.

Throughout the season individuals quoted as umpiring were Ted Dickinson, Len Leworthy, Peter Hobbs, A. Rich and S. Vincent; while for the first time Esme Kingdon was noted as scoring whenever her husband Bert, or son Malcolm, were playing in the thirds.

A brief article in the Torquay Times early in 1972 reported that the Corporation's Parks Committee were "looking into the Bay's sporting facilities and hoping to agree to a request to charge reasonable rents". If the Council agree with the Park's working committee it will then examine the rents and existing leases, it was stated. However in early discussion it was reported that Councillor Robert Hunt said, "the Council are already wet nursing local clubs", to which Alderman Ken Bryant replied, "to impose economic rents would give incentive to senior sport and do think of the publicity it does bring to the area". The Parks Committee eventually agreed to recommend that the general policy of the Council be relaxed, as far as amateur sports grounds were concerned, and reasonable rents be charged. Now, 30 years later !

A review of the 1971 season at the A.G.M. (March '72) held at the Queen's Hotel showed the club had made a working profit of well over £200 thanks mainly to a record turnover at the bar. The treasurer, Ken Peppiatt, did warn members that the assets had been reduced by £600, due to the payment made to the contractor after the completion of the pavilion improvements. Roger Matthews was elected secretary following the resignation of Tom Stranger, due to his ill health. Bob Hill was applauded for the manner in which he had managed the new bar and for the numerous jobs he had done within the pavilion. Details of the season were,

	Played	Won	Lost	Drawn	Abandoned.
Saturday X1.	17.	6.	2.	6.	3.
Mid-week	35	12	6	16	1
Sunday X1	6	1	0	5	
League/Cup	14.	7.	4	2.	1.

Barrie Matthews in 41 innings had scored 1408 runs and Vaughan Hosking in 56 visits to the crease had accumulated 1254. The bowling had mainly fallen on the shoulders of Roger Matthews, who in 546 overs had taken 93 wickets, supported by Alan Norman whose 350 overs claimed 60 victims.

The last item on the Agenda was the approval of the Committee's recommendation that subscriptions be increased. Senior players were to pay £5, under 21's £3, and under 18 years old £1.

THE DEVON SENIOR LEAGUE

The new Devon Senior League, different from the Shiphay Manor, was to commence in May, games were to consist of 46 overs a side, as opposed to the 44 overs in the Shiphay Manor League. Five points were to be awarded for a win, three for a winning draw and one for a losing draw. There were to be no restrictions on the number of overs a bowler could bowl. Since all the teams would not play the same number of league games in the first season, due to long standing fixture commitments, the table would be worked out on a percentage basis. For the first season the teams participating were to be:
Exmouth, Exeter, Sidmouth, Plymouth, South Devon, Paignton, Plymstock, Chudleigh, Yelverton, Exeter St. Thomas and Torquay.

In a pre-season interview with the captain, Barrie Matthews, a local reporter stated that Matthews was eagerly awaiting the start of the new season. He was anticipating the return of Paul Dunkels and fully expected Mike Goodrich to be available for more games in the coming season. With the arrival of Gerry Kendrick, a wicket-keeping batsman from Paignton and a talented teenage batsman from Cockington Corinthians Hiley Edwards, Matthews was quoted as saying, "Torquay will be out to win, and whatever the game, we will dish up the sort of cricket spectators enjoy". With the new league there would only be three Saturday games against the usual touring sides but some attractive fixtures had been arranged for Sundays.
Even before the season began Paul Dunkels, the 6'-10" fast bowler that Matthews had such hopes for, signed a two month contract for Sussex and was to play in a new competition, for uncapped county players, in the under 25 age group.

In an early season game against H.M.S. Thunderer the 17 year old former Babbacombe bowler, Martyn Goulding had his chance in the first X1 and seized it by taking 5 for 5 with some accurate bowling. Against Barton, in a Sunday match, Torquay appeared to be in dire straights taking over two hours to score just forty five runs. As it happened the wicket was difficult but all the bowlers were on form and after Barton had scored twenty for no wickets they were all out for 35, Tim Price was their top scorer with 15 runs of the overall total.

Torquay's first success in the new league came against Chudleigh at the Recreation Ground on a Sunday. The young Hiley Edwards was promoted from the seconds and scored 56 in the total of 167 for 8. Interestingly Edwards began his Torquay career like so many other better players with, not the usual one, but three ducks! Despite the constant drizzle throughout Chudleigh's innings Roger Matthews took 5 for 18 and Clive Cole 3 for 18 to have the visitors all out for 69. In the week that followed there was an unusual report of a Colts game. Barton Colts had made 140 for 8 and Torquay's lads had only made 115, however Bill Soper had scored exactly 100 of that total and had made his mark as a future prospect.

Reading through some of the team sheets for that time one is amazed at how players went from Saturday 3rds to Sunday 1sts or Saturday 2nds to Sunday 3rds. It had to be as a result of the difficulties, mentioned earlier, of the strong Saturday fixtures, the league matches and availability of Sunday players. Leo Matthews must have felt a father figure when on one occasion he had the Haly brothers playing in his team along with Bert Kingdon, his son Malcolm and Bert's wife Esme actually scoring.

One of the Saturday touring side fixtures was lost to the weather while the Sunday and Monday games against Bovey Tracey and St. Luke's were both drawn. The second X1 paid, what is believed to be, the first ever visit to Kelly College at Tavistock that season.

By June Peter Anderson, a police inspector, had been posted to Tavistock and had resigned from the Torquay club. In the same month, during a Devon League encounter with Paignton at Queen's Park, both Martyn Goulding and Barrie Matthews were in fine form. Goulding took 4 for 12 and Matthews 3 for 5 before the latter then scored 76 not out of the necessary 97 runs required to win.

Following a winning draw against South Devon, where Cole was outstanding scoring 64 in the 154 total and then obtaining 3 for 8, it was onto the Rothman Cup. Chelston were the opponents and were all for brighter cricket, in every sense of the word. Bill Traylor, their captain, was a man before his time. Years prior to the "pyjama game" of modern one day cricket, he had his men paint their pads pale yellow with a black band across the foot and over the knee. He had tried to obtain coloured shirts, without success, but apparently the coloured pads were sufficient to upset Torquay since they lost once again, albeit on the number of wickets lost since both teams had scored 103 runs. Steve Lang, an 18 year old hit 60 not out of Chelston's total, however they lost to Barton in the next round, who themselves had defeated another senior side, Paignton.

During June there were numerous games with the East Devon clubs, maximum points against Sidmouth, a complete wash-out at Exmouth and then losing to Seaton. The home side were 131 for 8 at the end of their allocation of overs but had Torquay all out for 88. Hosking and Barrie Matthews contributing 60 of that total and the reporter saying, " Seaton spinners had help from a drying wicket".

It was interesting to note that by the mid-season Bill Soper, the earlier mentioned colt with the century, was in the second's and on odd occasions the Sunday X1. He had several partnerships with Ken Creber that helped the teams they were playing for to victories. Richard Turpin was playing more regularly while Ken Peppiatt's name kept cropping up with bowling figures for him to be proud of.

A visit by Exmouth in July was almost spoilt by heavy morning showers which had left the main square unplayable. While it is hard to picture a present day league match taking place at the sea end, on that day it did. Martyn Goulding's 5 for 16, being mainly responsible for Exmouth's dismissal for 62, before Torquay too found runs hard to obtain. The scoreboard showed 51 for 6 when Peter Goodrich went out to bat but he quickly finished the game, and with a final hit for six.

Exciting cricket at Peverell Park almost saw Plymouth snatch victory rather than the losing draw they had to endure. Torquay declared on 192 for 4, Barrie Matthews 85, Clive Cole 45 and Paul Cullis 40. Plymouth batted well and needed nine to win off the last over. They managed to score only seven and had to be content with the one point after a very entertaining contest.

By August Paul Dunkels was back playing for the club, and was a member of the team that took the full five points at Paignton. Having declared at 169 for 8 Torquay then had Paignton all out for 132. Paul Dunkels then had 5 for 37 against South Devon but it was not sufficient to prevent them winning and collecting the points. The captain admitted he made a mistake by putting the home side in and although 137 did not appear a big total to chase, it was. Only Hosking 12 and Sibley 10 managed to get into double figures while South Devon's Bill Jordan was taking 7 for 29.

Matthews, Dunkels, Cole and Michael Goodrich were away with the Devon team when Exeter came to the Recreation Ground so Alan Sibley captained the side. Asked to bat first Torquay were 196 for 6 with Cullis 40, and Hiley Edwards 39, the top scorers. With inadequate bowling resources Sibley put Alan Norman on to seal one end and he returned figures of 2 for 43 off his 23 overs. Exeter at the close of play had scored 130 for 6. As time went on it became more and more normal for a stock bowler to seal one end in that fashion. That same weekend Buckfastleigh came for their match and were 172 for 1. To those old enough to remember George Cowan it will be no surprise that he had an entertaining century to his credit , while Torquay had a mere 61 for 7 on the scoreboard when time was called.

Devon's seven wicket victory over Cornwall at Falmouth had little local coverage except to state, "Barrie Matthews had a dazzling, chanceless 103 not out in a second wicket partnership of 95 in 61 minutes with Paignton's Terry Friend (51)".

While in those far off days it was most unusual to see a Third eleven on the main square it did happen that season and on a Sunday, to supporters' consternation. The Sunday side were due to play a Show –Biz X1 which was cancelled at the last minute and Leo Matthews's side were able to play, and defeat Buckfastleigh. .Matthews and Clive Haly were responsible for most of the runs while Harvey, 3 for 8 and Kingdon 4 for 37, took the wickets.

Following a Sunday victory over Chelston the President, Ken Bryant ran up a new flag that had been presented to the club by playing member Ken Creber. Over a number of years Creber did a tremendous amount of work for the club behind the scenes, apart from being an eager playing member. As a point of interest too, up until about 1990 no game was ever played without the club flag flying proudly, mainly due to Secretary Harry Ball and Bert Kingdon.

The latter part of August and early September were hectic times for the Torquay team that were endeavouring to win the league in its first year. Only picking up a single point from the game against Exeter St. Thomas they were faced with away games on consecutive days, against Tavistock and North Devon. Following the North Devon match 15 players were then off for an overnight stay at Salisbury, prior to moving on to Brighton for a tour. Most of the touring party were first team regulars and would not be back in time for the last double weekend against Yelverton and Chudleigh. Vaughan Hosking skippered the team against Yelverton and included second team players R.Haydock, R. Dickinson, R. Walworth and "in and out" of the first team D.Merrikin. As that result was a losing draw it meant that all five points were needed on the Sunday if Torquay were to capture the title. Fortunately several players did arrive back for the Sunday and strengthened the side, although it was Alan Norman who mainly restricted Chudleigh to scoring 111 runs with bowling figures of 4 for 31. Torquay lost five wickets in obtaining the necessary runs but a captain's innings by Barrie Matthews of 86, the only score that reached double figures, saw the first league title for his team.
There was a certain amount of sympathy for Chudleigh since they really had a bad week-end. Having led the Shiphay Manor league for most of the season, besides playing well in the Devon Senior league, not only did they lose to Torquay but they were beaten by Buckfastleigh on the Saturday who then carried off the other title.

Barrie Matthews had scored over 1600 runs during the season and Clive Cole well over a thousand. The latter, with Alan Sibley had each scored a century while Michael Goodrich had obtained his highest number of wickets in a season, 83. Five players had represented Devon, Barrie Matthews, Clive Cole, Michael Goodrich, Paul Dunkels and Alan Sibley.

At the A.G.M. in March 1973 it was officially confirmed that since Peter Anderson had left the area Michael Goodrich was to be the vice-captain. A newcomer to the club was Graham Gardiner, a wicket-keeper batsman from the Maidenhead area and there was the first mention of the Reverend Kenneth Warren. Warren was to be seen frequently umpiring for the club before eventually taking up the position of secretary with the Devon County, a great character in his own right.

When the season began changes to the Shiphay Manor League rules saw it come into line with the Devon Senior League, inasmuch as 46 overs had to be bowled and the nine over limit for individual bowlers was removed. Since Bovey, Chudleigh and Buckfastleigh were in both of the leagues their games could count for both competitions.

Torquay began the season with a couple of defeats but when Exeter University quickly accepted a fixture, following the cancellation of the proposed visit by Gloucester Casuals, batting confidence returned. In an interesting game Torquay batted first and declared on 201 for 3 with Dave Traylor 80 not out, Barrie Matthews 67 and Hiley Edwards 30. The University were never in any real trouble being 160 for 7 at the close, even with Roger Matthews taking 5 for 60. The Second X1, thanks to the bowling of Alan Smith and Derek Merrikin, easily defeated Stokeinteignhead in the first round of the Narracott Cup.

The weather spoilt the local derby against Paignton in June, after the visitors had amassed 232 for 3 in just 42 overs. Torquay were six for none when heavy rain washed out further play, whereas at Paignton the Second X1 were able to complete their game, and win. Later in the month, chasing 170 at Exmouth, Torquay looked well on their way to victory at 150 for 4. Matthews had set the scene by hammering a great 96 but, "the fat lady appeared early", and six wickets fell for just twelve runs. The skipper was not a happy man and was then left contemplating changes after also being beaten by Seaton. Declaring at 166 for 8 his bowlers were unable to utilise the wicket as Seaton's had done and the necessary runs were obtained with ease.

Barrie Matthews went off to Instow to lead Devon for the first time in the county's first ever encounter with Shropshire, so Michael Goodrich took the Torquay side to Sidmouth. The man himself took 3 for 11 and Vaughan Hosking 6 for 35 thus reducing the home team to 93 all out. David Traylor 57 not out, ensured Goodrich returned with all the points.

Peter Hobbs was noted as either umpiring or scoring throughout this season along with Terry Hubbard. For the first time George Clake was noticed umpiring for the Second X1 and Esme Kingdon a permanent scorer for the Thirds.

With such in and out form supporters wondered just how the team would perform when they went off to play Exeter. As it transpired the team had one of their better days and reports of the game told how well Mike Goodrich bowled. In 14 accurate overs he had taken 7 for 26 and only three of his own batsmen lost their wickets in passing Exeter's all out score of 107.

Following Devon's eight wicket defeat by Shropshire, under the captaincy of a local man skippering the county for the first time, it was only natural that the press wanted a story. Matthews told them of his disappointment and went on to explain that with the selectors approval he was going to try out a number of players. The intention was to build and mould a competitive side for the future. Quite a number of changes were made in the team for the game at the Recreation Ground against

Berkshire but rain prevented a result. Devon had obtained first innings points after Matthews had contributed 40 in their declared total of 140 for 7 and Yeabsley (Exeter) had 8 for 28 in a total of just 60 by the visitors.

Torquay was chosen to stage yet another big game when The Minor Counties played the West Indies Touring X1 at the Recreation Ground. Details of the organisation and the work necessary to bring this about were, unfortunately, not recorded but it must be appreciated that behind the scenes somebody had to work really hard to obtain such a fixture .Overseas tourists always need to have their expenses guaranteed, wherever they play, so who found the guarantors and who they were could have been another paragraph.The Minor Counties played the West Indies Touring X1 led by Lance Gibbs and large crowds were attracted to the ground. Batting first the Minor Counties declared on 300 for 8 with Warrington (Suffolk) bowled by Holder when he had scored 92.The tourists declared on 294 for 8 with Foster on 83, just six runs behind with Bradley (Shropshire) the best of the bowlers with 3 for 55.The Minor Counties closed their second innings on 242 for 6 leaving the West Indies to get 249 runs in three hours. Initially they went for the runs but with Fredericks, Rowe and then Clive Lloyd back in the pavilion it was Maurice Foster who again took the eye with 79. Murray had 59 before he and Holder were dismissed and stumps were drawn with the total on 202 for 8. One account read, "Many spectators felt the Minor Counties might well have won had not Bradley damaged his hand in taking a full blooded drive to caught and bowl Clive Lloyd".As it was he had 4 for 57 to go with his first innings haul.

I am not sure what would happen in this day and age if a club turned up an hour late for a league match! Torquay did that season after being stuck in the holiday traffic. However they quickly bowled out Exeter St.Thomas for 99, Norman 4 for 18, Barrie Matthews 3 for 42 and Smith 2 for 13. While three wickets were lost rather cheaply Hiley Edwards and Vaughan Hosking saw Torquay through to victory.

A strong M.C.C. side attracted a large attendance to the Rec. for a mid-week game where Torquay had the better of a drawn match. Included in the visitors were Len Coldwell (England/Worcester), Alan Moss (England/Middlesex), Derek Cole (Minor Counties/Torquay) Chris Greetham (Somerset) Bob Gale (Middlesex) and Torquay's Sunday captain, Ian Scofield. Torquay lost four wickets in accumulating 201 runs while the visitors were 169 for 6 at the close. Michael Goodrich had 3 for 51 and Roger Matthews 2 for 31 of the wickets that fell.

Late August saw an exciting county game against Cornwall when both captains played their parts in declarations. One of the newcomers in the Devon side was 15 year old wicketkeeper Mike Garnham (North Devon). Cornwall had declared at 233 for 7 to which Devon replied with 222 for 8. Cornwall gave Devon 90 minutes and 20 overs to get 179 after declaring for the second time, on 173 for 5. Matthews and Traylor put on 78 before Matthews was clean bowled while Traylor went on to hit 77. To keep up with the required run rate the middle order batsmen took chances and lost wickets. In the last over Devon needed ten runs to win when Considine was bowled and out to the wicket went the 15 year old Garnham. He did not lose his wicket and thus ended an exciting county game as had been seen for some time.

September saw a Saturday league game at Tavistock where Peter Anderson, with a top score of 48, helped his side to a 12 run victory over his ex-colleagues and effectively put paid to Torquay's hopes of another league title. However, with a tour commencing on the Sunday there was little time for recrimination. Mention of tours! over the years there have been so many 'yarns' around the clubhouse of happenings and incidents. Not all are fit to print but one or two gathered second hand from those involved had to be worth a mention as already recorded. Sorry Jane/Ted, (Full permission from J.E.Dickinson to quote same long before he sadly died)

The Paignton Cricket Club held their annual dinner at the Redcliffe Hotel in March 1974 and the Torquay Times reporting made mention of a speaker, Mr.A.Hitchman expounding on, "the wind of change that has gone through Devon cricket thanks to Barrie Matthews of the Torquay Club"..

Roger Matthews retired from the position of Secretary when the 1974 A.G.M. was held and John Evenett succeeded him .Len Leworthy, who had been umpiring for much of the previous season, was elected on to the committee. During discussion Barrie Matthews told members he was disappointed that 13 of the midweek games had been lost, and in an attempt to better a poor record the club intended appointing match managers. The club felt it was essential to have good sides representing Torquay, not only for the members enjoyment, but to attract other spectators, who in turn helped to ensure that gate monies, refreshments and bar takings were upheld. Members were told that Somerset were to stage their Sunday Players League game against Lancashire on August 11th at the Recreation Ground as well as their Benson and Hedges Cup encounter with Minor Counties South. It was the intention of the club to arrange a benefit game during August for the Leicestershire and England player Jack Birkenshaw.

Before the season began Barrie Matthews announced to the press that he had a new wicket-keeper for the club and whereas it was great news for Torquay it was rather a shock for Paignton. Brian Sambrook, after ten years playing for our rivals across the Bay had joined Torquay. An Ivybridge schoolmaster who had already played for Devon, Sambrook was considered a real capture by Matthews who said, "Graham Gardiner had done a good job behind the stumps but he felt that since Jack Fox had left the club had missed a class keeper".

The season began with a fine victory over the title holder's Plymstock and followed on the Sunday with a win against Westward Ho! However, the usual May weather played havoc with a number of games before the months end. Doug Yeabsley and Barrie Matthews were the two Devonians chosen to play for Minor Counties South against Gloucestershire but Matthews elected to go on a club tour of Leicestershire. The same two players were selected again for the Minor Counties when they played Somerset at Torquay on the 1st. July.

Prior to that cup encounter Torquay endured a frustrating weekend. Going off to Dean Cross most supporters were anticipating another victory but it was not to be and a drawn game resulted. The Sunday match was away against Bovey Tracey where, having scored 179 for 6 the bowlers could do no better than reduce the home side to 150 for 7 for yet another draw .A five wicket victory over St.Luke's College on the Monday did little to make up for the loss of league points over the weekend.

Brian Close, ex-Yorkshire and England, led the Somerset X1 which included Tom Cartwright and an "exciting discovery from the West Indies", Viv Richards. Well that's how the papers of the time described him. Expectations were high but the chances of an upset were not realistic. Moseley, a West Indies quickie, and Jones opened the bowling for Somerset and in the first ten overs only eleven runs were scored. After Cartwright had taken Barrie Matthews wicket for 6 runs other batsmen's wickets tumbled and spectators envisaged an early finish. Lunch was taken at 82 for 4 and while there was another hold up for a short drizzle the end came after 49 overs, all out 118, a total the professional county passed with ease.

Early in July the captain called a players meeting as he was far from satisfied with on the field performances. The local reporter of the time had an article on his meeting with Barrie Matthews and they were eye catching headlines. He stated how the skipper had quoted losing to Exmouth by eight wickets and even with three Devon bowlers in the team they had only taken two wickets! How the fielding was letting down the bowlers and the batsmen were not grafting for runs when necessary, it had to be consistency or heads would roll. The paper, and the reporter, certainly made the most of that interview.

The result of the players meeting certainly had an effect as there were subsequent victories over Exeter, South Devon and Paignton, even when numerous players were away on county duty, which saw the team showing the consistency the captain had requested.

With both the first and second X1's in action an Over 25s side was chosen to play an Under 25s X1 one Saturday and to show the strength of the club at that time the sides are quoted.
Over 25. B. Kingdon (captain), R.Lear, G.Baker, S.Smith, V.Goulding, S.Keeley, F.Craxford, K.Peppiatt, M.Pavey, R.Holloway and P.O'Donoghue.

Under 25 J.Haly (captain) C. Haly K.Creber, S.Craig, R.Harvey, B.Roper, C.Johnson, C.Fletcher, B.Bettesworth, H.Stevenson and M.McMurray.

By the beginning of August Torquay were clawing their way back to the top of the league table again. Although the home game against Exeter was rained off, a winning draw against Buckfastleigh and a crushing ten wicket defeat of Plymouth saw the club with every chance of regaining the title. Plymouth took 46 overs to score 72 for 9 with Hosking taking 4 for 29, Goodrich 2 for 15 and Alan Smith 3 for 23. Matthews 68 and Clive Cole 23 obtained the required runs without even losing one wicket.

Despite overnight rain and early morning showers some 2000 people were said to have paid to watch the benefit game arranged for Leicestershire's Jack Birkenshaw. The Tolchard connection, Ted Dickinson's contacts, and the holiday season were sufficient reasons to have such a game so far from Leicester. A strong Leicester side made 214 for 5 in 40 overs while Torquay could only muster 149 for 6 in reply.

The paper described the number of people attending the John Player game between Somerset and Lancashire as a "huge crowd" but the rains came and spoiled the whole proceedings. The "Cider Boys" were 167 for 9 after their allotted overs with Burgess and Close 54 and 39 not out respectively. Lancashire had scored 36 for 1 when the game was literally washed out by torrential rain.

That same weekend it was announced that Barney Bettesworth had decided to join the Cockington Corinthians and he scored 38 of their 115 runs in their victory at Buckfastleigh.

Ian Scofield led another M.C.C. side during August but an entertaining afternoon ended with a drawn game. Torquay had declared on 201 for four wickets with Roger Matthews 54, Vaughan Hosking 52 and Hiley Edwards 52 not out. When stumps were drawn the M.C.C. were 169 for 6, George Cowan with 55 and Ian Scofield 34 not out.

Ray Tolchard, a teenager and a brother of the Leicestershire player, was in the Sunday side that defeated Buckfastleigh and it was felt that he too was designated for a career in the game. On that day however, it was Bill Soper who caught the eye with a superb 91 not out in a Torquay total of 190 for 4.

Barrie Matthews grabbed the headlines in mid-August when his Devon team won their first match for the season, against Oxfordshire at Sidmouth. Devon had once again obtained first innings points, but had then been left to chase a declared total of 171 for 9. Devon lost early wickets and were 48 for 3 when Matthews went to the middle. Hitting loose balls around the ground, including twelve fours and two sixes, he quickly scored 81 before being stumped. Peter Anderson 21 not out, and Bob Harriott then went on to win the match with an over to spare, Harriott finishing with four, six and another four off consecutive balls. The hard hitting Harriott (Exmouth) followed that knock with 85 not out against Somerset 2cds at Taunton but that was a drawn game. Chasing 190 the Cider-men were 34 for 4 when the shutters went up.

Scoring for Devon had been Ralph Haly, the long serving Torquay club secretary who invariably travelled in the car with Ted and Jane Dickinson. Going on to the next county fixture, at Shrewsbury, Jane turned to speak to Ralph sitting on the back seat and had Ted stop the car immediately. Ralph Haly had died quite peacefully, with long standing friends but so far from his family. Teams stood for a minutes silence at the Recreation Ground at the next home match in memory of a great clubman.

At Shrewsbury Barrie Matthews gambled after winning the toss and asked the home side to bat. Runs proved hard to come by and Shropshire were all out for 162, John Childs 4 for 20 and Ian Roberts (Plymstock) 4 for 40 taking the bowling honours. However Devon were only able to total 129 in reply. Shropshire, in their second innings, declared at 173 for 4. Devon fared no better in their second knock and were all out for a mere 138.

Included in a review of the season there was an interesting paragraph on the Colts. It mentioned how they had won seven out of eight games against other Colts teams and had a tied match with the South Devon Fire Service. The best bowlers had been Bob Holloway and Chris Fletcher while the captain, Malcolm Kingdon, with a batting average of 30 was a fine prospect for the future. It went on to say he had played in the Sunday X1 and records show that mother Esme had scored for the side.

The beginning of 1975 saw the arrival at Torquay of a young player who was going to have a huge influence on the club and Devon cricket. Gary Wallen had been a member of the Exeter St. Thomas club and Barry Matthews had witnessed his capabilities when playing for Devon. As fate would have it the first league game of the season for Torquay was against the St. Thomas club and while Wallen did not play Torquay actually lost by seven runs. Chasing a meagre total of 125 for 7 Torquay were all out for 118 with only Brian Sambrook 32 and Martyn Goulding 20 not out showing any form at all.

Before the end of May Gary Wallen had made his first century for the club, against St. Luke's, in a game where Torquay had lost two wickets for one run. Wallen and Hosking had taken the score to 222 when Wallen was out to the last ball of the allotted overs. Hosking went on to take 5 for 30 but it was a drawn game. Before the next weekend Wallen was off to play for Somerset Seconds against Warwickshire.

After previous poor results at Cockington the first eleven made no mistake in the first round of the Devon Cup, while the Third X1 easily eliminated Babbacombe 2cds from the Brockman competition, with Ken Creber and Bert Kingdon leading the run scoring.

At the end of May spectators had an exciting week-end when Torquay played Paignton in the league and the club entertained a Devon X1 on the Sunday. The Paignton captain, Graham Ashworth, won the toss and asked Torquay to bat which looked a good decision when Friend took four quick wickets. Traylor, Gardiner, Wallen and Hosking lifted the total to 209 for 6 by the close. At 159 for 4 with Markham 61 and Friend 37 Paignton were very much in command but then Matthews took the ball. In ten overs he claimed 5 for 33 and the last pair played out the remaining overs to leave Paignton 193 for 9, an exciting end to a drawn match.

On the Sunday Torquay decided to include the youngster Malcolm Kingdon and it was he who had the headlines in the Monday cricket news. The Devon X1 was all out for 116 with Paignton's Mike Stumbles the top scorer with 46. When Kingdon went on to bowl for Torquay he took five for twenty eight in twelve overs, after which the batsmen then saw Torquay through to a comfortable victory.

By mid-June the league table was looking like a 'one horse race' as Exeter had not lost a game nor had a losing draw in their points tally. Michael Goodrich could not understand why so many players performed well midweek and on a Sunday, but indifferently in a league match. A victory at Exmouth had taken the club to fourth place even though top scorer Roger Matthews, with 53, had been dropped six times so the papers reported. Exmouth were all out for 187 chasing 202 and while the skipper's bowling returns of 4 for 57 looked good, all four wickets had been taken in his last two overs. The return game at the Recreation Ground was even more frustrating, having knocked up 206 runs and had the visitors 26 for 3 at one stage the match ended in a draw with Exmouth on 133 for 8. Chasing just 101 at Tiverton eight batsmen were back in the pavilion before Gardiner took command and saw the win achieved.

Papers of the period rarely gave coverage to the games of junior sides from senior clubs, unless it was a cup competition. Consequently it was interesting to see an account of Torquay 3rd X1 against Brixham where Ken Creber with 60 and John Haly 39 were the heaviest scorers in a 200 total. Dick Lear, 5 for 30 and Derek Merrikin 4 for 41 had ensured a comfortable victory.

Torquay went off to the Exeter County Ground in mid-July hoping to reduce the lead the Grecians had in the league. Exeter made an excellent start and recorded 231 for 5 in their overs while Matthews 63 and Traylor 47 gave a positive start to Torquay's reply. Hiley Edwards continued the chase with a top score of 69 but nine runs were needed off the last over. Only three were obtained and at 227 for 7 it was a nerve racking end for both sets of supporters but great entertainment for the neutral observer.

The end of July saw another of those 'cricketing episodes' that defy explanation. Four days after South Devon had sent Torquay crashing out of the Devon Cup the teams met again at Newton Abbot. Following the cup defeat and the string of disappointing league results the odds were on South Devon. Torquay's 158 for 9,

Ray Tolchard 42 and Graham Gardiner 42, looked well within reach until Allan Smith went on to bowl. South Devon's collapse was unbelievable, all out for 53 and Smith had figures of 5 for 17, the fascination of cricket.

Bill Soper started August with a century against the tourists, Malcontents, but had been in and out of the first team, as had Roger Walworth. Both felt they needed regular first team cricket and as Soper said, "with Torquay mid-table in the league and I cannot get a regular spot", it was off to Buckfastleigh for both of them. When talented youngsters are coming through it is difficult for a club to ensure everyone's ambitions are fulfilled, and especially when the individual thinks the time is 'right now'!

Soper and Walworth were both in the Buckfastleigh side later when Torquay were involved with a double weekend, against Exeter and Buckfastleigh. Against Exeter Garry Wallen had 98 in Torquay's 193 for 4 and the City could only muster 168 for 8 in reply, with Barrie Matthews having the best bowling figures of 4 for 24. Nerves were very evident at Buckfastleigh where Torquay fielders managed to drop seven comfortable catches while the home side were accumulating 128 all out. Despite the fielders errors Alan Smith returned figures of 5 for 33 and Mike Goodrich 3 for 53. After a reasonable start Torquay's reply went from 96 for 4 to 101 for 9 and it looked as though Soper and Walworth were going to have the last laugh. Like a good captain Michael Goodrich, together with Brian Sambrook, stayed long enough to get the necessary runs for victory.

Monday's sporting headlines were more about Martyn Goulding, as an individual, rather than the weekend cricket. He had failed to play for Torquay and had not made contact with anyone at the club so Mike Goodrich said he would not be selected for any team until he did so. Since the next league fixture was against third placed Plymouth and the club would be without Paul Dunkels, away on a tour in Holland, Alan Smith off on holiday and Ray Tolchard at the Cricket Cup final in London, it was as well that the game was actually rained off.

When Torquay played Bovey Tracey during the August the Moorland side were 90 for 7 with Nigel Mountford 45 not out. The son of former Devon wicketkeeper Stuart Mountford, Nigel was called into the Devon side the following week to face Somerset 2cds at the Recreation Ground as a replacement for Bruce Coleman who had been injured. Nine of the Somerset team had first class experience and it is worth recording the names to appreciate what the Devon players were up against. Cartwright, Gard, Hook, Jennings, Burgess, Roebuck, Rose, Slocombe, Clapp, Marks and Breakwell. Batting first Somerset raced to 213 for 4 with Burgess getting 73 before the declaration. Only Staddon and Moylan-Jones were able to cope with Breakwell, 6 for 41, and Devon were all out for 136. In their second innings each Somerset batsman went for the runs and lost their wickets after scoring between fifteen and twenty. Cartwright declared at 137 for 7 leaving Devon to get 215 in some 185 minutes. Three wickets down for seventeen became 44 for 5 before Hiley

Edwards and Garry Wallen set about the bowling. Wallen 32, Edwards 25 and a grafting 40 from Doug Yeabsley brought respectability but it was not sufficient. Two weeks later the return match was played at Bath and even though Peter Roebuck had a personal total of 146 the game was drawn.

Prior to the end of the season Torquay lost the services of wicketkeeper Brian Sambrook who had accepted a new post in Kent, so, once more it was a case of 'looking for a man for behind the sticks'. Ken Creber stepped into the breech and was top scorer with 24 out of a pathetic 63 total at North Devon. The home side had declared on 122 for 8 with Malcolm Kingdon taking 7 for 48. Unable to beat Chudleigh in the last match Torquay finished fourth in the league behind Exeter, South Devon, and Paignton.

Mention must be made of the Devon captain, our own stalwart Barrie Matthews, sadly completely ignored in the production of the centenary booklet. He had set himself a target of five years to lift the standing of Devon's cricket in the Minor Counties. At this point, the end of the third season, he told the press how disappointed he felt to finish sixth from the bottom of that league. He had come to realise that with the County Programme mainly taking place in the two months of July and August, just how few players could take the necessary time off from whatever business they were employed in. Only three players had managed to participate in every game so, after discussion with his committee, it had been decided that in future Shropshire would be dropped, and the county would have ten games rather than twelve. Matthews told the press that he felt some players might be putting club before county. The writer while researching for this book spoke to individuals who made it clear they all had wanted to play for the county. There had been misunderstandings, an individual was not available when asked initially, so another player was invited, then, when the time came for the week away the first individual is free to travel. Very difficult for the captain, he wanted his best side but also frustrating for the player who is 'jocked off' after arranging time off, and reading in the press Matthews's statement that, "we have a great number of players of very similar ability". As will be seen later the "five year plan" did come to fruition but one can appreciate the snags along the way for both the captain, and the players involved.

Not part of the club's history but certainly of local interest. Because of the success of the league at the end of the 1975 season Barton's Peter Cassells sent letters to numerous clubs, with the permission of the leagues secretary, Graham Shears, in an attempt to form a "B" Division of the Senior League. Some clubs never bothered to reply and others pointed out they were already in local leagues and it was to be some time before the Devon League really expanded.

Following the departure of schoolmaster Sambrook to Kent the question of who was to keep wicket was answered before the start of the '76 season with the arrival of Nigel Mountford. Sad for Bovey Tracey, since the family connection had been there for many years, but a great fillip for Torquay's Michael Goodrich. Mountford had impressed Devon skipper Barrie Matthews on his debut for Devon and, rightly or wrongly, supporters felt he had something to do with the transfer.

The first league game was an easy six wicket victory away at Exeter St. Thomas with Ray Tolchard and Hiley Edwards quickly into form with the bat. Other early season wins followed, mainly due to the consistent batting of Traylor, Matthews and Wallen while Alan Smith and Mike Goodrich were constant wicket takers. Victories over Buckfastleigh, Plymstock and Sidmouth satisfied the supporters and the captain. Garry Wallen was also having the odd game for Gloucestershire 2nds which many supporters were expecting to see turn into a departure to the professional game.

An almost unbelievable game took place at Exmouth in the June of that season. Arriving some forty five minutes late, due to the heavy holiday traffic, Torquay were penalised 16 overs. The batsmen really had to go for the runs in those circumstances and Dave Traylor had 50 in just 52 balls. Hiley Edwards had 49 and with Tolchard and Gardiner adding 18 and 16 not out respectively, Torquay went on to record 176 for 4 in their 30 overs. Exmouth's Tozer began well but when he had scored 40 the total was 68 for 3 and a collapse to 84 for 8 followed. Despite a stubborn 50 from Allum Exmouth were all out for 144 and it was interesting to see that the 'promising Colt' of '74, Chris Fletcher had taken 3 for 25 and Goodrich 4 for 57.

When in July Torquay went to play the title holders at Exeter the home side had lost only one game while Torquay were unbeaten, and, with three games in hand, were only three points behind the leaders. Mike Goodrich said later he was pleased he lost the toss when he saw Wallen crack 91 off 100 balls while Traylor, Matthews and Edwards pushed the total to 201 for 6. Exeter struggled to 118 for 7 with Mike Goodrich taking three wickets in a marathon bowling spell of 23 overs for 49 runs. Wallen had 2 for 7, leaving Exeter with the knowledge that they were going to have to work hard to retain the title.

The writer found the research as well as the history fascinating. Mention of the ex-Colt Chris Fletcher has already been made and this particular season his name cropped up more and more. Checking back on the previous season his form had suffered, according to the statistics, while a small paragraph related how he had spent part of the winter at Peter Wight's cricket school at Bath where his run up had been "sorted out" without losing any pace.

While Barrie Matthews had passed his thousand runs for the season David Traylor was expected to obtain the forty he needed when near bottom of the league Yelverton were played. Cricket being the game it is Traylor was out first ball in that match, but in the mid-week fixture following he hammered the Hayward Heath bowling and passed the four figure total.

By the end of August the league title had been won by a massive 24 point margin, thus making the season one of the best up to that time. Unbeaten and not even a losing draw to blot the league results! The last game at the Recreation Ground against Exeter St. Thomas had been won by an incredible margin with the visitors all out for FIVE runs in 11-1 overs. Michael Goodrich had completely destroyed the batting taking 7 for 4, while Alan Smith had 3 for 1. When the reporter phoned in his copy for publication it took a while for it to be believed. Goodrich had taken 67 wickets in the league that season and Smith 40.

Throughout the season, in league and club games, Barrie Matthews had scored 1674 runs, David Traylor 1427 and Ray Tolchard 1059. Skippering Devon, Matthews had been supported in numerous games by Torquay colleagues D.Traylor, G.Wallen, R.Tolchard, M.Goodrich, G.Gardiner, V.Hosking and C. Fletcher.

Reviewing the season R.G.Hill at the A.G.M. of '77 also paid tribute to Ken Creber for the organisation of, and the work that had been done during the winter in the pavilion. The showers and dressing rooms had been improved and there was now bench seating against the pavilion under cover. Mr. Hill went on to point out that for years the clubs deckchairs had not been replaced when damaged or broken and he asked that any member who felt he could donate a chair to do so. Ken Creber, like many a club worker, was quite outspoken at times but a staunch member of whichever team he played in. The younger players who came through the thirds and seconds to reach the first eleven owed a lot to such stalwarts as well as to Leo Matthews, John Neville and Brian Jones.

The old saying, 'After the Lord Mayor's Show' was certainly true of the Torquay Cricket in 1977. Winning the league by such a margin and the next season struggling to stay in the top half of the table was puzzling, and beyond understanding for most supporters. In his third season as captain Michael Goodrich said prior to the start he could not see any team, other than Exeter, really challenging Torquay. With two newcomers, John Billings from Staffordshire League and Bill Hatchett from Ealing, backing up his already strong squad supporters could understand his confidence. However, cricket being the game it is, the season's games did not run according to expectations.

Early season non availability of Garry Wallen, Barrie Matthews and the skipper himself saw several second team players getting promotion and Vaughan Hosking captaining the side. Bobby Coombe, Rees Price and Terry Hubbard were in and out of the first eleven during the changes. During a double weekend, Buckfastleigh and Chudleigh, Hosking took the unusual step, after being asked to bat, of declaring after just 40 overs. Torquay were 171 for 8 with Barrie Matthews contribution 75. Rees Price took two quick wickets and then Hosking, with 4 for 4, soon had Buckfastleigh all out for

92. On the Sunday Chudleigh were all out for 145 and with Ray Tolchard making 53 Torquay managed 146 for the loss of 7 wickets.

A Sunday game against Callington included a brilliant exhibition of batting by Garry Wallen. Chasing 184 for 4 he led Torquay to a comfortable victory with 121 not out, scored off 92 balls in just 89 minutes, ably backed up by Hiley Edwards with a solid 50. The latter was also in great form at Exmouth and won the game with another fifty off forty six balls. Mike Goodrich had taken 3 for 14 in ten overs to restrict Exmouth to 163 for 7, but things did not look good when both Barrie Matthews and Dave Traylor went for two runs. Garry Wallen 40 and Ray Tolchard 46 began the recovery.

During July while Matthews, Wallen and Tolchard were at Exeter ensuring Devon beat the Royal Navy in a 55 over game, Dave Traylor was scoring 93 in a victory over Tiverton Heathcoat. Yes dear reader the author has recalled the good results and would point out that at this stage of the season Torquay were sixth, eight points behind Paignton, in fourth position but thirteen points adrift of Exeter in first place.

Also during July there was another 'holidaymaker story' when an Australian asked for a game and said he "bowled a bit". He certainly did, playing in the mid-week X1 against Sheffield University he took 7 for 17 and thereby cut short the afternoon's entertainment for the faithful.

Team selection is often beyond the understanding of supporters and the dropping of Nigel Mountford for the Exeter game that year was more than a surprise. Torquay's 190 for 4, Matthews, Traylor and Wallen all well into the forties, looked quite good when Exeter were 104 for 5. The bowling then lost its cutting edge and only one more wicket fell before Exeter won the game. With Malcolm Kingdon returning from his college in Portsmouth, the selectors then decided the next team, to play against Plymouth, would not be chosen until he had played midweek. Kingdon played against Worsley, a touring side from Manchester, and took 4 for 32. As a result Goodrich decided his form was right for the first team. He told the press, "I must make changes we have not been getting the early break through". The discarded bowler was Rees Price and within a short time he took the same route as Terry Hubbard had taken after his demotion, the road to South Devon. Whether it was because of the chopping and changing of the players or general disappointment of the season, but Bill Hatchett also left after being taken off in a game where he expected a much longer bowl. Fortunately Alan Smith was back on holiday and he made himself available whenever needed.

Amazingly Terry Hubbard's first game for South Devon was against Torquay and it was noted for runs rather than wickets. Torquay's 209 for 3, Matthews 50, Traylor 46, Wallen 58 and Edwards 37 not out. Then South Devon's 209 for 7 saw that rare result, a tie!

The Devon Cup quarter final against the Cockington Corinthians deserves mention for the ridiculous conditions in which it finished. The game was completed at 9-25 p.m. with the scorers having had to adjourn to the pavilion, since there was no electricity in the score box in those days and they were unable to see! A press report best sums up the fiasco, "Cup cricket at its best in conditions at their worst. Torquay winning because Goodrich won the toss and Alan Smith only conceded 13 runs off four 8 ball overs."

The semi final was against Tiverton Heathcoat and resulted in a comfortable victory. Traylor and Matthews gave Torquay a good start, 41 and 32 respectively and the total eventually attained was 141 for 5. Tiverton were restricted to 90 for 5 by some very accurate bowling.

 Exeter, who had reclaimed their League Champions title again were also favourites to win the final. Batting first they had scored 129 for 6, with John Tolliday cracking 63 not out off 74 balls. If Torquay were going to win they needed a hero and on the day it turned out to be Garry Wallen. With two, 8 ball overs left, thirty runs were needed to win. Wallen hammered three sixes and ran a three off the last ball of the penultimate over. Eight balls left and nine runs required, nail biting entertainment that Wallen finished with two balls to spare. To win against the league champions, who had deposed them, was most satisfying and a little comfort to Michael Goodrich who endured a difficult season, which, rather sadly included personal criticism on occasions.

Fifteen year old John Gerard and Steve Craig had odd Sunday games during the season and during September were chosen for the last of the first team league matches. With Malcolm Kingdon in the first team, mother Esme took over the scoring for that side, while George and Muriel Clake became the permanent dual, umpire and scorer for the seconds. Few people realise George Clake's contribution to the club both on and off the field. If a fast bowler split a stump George would expect to return the next time with same repaired and if that was not possible there would be another set of bails made from the wood. Many players were saved the expense of a new bat with his mending of their damaged article.

Reviewing the County Scene Barry Matthews was delighted that he had guided Devon to its first Gillette Cup place for eight years. When all games were completed Devon were fourth in the Minor Counties League and he went on to say that Bob Cottam, the first professional that the county had for many seasons, had made a significant difference. Robert Cottam had been a right arm fast bowler and batsman for Hampshire and Northants during his first class career which had included four Test match appearances. Matthews said he was disappointed in the Gillette draw since it was only Staffordshire Devon were to entertain and not quite the "money spinner" everyone had hoped for, but playing another Minor County there was a chance of reaching the second round.

March 1978 saw the A.G.M. held and Ken Peppiatt announcing a deficit of some £700. The difficult season had seen bar and refreshment takings well below the average since attendances had dropped. The club had purchased a number of deckchairs which had cost some £350 thus reducing the "balance in hand".As a result players subscriptions were raised to £10, from £7:50 and the 'fund raising member', Mike Goodrich asked everyone to make a special effort to get new members. He himself had, at an earlier players meeting, resigned from the captaincy after three years and the players new choice had been Vaughan Hosking. This was endorsed at the A.G.M. with Hiley Edwards confirmed as his vice skipper. After umpiring the majority of the first team matches The Reverend Kenneth Warren became the fixture secretary while John Haly, Braham Fredman and Stuart Mountford became new committee members.

After the meeting, but long before the season began, rumours were rife regarding an overseas player and thanks to the writer being able to borrow scrapbooks, carefully kept by a dutiful wife of the time, details were easy to follow. A 21 year old Indian player who was expected to be in the Indian squad to tour England the following season, wanted to experience conditions here this year. Rajuvendra Jadeja was reported to be an all rounder and was strongly recommended to Torquay by their ex-professional, Derek Semmence .Garry Wallen had not obtained the expected contract with Worcestershire and would still be available to play, while the news that Bill Hatchett was to rejoin put Hosking in great heart for his first season as skipper. It had been a tight contest with Edwards for the captaincy and while Edwards would be the vice-captain he would actually skipper the Sunday X1. A local reporter at the time wrote, "Hosking is a harder cricketer than Goodrich and can be expected to crack the whip if anyone does not play the game his way. Torquay have won the league every other year and consequently are due to take the pennant again this summer".

Prior to the first match off went Vaughan Hosking to Heathrow to collect Jadeja, but returned with Chandresekar Bukshi! The story was that Jadeja had fallen foul of Immigration and would not be arriving for a few days. By the time of the first week-end of the season Hosking had recruited yet another bowler, Robert Worthy from St. Luke's College Exeter. An easy victory over Plymstock in the opening game was mainly due to Bill Hatchett who had bowling figures of 5 for 8 and it did look as though the skipper might have difficulty keeping all the players happy. A very different team on the Sunday however had to struggle against the Cockington Corinthians. The home team had scored 119, with a young Chris Edwards, giving notice of his potential, with a knock of 40. Torquay were 108 for 6 when stumps were drawn.

Interestingly the week the first X1 were due to play Buckfastleigh the respective seconds should also have met each other. However it was the Rugby League Cup Final at Wembley and the Bucks. Second's could not raise a side with so many players off to London for the weekend. Torquay's captain, Ian Scofield could see he was only going to get two points for the cancelled match and was expecting six against a weakened side so he decided to campaign to get the ruling changed. His plea was, "one of these days a league title could depend on such an occurrence".

Irrespective of Graham Hull returning to the club, plus all his bowlers taking wickets Hosking sat down to talk to his great friend and colleague Barrie Matthews. Always able to "turn his arm" with great effect, and one of the fastest bowlers in the club when he did bowl, Matthews liked the suggestion of his bowling a bit more. He was always thinking about his county responsibilities, and with the Gillette Cup game in the offing, he agreed with Hosking that if he did have short spells for the club he would then be ready if one of his mainstream bowlers in the county side had an off day. The next match, against Chudleigh at the Recreation Ground, Barrie Matthews opened the bowling. He took 3 for 10, Bill Hatchett 4 for 26 and the visitors were all out for 78, another victory was obtained in just 16 overs and by 10 wickets.

With three league games played there was still no sign of Jadeja and each time Hosking was asked he replied with one word, "Immigration". He did however keep reiterating to everyone that he wanted to be on top of the league and well clear of any other side by July. Hosking went on to explain his reasons. Looking at the Devon cricket fixtures he expected to not only to be without the services of Barrie Matthews, Devon's captain, but at least three of his players in addition and there was also the possibility it could be more.

At the end of May Hosking did eventually welcome the overdue arrival of Rajendra Jadeja and he went straight into the midweek eleven to play against the regular tourists Ashford. A delightful knock of 69 saw him chosen for the Saturday side and Chandreseka dropped to the Second X1. Naturally there was much interest in the new arrival but he found bowling conditions very different to those he was used to and did not impress in that department. Exmouth were all out for 204 while Torquay could only muster 148 for 9 with Hosking 42 and Jadeja 43. Barrie Matthews had registered Jadeja for Devon during the waiting period, and, after his innings at Exmouth, included him in the following day's Devon team. This game was against Cornwall in the Peninsular Cup at Troon and again there was great interest as to how Jadeja would perform. Devon lost but the Indian took 1 for 25 in his nine overs and scored 55 in a total of 163 for 6. During the following week he had games for Torquay and his name was in the Friday nights paper for the Saturday match. He failed to appear and a visit to his "digs" resulted in the enquirer being told he had left with all his belongings!

There was no contact with the club or with the Devon authorities which left people mystified and fuming. When the news did break that he had gone to join a club in the Lancashire League the local feeling really did turn to anger. The whole incident was at the same time that the unfortunate death of Bob Bridges the County secretary occurred, or one can imagine the entire matter would have been properly pursued. The Torquay club were just relieved that they had not been financially involved since his sponsorship had been arranged by the Indian Cricket Board.

A week before the Gillette encounter with Staffordshire Devon arranged a warm up game with Gloucestershire consisting of 60 overs each. Garry Wallen had injured himself and was not available while right up until the start of play Bob Cottam was doubtful. The game was great entertainment for the crowd with Matthews scoring 103 and Tolchard 50 in Devon's total of 255 for 5. Gloucestershire were 187 for 5 with Barton's Martyn Goulding taking 4 for 22 and Cottam 2 for 22.

There was a lot at stake when the big day arrived since the winning side would have a home match with Sussex, which would be a great attraction with their array of top class players. A good crowd saw an entertaining game but all too sadly for the Devonians it was the wrong result. Devon scored 205 for 8 with Barrie Matthews 66, Ray Tolchard 40 and Doug. Yeabsley 22 not out. Staffordshire passed the total with the loss of six wickets, Goulding having two of them in his twelve overs.

By the middle of July Torquay were sitting on the top of the league, just as Hosking had wanted, but only with a four point advantage over Exeter. Bill Hatchett had a shoulder injury which had kept him out of the game for two weeks, before he then advised the captain he would be out for the rest of the season, on medical advice. Matthews, Wallen, Tolchard and Edwards were all in the Devon side, as Hosking had predicted, and he was keeping his fingers crossed there would be no more sudden injuries. During July there were victories over Plymouth, Chudleigh and South Devon., with batsmen and bowlers sharing the honours with their respective performances. Hosking and Traylor were in great form with the bat, while when they were not playing for Devon Matthews and Edwards were scoring runs at will. Defiant Ken Creber had 51 out of Chudleigh's 110 but Malcolm Kingdon's 7 for 53 made sure of the victory and an early finish. While South Devon were left to chase the highest league total posted at the time, 253 for 6, it was another sad day since John Billings had also opted to join the Newtonians, he felt he was not getting enough opportunities because of the excellent form of Nigel Mountford.

The second eleven had won the Narracott Cup but of greater significance was the third's first ever victory in the Brockman Cup. Captain, Leo Matthews, who lifted the trophy told the spectators he had played in his first Brockman tie at the age of 12 and now thirty years later he had at last got his hands on the cup. Beating the Police with just six balls to spare completed quite a tussle. In their allotted overs the Police had 59 for 5 with Vernon Goulding, father of Martyn, taking 2 for 6. Torquay's reply was 60 for 7 with Stephenson hitting Neil Stanlake's last ball for a boundary. The traditional match between the Brockman and Narracott winners for the Kendall Meek trophy was then to be played between the Torquay club's junior teams. That naturally resulted in a certain amount of leg pulling within the club, but the encounter never actually took place.

After the cup success of the 2nds and 3rds the first eleven beat Budleigh Salterton to go through to the semi-final of the Devon Knockout Cup. Only chasing 93

Torquay still needed 16 runs off the last two overs and had lost six wickets including Garry Wallen who had scored 31 out of the 77. Hiley Edwards and Steve Smith saw the necessary runs scored but with only three balls left skipper Hosking thought it "far too close for comfort". .

Devon played Oxfordshire at the Recreation Ground and had a hoped for, but really unexpected, victory. The visitors declared at 266 for 7, and Barrie Matthews in turn declared Devon's innings over at 217 for 7. Then the excitement commenced, Michael Goodrich and Tony Allin swung the game in Devon's favour taking 6 for 34 and 2 for 21 respectively. 170 in 150 minutes was the target and with Garry Wallen leading the charge and getting the luck needed, dropped at 30, he went on to hit 89, ably supported by Bob Harriott, not out 38. After the victory Barrie Matthews was "over the moon" and telling the press that he felt Devon were now the favourites to win the Minor Counties Championship.

Research is interesting and fascinating but there are times when it is also so frustrating. All the writer can record is that another big game was played at the Recreation Ground during the beginning of August and the cricketing public were fortunate enough to see yet another overseas touring side play a Minor Counties X1. Knowing the work that is necessary to go into obtaining a fixture of this nature and the early planning to obtain the financial guarantees required it would have been interesting to learn who was responsible. The New Zealand tourists certainly played their part in an entertaining match declaring their first innings closed on 117 for 3. The Minor Counties in turn also closed at 82 for 2 whereupon the tourist's captain, John Parker, had his team go for quick runs. Edwards 46, Congdon 42 and Anderson 35 enabled him to set the Counties 211 to win in 160 minutes. The chase was taken up and the temptation was evident as Parker kept his spinners turning their arms. Five runs an over were scored off the last twenty and from the final over eight runs were required to win. The ultimate blow was a huge six by Frank Collyer (Hearts) in his 35 not out, after Ikin, Kippax and Norton had started the initial onslaught. An interesting point to emerge was that Bert Flack, at one time the most famous groundsman in the country at Old Trafford, living at Willand, near Cullompton in his retirement, had been down to help in preparing the wicket.

When Paignton came to play at the Recreation Ground their new player made his debut in Senior League against his brother. Chris Edwards, who had played so well for the Cockington Corinthians was now about to come face to face against Hiley. All too sadly the game received a scathing press by a reporter who had been advocating a different points system for two years. Paignton won the toss and asked Torquay to bat and they did so to the tune of 194 for 5 wickets. Paignton were just 18 for 3 when apparently the shutters went up and stayed that way while another three wickets fell. The last wicket, at 83 for 6, actually fell to Garry Wallen in the 46 over who bowled UNDERARM to snap up Mahes Naran for 41, the only other batsman to get double figures was, Chris Edwards.

Before Devon went on their week long tour they had an important game against Somerset 2nd and with Barrie Matthews getting his first county century for a while and Garry Wallen hitting 90 not out, a declaration had been made at 258 for 2. Somerset in turn declared on 211 for 5 and heavy overnight rain left the game wide open. Devon managed only 82 runs in their second innings with Garry Wallen the top scorer with 20. At 60 for 1, and only needing 132 to win, it looked odds on that Somerset would be victors. Tony Allin, the Bideford bowler, then had the spell of a lifetime, he took 8 for 51 and the Cidermen were all out for 100. Allin was awarded his county cap and well did he deserve it. For the tour Matthews had the same old problems of availability since, with the exception of Cottam, they were all cricketers and not professionals. Paignton's 18 year old Keith Benton was drafted into the squad and made his debut for Devon in a game when Michael Goodrich was unavailable. A draw against Dorset, a ten wicket victory over Oxfordshire, where Doug Yeabsley took 13 wickets for just 64 runs, and a draw with Berkshire meant Devon were well placed in the title chase that Matthews coveted.

While Devon were engaged against Somerset Torquay had a most important fixture against Exeter. As Torquay were minus Matthews, Wallen, Edwards and Tolchard whereas only two of Exeter's side, Picton and Walker, were in the county team, the game promised to be a struggle. Second team captain, Ian Scofield, was drafted into the first eleven as were Alan Smith, Mike Whitney and Steve Craig. The strength of the club in depth was emphasized by the nine wicket victory in which Steve Watt-Smith took 6 for 6 reducing Exeter to 73 all out whereupon Nigel Mountford and Steve Craig 34 and 36 not out respectively scored the necessary runs.

By early August Hosking was anticipating the League title coming back to Torquay and remaining undefeated for the season. However, in the double week-end, against Plymouth and Yelverton, the defeat came but so also did the title! The usual four batsmen were away with Devon when the Plymouth match was played at the Recreation Ground and, put into bat, only Nigel Mountford with 38 not out brought respectability to the total. However, it was far from enough runs to prevent Plymouth winning by seven wickets. On the Sunday, against Yelverton, Ray Tolchard and Hiley Edwards returned from their County exploits and played their part in the run chase. Steve Watt-Smith was mainly responsible for reducing Yelverton to 130 for 8 with bowling returns of 5 for 56, while Traylor 30, Tolchard 24, Edwards 28 and Hull 23 gave Hosking his five wicket victory.

The last league game at Sidmouth saw the title celebrated in style with a new record score of 310 for 5, with Dave Traylor 111, Hiley Edwards 65, Garry Wallen 51 and the skipper himself 37 not out. Unfortunately the teams bowlers were not in such good form and the Sidmouth team were able to hang on for a draw with a score of 143 for 5.

Torquay reached the semi-final of the Broseley Homes sponsored Devon Cup but were again to suffer defeat by Plymouth. Chasing 152 for 8 Torquay were all out for 138 and Plymouth went on to beat Paignton by the same number of runs in the final.

With the excitement of winning the League title over supporters nerves were tingling with Devon's possibilities. At the beginning of the season Barrie Matthews had intimated that it could be his last as captain but as time went on and his "troops" did the business, and with qualification again secured for the Gillette Cup, people began to "work on him" to reconsider. After a six wicket victory over Oxfordshire at the Rec. Matthews told the press only Durham or Suffolk could prevent his team from winning the championship. Oxfordshire had declared on 266 for 7 and Matthews had closed Devon's reply 217 for 7. The second Oxford innings was an entirely different affair, Mike Goodrich with 6 for 34 and Tony Allin 2 for 21 had them all back in the pavilion for 120, leaving Devon with a great chance to get ten points. Garry Wallen began the chase for the necessary 170 runs in about even time, and had fifty in fifty minutes and 89 to his credit when he was out. A 38 not out from Bob Harriott, with contributions from Ray Tolchard and Tony Allin, got the runs and obtained the points which delighted Barry Matthews and the Devon supporters.

Two days later a rather different team faced Cornwall at Sidmouth but with a similar result, which pushed Devon even further towards that title. The last area game was against Somerset and although it ended in a draw there was a time when the supporters felt they might be witnessing the first defeat of the season. Batting first Devon had made 299 for 5 before declaring with Wallen 87 and Matthews 81. Somerset's reply was 240 for 8 with the young Keith Benton taking 3 for 60. As in the first innings Matthews and Wallen enjoyed their batting, hitting 83 and 73 respectively, with Harriott 57 not out in the total of 248 for 5. Set to score 308 Somerset had sped along at over six an over for the first sixteen overs and Mervyn Kitchen was well in command. Martyn Goulding was put away to the boundary for twenty in his first over but he then took three quick wickets. Michael Goodrich had Kitchen caught behind and eventually bad light brought a finish to the game which had seen Devon obtain three more precious points.

So, well into September the challenge of the professionals from Durham was faced at the Exeter County Ground. Devon did not have to win to ensure they would be champions, but they did have to ensure they did not lose. Batting first Durham scored 301 for 6 with Kippax not out 134. The Durham bowlers soon had Devon in deep trouble and only an amazing century by Ray Tolchard saved the day. He was the last man out with the total at 212 and Devon had created a record for the longest time an innings had lasted in the championship. Due to the amount of time Devon had managed to occupy the crease Durham declared their second innings closed on 71 for 1, leaving Devon to get 161 in 50 minutes and twenty overs. Exeter's Holliday began well but was adjudged lbw when he had 24, then calamity as Wallen went for a duck. Tolchard, tired after his first innings marathon, did not last long and was soon joined by Picton and Harriott back in the pavilion. After forty minutes of determined batting by Matthews the score had increased very little and eventually the captain was out before he reached double figures. At 42 for 6 things were desperate and wicketkeeper, Jeff Evans, was sitting with his wrist in plaster hoping not to have to further risk his injury. Eventually Devon was relying on their two bowlers, Martyn Goulding and the young Keith Benton, to play out the remaining ten overs and save the day. To their great credit they did, and for the first time in their 130 year history Devon won the Minor Counties Championship.

The writer makes no apologies for the space given to Devon cricket in these years' records since the County Club was founded by the forerunners of our club. Devon had been captained by Barrie Matthews who had lifted the County from obscurity to note and he was a Torquay player. He had captained the County for five years and had still contributed his thousand runs for Torquay each season but was sadly ignored when the club celebrated their 150 year. Achievements and records should be recorded or they are forgotten in the passage of time and club history is lost. Committees come and go but the club goes on and on.

During the winter of 1978 Ted Dickinson, with former captain and at that time skipper of Paignton Paul Twose, were busy organising events for Roger Tolchard's benefit season in '79. Leicestershire's Tolchard, was away on the Ashes tour of Australia where a short ball had risen and smashed his cheek bone, cutting his participation short.

After some forty years as player, umpire and eventually Chairman, Ted Dickinson retired at the Annual General Meeting in 1979. He said "it was time to sit back and take things easy", whereas it was another five years or so before his wife Jane and her helpers were to stop serving teas every afternoon .The writer pulled Ted's leg over this when discussing this history and he had a good chuckle. Ken Peppiatt took over the Chairman's mantle while Rowland Gerard, better known as Tony, was elected Treasurer. The members confirmed the captains and deputies as, 1st X1, Vaughan Hosking and Hiley Edwards, 2cd X1, Ian Scofield and Derek Merrikin, 3rd X1 Leo Matthews.

The Devon League brought in a new points system which still did not meet the approval of all players or supporters. It was as follows

    10 points for a win 6 points for the side with the most runs if the game is not complete with 2 points for the opponents.

    1 batting bonus point to be added for the first 100 runs and 1 point for every 25 after that up to 200.

    1 bowling point for every two wickets taken.

    1 point to be awarded to the winning side when batting second for every two wickets still standing at the end of the game.

    5 points for a tie, when the scores are level.

    6 points for an abandonment or cancellation.

Hence the system that brought about the amazing anomaly, and corruption of the English language, introducing 'winning and losing draws'!

Before the season began Ray Tolchard left the club and signed for Barton who had raced away with the Second Division of the league and obtained promotion to the First. However, Clive Wallen, brother of the prolific scoring Garry had joined, Bill Hatchett was fit again and Terry Hubbard had returned after his season with South Devon.

When the league season got under way Torquay had little trouble in picking up 18 points at Plymstock. Bill Hatchett quickly obtained the first three wickets and Mike Goodrich took 4 for 13 before Garry Wallen finished off with 3 for 2. Torquay did lose four wickets in knocking off the eighty odd runs required but Plymstock's early loss of wickets really killed the game. Ken Warren umpiring and Esme Kingdon scoring, which had become the norm for Torquay, as was George Clake and wife Muriel for the second X1 who quickly became established in their respective roles. Torquay's early season game, against newcomers Barton, was eagerly anticipated but on the day they were under strength with Socha and player-coach Tolchard not available. Barrie Matthews was in great form and hit 107 out of the 182 for 4 that skipper Hosking declared on. Martyn Goulding bowled unchanged for 23 overs but was unable to stop the run flow. The Barton batsmen were all back in the pavilion for 35, Malcolm Kingdon 5 for 12 and Michael Goodrich 5 for 22 doing the damage.

When Devon defeated Cornwall in the annual game for the Peninsular Cup Malcolm Kingdon made his debut for Devon and took 2 wickets for 23. The Cornwall side were all out for 105, with Exeter's Picton and Tolliday getting the necessary runs without losing a wicket.

During June the club hit somewhat of a purple patch and it was badly needed. Matthews and Coombe were mainly responsible for the total of 125 on a very soft wicket against Exmouth while Goodrich with 5 for 43 and an economical Kingdon, 3 for 37 in 20 overs, ensured a winning draw. Away at South Devon their captain, Barton Sewell, got 55 out of their total of 173 for 8 but led by Matthews, with 88, Torquay passed it with the loss of only three wickets. At the Recreation Ground another nineteen points came from a victory over North Devon. Ex-colleague Alan Sibley contributed 63 out of the 128 total of North Devon while Mike Goodrich with 7 for 45, literally destroyed the visitors main batting. Torquay's reply was 129 for 3 being largely based on Dave Traylor's 72.

Before Devon's Gillette Cup game with Leicestershire two warm up games were arranged, against Cornwall and Torquay. In the Cornish match Bob Sylvester (Paignton) damaged his rib muscles and missed out while in the game against Torquay only six Devon county regular players were available. Even so Devon were more than surprised to get skittled out for 83! The damage was done by Malcolm Kingdon taking 6 for 33 in 17 overs.

While it was one more experience for Matthews and his Devon side when they played at Grace Road, all so sadly, no one played to their potential when the big day arrived.

Jeff Tolchard was anticipated as being the Devon anchorman around whom their innings would be built. Unfortunately he was caught out early on in his innings by his brother Roger. Things went from bad to worse and from 57 for 6 Picton and Wagstaffe managed to reach the luncheon break with 83 runs on the scoreboard. Allin got a late 17 but a total of 111 against a team of county professionals was never going to give the bowlers a chance. Leicestershire lost one wicket in getting their 114 with Steele 76 not out.

Mention has been made of teams playing at the sea-end and during the summer of 1979 the Torbay Ladies X1 played on that area. Irrespective of the cricket they were quite an attraction in their short white shorts or tiny skirts!

In the quarter final of the Broseley Homes Cup Torquay played Paignton at the Recreation Ground and one of the most exciting local derbies was enacted. Batting first the home side had 143 for 7 on the scoreboard at the end of their allotted overs, eight ball overs in that competition. Roger Mann had been called into the Paignton team for the game and in four overs had taken the wickets of Barrie Matthews and Garry Wallen for just 21 runs. Dave Traylor held the innings together scoring 62 before falling to Chris Edwards who had also taken the wicket of his brother Hiley. When Paignton batted they quickly lost the wickets of Ashworth and Chris Edwards, the latter to brother Hiley! Partnerships between Friend and Sylvester, and then Newcombe and Marcombe took the score to 125 for 5 when Matthews obtained two quick victims. A run out then left Mike Stumbles and Keith Benton needing eight runs off the last over, a run per ball. Despite his young age Benton had experience having toured India with the England U 19 side and played for Devon, while his partner Stumbles was an 'old hand' in the game. Two runs were needed off the last ball and nerves were on edge but Benton cracked a four for a dramatic victory.

Not long after this cup encounter Torquay were over at Queen's Park for the return league fixture and Vaughan Hosking was not a happy captain. Mike Goodrich had taken 6 for 87 in Paignton's total of 170 but the slow batting of Torquay saw them only reach 168 with five wickets in hand. League points "thrown away" he said, but for the supporters, two losing draws and a cup defeat against Paignton was most painful!

The following day at Taunton, Barrie Matthews had his Devon side facing Somerset 2nd in another Minor Counties game. Declaring on 211 for 2, scored in just 55 overs, Somerset then proceeded to bowl out their visitors for 192. The completion of the two innings in one day augured well for the spectators actually seeing a positive finish. Allin, Goulding and Harriott were in better form with the ball in Somerset's second innings and had the Cidermen all back in the pavilion for 140. Picton 42, Tolchard 36 not out and a Matthews innings of 34 ensured the third victory in four games for Devon.

During August, with several players off again on County duty, many people expected that the two games against Barton and Plymouth would see more defeats but as ever, cricket always has a surprise. Nigel Merrikin 3 for 22, Steve Watt-Smith 3 for 13 and Malcolm Kingdon 3 for 31 had Barton all out for 97. Torquay lost their first five wickets but Kerslake and Hosking, 30 and 28 respectively, saw the side safely through to victory. However, the following week Plymouth came to the Rec. and inflicted a crushing defeat much to the disappointment of supporters who had witnessed the Barton episode. The season ended with the match at Yelverton being called off due to the ground being unfit. With the six points for the abandonment Torquay finished second in the league, a very disappointing 33 points behind Exeter.

Before the end of the county scene there were some amazing happenings and results with Oxfordshire. Due to the weather in the first game both captains declared their first inngs closed at 30 for 0 and Devon went on to win. In the return game Oxfordshire had Devon all out for the total of 75, of which two men were responsible for 50 runs, Tolchard and Wagstaffe. Oxfordshire themselves were in for a shock when they began batting and were all back in the pavilion for 84, Doug. Yeabsley taking 8 for 36. Devon managed 123 runs in their second innings but Oxfordshire lost only one wicket in obtaining the necessary runs for victory. A further loss at Exmouth to Cornwall saw the previous seasons champions finish in fourth place in the Minor Counties table. For the first time ever though both Devon and the Dutchy had qualified for the Gillette Cup.

THE 1980 - 1990 PERIOD

At the A.G.M. in March 1980 it was confirmed that the financial slump, reported the previous year, had been rectified with bar takings back to a respectable figure and the overall club profit quadrupled. A keen supporter, Arthur Read, had also left the club a legacy of £2500. Mr. Read, a retired sports master at the Torquay Grammar School is still affectionately remembered by the longest serving member, Wilfred Hore(2003), who says Read was a "sports fanatic". Treasurer Tony Gerard told the meeting the four new sight screens had cost £2000 while secretary Bob Hill pointed out that discussions were being held by the Committee regarding interior pavilion alterations which would need considerable expenditure. Vernon Goulding was elected to take over as the fixture secretary since the Reverend Ken Warren had been appointed Devon's secretary.

At the beginning of the 1980 season the captain, Vaughan Hosking realised he was in for a difficult campaign. In an interview with the local cricket reporter he admitted that while in the past Torquay had little trouble recruiting players it had been completely different during that closed season. Having been told that Steve Watt-Smith was moving out of the area, Bill Hatchett had decided to retire from cricket and Malcolm Kingdon would be away at college, he had spent time, unsuccessfully, trying to persuade bowlers he wanted to come to the Recreation Ground. Hosking went on to explain that change, or occasional bowlers, were going to find that they would be called on more frequently, and for longer spells, so they would have to be really fit for the coming season.

After opening with a winning draw against Plymstock, the first of the five games they were to win throughout the season came against Barton. In their first match Barton had actually beaten the champions Exeter and had high expectations of another victory. Barrie Matthews and Bob Coombe, 46 and 38 respectively, were the main run getters in Torquay's 154 for 7, while Goulding had taken 5 for 36 of his ex-Torquay colleague wickets. Barton could only muster 73 runs in reply with Matthews taking 4 for 9, Hiley Edwards 2 for 9 and Coombe 2 for 1.

Even though Vaughan Hosking took 9 for 69 against Paignton the result was a losing draw, as was the encounter with Tiverton Heathcoat. Away at Exmouth the home side won with ease, Considine took 5 for 25 and Torquay were all out for rather pathetic 90. That total was quickly passed with the loss of only two wickets.

When the team went to Chudleigh the interest was to see the home side's new bowler who had played for Lancashire 2nd's. Martin Taylor, a policeman, did take 3 for 21 but Torquay's 141 proved too many for the Chudleigh batsmen. Mike Goodrich had 6 for 36 and Garry Wallen 3 for 25 while Hiley Edwards took five catches that afternoon.

Early in June Hosking had another 'bitter pill to swallow', Barrie Matthews who had struggled through games with a troublesome rib injury, told the skipper he needed to rest and be fit to lead Devon. He even opted out of the Devon side which was to play a Select League X1 in a trial, Garry Wallen took over the captaincy and his brother Clive replaced Matthews in the side. The county won this game, as they did the warm up match against Gloucestershire 2nds, played prior to the Gillette Cup round.

As Cornwall had beaten Devon in the final Minor Counties game at Exmouth the previous season their expectations were high when they assembled at Exeter for the Gillette. Knowing that the next round would see the victors playing Warwickshire the Cornish authorities had booked further hotel accommodation, such was their belief in the team that they would be victorious!

Barrie Matthews was just as confident however and had told the local press "the two counties are poles apart". Batting first Devon scored 229 which at that time had been the highest score in the competition by a Minor Counties team. Jeff Tolchard went in the first over but Matthews and Wallen then stayed together until lunch when the scoreboard read 110 with twenty overs to go. Matthews, struggling to find his usual county form, was eventually out for 32 but Wallen went on to get a great century, 104. Brad Green, an Australian studying at the Exeter University and playing for the city, hit 54 off 51 balls and, with Wallen, put on 82 runs in 14 overs to take Devon to their total. Barton's Martyn Goulding shattered Cornwall's batting with some superb fast bowling taking 5 for 21 in ten overs. Doug. Yeabsley, in his twenty third year of playing cricket for Devon, had the bowling analysis of 7 overs, 5 maidens, 2 wickets for 5 runs!

Garry Wallen won the 'man of the match', and the £100, but while some supporters thought he was fortunate to be chosen, his own comments later that, "there was not much of it left the following morning", left one feeling the whole team shared the winnings!

While Devon were going along very well as regards the Minor Counties competition Torquay had slipped down into the bottom half of the league. Losing to Exeter, Chudleigh and Paignton, before picking up winning draws against Plymouth and South Devon, meant insufficient points were obtained for them to keep up with the pacemakers. Sadly too many of the midweek games against long time tourists were also being lost, although numerous youngsters were being given the opportunities to vie for places. A few did make the grade and that season Rob Cameron, a fifteen year old, and another schoolboy, John Gerard, went quickly into the seconds, after midweek success, before both had the odd first eleven game. A father and son combination took the eye on more than one occasion when Derek and Nigel Merrikin gave sterling service to whatever team they played in.

In a season when Torquay followers had little to shout about the Devon Cup did provide a certain amount of cheer. Wins over Barton, South Devon and then Sidmouth saw the team into a semi-final against the old enemy, Exeter. Hiley Edwards scored 51 in Torquay's total of 141 for 5 and Exeter finished on 110 for the loss of seven wickets. Once more the neighbours across the Bay put paid to Torquay's hopes of lifting the trophy. Chasing Paignton's total of 142 for 4 the batsmen were only able to manage 137 for 6.

A large following made the journey to Edgbaston to support Devon in the second round of the Gillette and while common sense told everyone the travelling was a vain hope, it was the experience of a lifetime. Losing both Barrie Matthews and Ray Tolchard when only five runs had been scored, Devon were eventually all out for 142. Brad Green had another excellent 59 but was one more victim of Dilip Doshi, who had 3 for 27 and, at that time, was the leading wicket taker in the County Championship. Lloyd with 81 and Amiss's 38 saw Warwickshire home after losing three wickets. Bob Willis, the Warwickshire captain, said later he felt that a Minor County should put their opponents in first, but had to concede when it was pointed out, that his own county had caned Oxfordshire for over 300 runs when told to bat first!

Victories over Tiverton, where Nigel Merrikin took 4 for 44, Plymouth, thanks to Mike Goodrich's 6 for 26 and a tie at Sidmouth, eventually saw Torquay finish sixth in the league table. Hiley Edwards had obtained 1116 runs for the club in all games and Michael Goodrich, after bowling 500 overs, had taken a total of ninety eight wickets during the season.

When Barrie Matthews returned from Devon's three games in a week trip, he described it as a disaster, due to the rain affected matches and the poor wickets. Later he did praise the wicket that Bovey Tracey provided when that club were hosting a Minor County match for the first time. Nick Gaywood had the distinction of playing for both Devon and Cornwall in that game since he was called upon to field for the two sides being the only 'twelfth man' available! Sadly, for the first time in three years, Devon had not qualified for the next seasons, what was to become known as The Nat West Cup Competition.

Before the 1981 season began the usual movement of players took place and the Wallen brothers went to Exeter. The local correspondent reported that Garry invariably did better for Devon than Torquay but that appeared rather a wild statement when checking records. Old timers around the pavilion tell stories of how Garry Wallen could "really bat when a certain committee man would tell him, a £5 for fifty today!"

A young pace bowler named John Smale joined Torquay from Buckfastleigh and Chris Edwards signed for the club, joining his brother Hiley. Chris had been vice-captain of the first eleven at Paignton until he had opted out part way through the previous season. He did tell the press he felt he had been under-used as a bowler and had not enjoyed his cricket as much as he wanted but did not confirm the reporter's expressed opinion, "that he did not get on with the Paignton captain"! Chris was certainly a 'capture' for Torquay and proved his abilities over many seasons.

Torquay began the league season at Plymstock and the press comments were scathing about most of the games played that day. The main criticism laid the blame on the officials who ran the competition, and the reporter implied that with the existing points system there was no real motivation for teams. It was pointed out that the one team that played with conviction, and went for runs, was the conqueror of Torquay! Plymstock had passed Torquay's total of 118 all out with four wickets in hand, but too many games for the reporter's liking had "fizzled out" since the incentive of "big points" was non existent.

The game against Barton was washed out after Torquay had lost four wickets for seventy runs, and then supporters had the experience of sitting through two losing draws, against North Devon and Exmouth. However the encounter with Exeter had been eagerly anticipated and especially so after the Wallen brothers had returned to that club. As it happened the match ended in a tie with each side having scored 146. Dave Traylor and Wayne Fox each scored 55 runs, while Hiley Edwards and Wayne Fox took the honours with their bowling, 4 for 35 and 3 for 50 respectively. Garry Wallen scored 43 of the Exeter total.

During May a special meeting was called of players and members as the Committee needed permission to borrow £10,000. It had been decided that a new kitchen and dining area was needed, an extension to the bar was necessary, improved toilet facilities and the club needed to convert the old kitchen into an office and umpires room. Interest free loans and donations were mainly required as well as various fund raising functions organised. (There are no known photographs that exist of the interior of the pavilion before the changes took place)

While Nigel Mountford played for Torquay he organised a midweek game each season against the South West Post Office employees with whom he worked. This was always an interesting encounter since he was able to call on some excellent club cricketers throughout the West Country. Torquay actually won the game this year but despite Barrie Matthews 105 not out against the regular tourists, Bristol Adders, that was another in the long list of midweek matches lost.

The first round of the Devon Cup saw Torquay at Newton Abbot to play South Devon and once more it was 'curtains' at the first attempt. Chasing a very modest total of 95 the side were unable to muster the necessary runs and finished on 67. Only the young John Gerard, Fox and Goodrich reached double figures, 10, 11 and 11 respectively.

By the middle of June Vaughan Hosking was a worried skipper since there did not appear to be any consistency in team performances whatsoever. Chasing Paignton's modest total of 136 Torquay were 51 for 8 with Mike Goodrich and Nigel Mountford playing out the last seven overs to frustrate the Paignton bowlers. The following day, Sunday, Hosking's troops had to play two games in the one day! At Babbacombe in the morning, Torquay played the locals in the Devon Cup and managed a victory. John Smale was the bowler of the morning taking 4 for 6, with the four wickets obtained in five balls actually! Barrie Matthews scored forty off his old club's bowling. The afternoon was a completely different story, Sidmouth left the Recreation Ground with another 18 league points to the good and local supporters really concerned. After nine league games Torquay and Barton each had 57 points, just five clear of the bottom side Chudleigh, and only South Devon in between. Another lost game followed, to South Devon, and then, for whatever reason things, began to change!

Tavistock were beaten after the game had been reduced to 40 overs each, and that was the first victory in eleven matches. Plymstock came to the Recreation Ground and with John Smale taking 7 for 41 and Chris Edwards hammering 83 not out, went home well beaten. A winning draw against Barton was obtained when Malcolm Kingdon was home from college and he took 7 for 23 in his usual twenty over spell. In the winning draw against North Devon Hiley Edwards hit 102 and was well supported by his brother Chris, also not out, with 53. A visit to Exmouth and Torquay had a victory at the Maer, Chris Edwards scoring 85 and Derek Merrikin taking 5 for 56. One press scribe reported, "Vaughan Hosking had been seen to smile of late while Torquay had been moving up the league after their very poor start". John Smale had a haul of five wickets for 49 in a good victory over Exeter, at Exeter, after which Paignton were beaten. "At last", someone was heard to remark when the result reached the Recreation Ground. The man mainly responsible, Malcolm Kingdon, who had taken 7 for 44! The Edwards brothers had most of the publicity when Torquay went to Sidmouth and won another game, with Hiley taking 4 for 15 and Chris hitting 69. While South Devon were defeated a slip came, in the last league match of the season, against Tavistock. Their bowler Bentley was in top form and whipped out eight of the Torquay batsmen for a mere twenty eight runs which enabled them to go home with the points.

Cricket being the peculiar game it is, the real difficulty in reviewing such a season as 1981 is where to begin the analysis. To have won only one game by the end of June, and then string five victories together in the last six matches takes some understanding. Added to which the latter games were won after David Traylor had walked out of the club, following his being dropped from the first team when the side were slipping down the table.

In all matches Hiley Edwards had scored 1353 runs for the club and his brother Chris, in his first season with the team, 1042. Nigel Merrikin had taken the most wickets, 63, while Wayne Fox had 50 and John Smale 47. Matthews, Edwards and Stopp had all obtained centuries during the season and it was noticed that Len Leworthy had taken over the umpires coat when Ken Warren had been off with Devon.

One reporter had been "delighted to see the Torquay / Exeter monopoly broken by Exmouth " but most of the local clubs were more disappointed to see Barton return to the Second Division so quickly, since derby games attract the crowds and are good for the bar takings.

During the season it had been interesting to see the publicity, in the National press too, that Torquay got as a result of a divorce! Mrs Mildred Rowley had been granted the divorce, after 17 years of marriage, because of her husband's devotion to cricket The 51 year old nurse told the court," Cricket is not his hobby but his obsession". He had left their matrimonial home and gone to live in the Stourbridge Cricket Club pavilion. On the day the decree nisi was granted Torquay were entertaining Worcester Marauders, the touring name of the Stourbridge club. While Mr. Rowley was quite happy with his freedom he was also delighted with the result! Marauders 189 for 5, Torquay all out 32 and only Paul Traylor getting double figures, 10…Shame the result of the game was in the press!

The 1982 season saw the arrival in the area of Ronnie Owen, a Lancastrian who had played a good standard of cricket in the Lancashire and Cheshire league and opted to join Torquay. Dave Traylor had settled his differences with the club and was once more available while the regular presence of Malcolm Kingdon's bowling was to be a plus factor for the captain. Teenager Nigel Merrikin, who had vastly improved toward the end of the previous season, was expected to take over Mike Goodrich's role since he was to devote more time to his golf. As it happened the club were most fortunate that before the season was very advanced Martyn Goulding returned from the Argentine and rejoined the club where his pace bowling was very welcomed.

A usual late April friendly game with the Exmouth club fuelled high hopes for the season but the reality of life returned when the first league game was played against Bideford the following week. Torquay's total of 166 for 6 being quickly passed for the loss of just two wickets. Unlike the previous season this reverse was rapidly sorted out and victories were obtained against Chudleigh, Plymouth and Exeter. A winning draw against North Devon, at Instow, saw the team again playing entertaining cricket and they were attracting good crowds wherever they went.

Unable to always field strong Sunday and mid-week teams saw the club beaten by Exeter St. Thomas, Ashford, Somerset Stragglers, Midland Bank and Nigel Mount ford's S.W. Post Office amongst many others.

Champions Exmouth came to the Recreation Ground where a young Nick. Folland had 77 not out in their total of 196 for 6. However, with the Edwards brothers scoring 61 and 42, Torquay soon had the winning points. Ted Dickinson got together a strong side for a Sunday fixture with the club and an entertaining game ensued. While older readers will remember the standing and reputation Ted had throughout the Devonshire cricketing fraternity it bears mentioning the calibre of players who supported his Sunday team. Wallen Considine and Dunk from Exeter, Twose and Benton from Paignton, Billings and Melhuish from South Devon, each man with county experience. Torquay's 163 certainly looked attainable but Martyn Goulding with 6 for 33 ensured another victory for the home side and it was 'roll on the next league match'.

So much for expectations as the game was a real upset, losing against Plymstock where only Ronnie Owen was able to cope with the bowling and score a few runs, 33. That surprise was followed by a match against the bogey team, Paignton, Martyn Goulding, always a good bowler but on occasions quite devastating, had a good afternoon and took 7 for 52 which was mainly responsible for the Paignton all out total of just 113. While the nerves of the Torquay followers were sorely tried, because four wickets went down very quickly, the Edwards brothers came together and saw the target safely reached. Hiley Edwards also had a good innings of 84 in the next game against South Devon, but on that occasion Torquay had to settle for a losing draw.

Once more the cup draw had thrown up an encounter with the Cockington Corries and since both Edwards began their careers at the club and would be playing against the third brother interest was high. Paul Edwards was a very important cog in the Cockington side and he was keen to see Torquay defeated. Torquay paraded their full first eleven and batting first the Corinthians had to face Martyn Goulding and Malcolm Kingdon. Stuart Gibson scored a few boundaries before Kingdon had him caught for 15. Paul Edwards and Peter Griffiths treated the bowling with little respect and skipper Hosking and Hiley Edwards had an over each in an attempt to slow the run flow but without success. Fox and Smale then took wickets but at the end of the allotted overs the total was 92 for 6. Barrie Matthews and Chris Edwards opened the Torquay innings and managed to score 13 and 10 respectively. Hiley Edwards 16, Ronnie Owen a 'duck', Vaughan Hosking 10, Martyn Goulding 13 and before the end only Nigel Merrikin troubled the scorers a little, with 7 not out. Total, 84 for 8! Paul Edwards was the top scorer of the night with 32 and Stuart Gibson with his 5 for 21 in four overs had 'seen off' the senior club.
Such games are part of our history and should not be forgotten. Throughout the years, and in this 21st. century we still hear silly remarks like, "with our strong batting!", whereas every game is a case of, 'on the day, on the field' and that's what makes cricket the fascinating game it is.

The loss of that game did not affect the overall application in the quest for the league title and only two more games were lost. Those two had to be Exmouth and Paignton .After the Exmouth result a double weekend saw some remarkable batting by several players and Dave Traylor in particular. Top scoring with 69 in a stand with Chris Edwards of 107, chasing 179 to ensure a six wicket victory at Plymouth, he then, the next day, had 101 not out against North Devon. That game at the Recreation Ground, saw Traylor and Matthews establish a then new record opening stand for the league of 158, but the visitors held on for a losing draw. After the league title had come back to Torquay Chris Edwards pointed out the four top batsmen had scored over two thousand runs while the two opening bowlers, Martyn Goulding and Malcolm Kingdon had taken a hundred wickets between them . His own total of 609 league runs had given him an average of 38 and relegated his brother to second place with 33:2. In all games for the club four batsmen had passed the thousand run mark, Barrie Matthews, Dave Traylor, Hiley Edwards and Ronnie Owen.

Throughout the season various functions were held to raise funds for the Pavilion alterations that had taken place. The last being a four course, roast beef dinner in the newly completed dining area organised by Sylvia and Tony Gerard before his retirement as the club Treasurer.

Torquay commenced the 1983 season under the captaincy of Hiley Edwards with the usual closed season of player movement. Ronnie Owen had returned to Lancashire but there had been the return of Ken Creber from Chudleigh, Ian Coulton had joined from Buckfastleigh and a promising youngster, Nigel Janes had arrived from the Cockington Corinthians. Supporters said, "If he turned out as good as the Edwards dual from Cockington he would be o.k". An Australian who wanted a season's cricket in England also joined, Ian Moore, and he turned out a very useful acquisition as well as a great ambassador for Torquay cricket when he returned to Australia.

The league "A" Division sides will remember the season for the introduction of official umpires. No longer would club members officiate for their home team, whether qualified or not, but league appointed umpires for every competitive game. Checking the Torquay score books it was unusual not to see Ken Warren, Len Leworthy or George Clake recorded as 'umpire' whereas later it was, Mr. Lewis, Mr. Fogwill, Mr. Miller etc.

During the 1982 season Barton had employed a former Pakistan test player, Agha Zahid, who had helped see them race away with their league and gain promotion. His diligence at training and in the nets had seen a number of young players develop and this time the Barton club were suggested as " the dark horses to be watched ", and no longer a bet to go down again. Just before the season began Torquay had a real surprise and a shock! Martyn Goulding left the club to join Barton, as their captain! , and with Zahid the two were to prove a formidable partnership.

Opening the quest to retain the league title Torquay had to be content with a winning draw against Plymouth and only when skipper Edwards took the ball did wickets fall, 3 for 19 but too late to get a result. Ian Coulton had gone into the first eleven but Ken Creber had reminded everyone of what he was capable of when in the Sunday First he had a game saving innings of 57 against Taunton St. Andrews. Two winning draws in the league followed and Ian Moore showed his capabilities with 90 against Paignton whereas it was the skipper who hit 78 against North Devon.

Nigel Janes had his first half century in a midweek game against Acton where he was well supported by Ken Creber with 47, but to no avail as the visitors went home victorious. Barrie Matthews and Chris Edwards made over half the team's total score of 107 against the Ashford tourists, but with five other players not troubling the scorer at all one feels 'it was one of those mid-week sides'! Paul Bowes was at it again when the Heffle Cuckoos arrived for their annual visit with another century to his credit, he appeared to enjoy batting on the Torquay wicket.

Exeter were soundly beaten in the league when Ian Moore had an excellent 75 in the total of 155 and Malcolm Kingdon wrecked the heart of the Exeter batting taking 5 for 34. That game was followed by the encounter with Barton and what a different story to the first season they were in the "A" division. Torquay's total of 166 for 9 was mainly due to Nigel Mountford 81 not out, the only batsman able to cope with the bowling of Goulding and Hudson. Barton lost seven wickets by the time the Torquay score was passed but it was another game lost for the club and the beginning of a series of surprising results between the two sides.

In his first season as captain Hiley Edwards was having all sorts of problems, including injuries to his bowlers causing him concern. A knee injury to Kingdon then left him with only one regular opening bowler, John Smale, and he was awaiting a call to take up a new post in Oxford. The quarter final of the Devon Cup had seen Paignton knock up 65 runs without losing a wicket, before rain prevented further play. In the replay Paul Dunkels was called up from the seconds but on the day required he was working at the Bodmin Crown Court, as a barrister no less.. Paignton were 141 for none when Hiley Edwards put himself on to bowl and proceeded to take 3 for 18, it was 183 for 4 at the end of the allotted overs, Ray Tolchard 75 and Keith Benton 59. With Barrie Matthews out first ball to Stuart Lott, Torquay struggled to 147 for 7 and once more were beaten by their neighbours across the Bay.

Before the end of the week Mark Clilverd, a medium pace bowler from Dartington, signed for the club and went straight into the first team for the double weekend. Hiley Edwards told the press that it was against the clubs normal policy but he was so short of bowlers it had to be done. At Sidmouth it was another lost game, while at home to South Devon a winning draw was attained, and that was mainly thanks to the skipper's innings of 99 , and most people said he deserved a century.

The penultimate game of the league season was against Plymstock, at the Recreation Ground, and the club included 16 year old Richard Turpin, the son of the earlier mentioned Richard Turpin, hotel trainee. A wicketkeeper batsman in the Colts, but with county keeper Nigel Mountford behind the stumps, Turpin was in the side for his batting. Up to that time only three Torquay players had managed fifties in the league, which was such a difference from previous years. Hiley Edwards had told the cricket reporter that he felt, "rock bottom had been reached when on an excellent wicket Torquay had only managed 119 for 9 after Exeter had scored 204". As it turned out Torquay had a winning draw against Plymstock, Hiley Edwards and Dave Traylor, 81 and 70 not out respectively, taking the total to 222 for 2. Chris Edwards with 7 for 62 reduced the visitors to 137 for 9.

The last game of the season was at Barton and papers of the time described it as the most exciting final weekend of the league ever. Throughout August the title had appeared to be heading for Sidmouth but Barton supporters knew they had a chance. Their expectations were lifted when the team had beaten Exeter and now they had to depose the existing champions and take the title themselves. The anticipation of seeing Torquay beaten and new champions crowned ensured a large crowd which the papers reported as "over five hundred". Torquay had included the young Turpin in the side and supporters wondered just how he would cope with the pressure that was undoubtedly on him and the whole team. Barton's Martyn Goulding returned figures of 8 for 44 but Turpin actually had the top score of 52, and was ably supported by Ian Moore with 47 in the all "out total" of 151. The lad had shown great courage and application in what was a cauldron of emotion. Then it was Barton's turn to see how their nerves would react to the pressure and at 82 for 5, with Agha Zahid run out, the tension began to tell. Chris Edwards had another afternoon of good bowling and took 6 for 40 but Barton achieved their goal with 118 for 8, a 'losing draw' but a title in the bag! Barton became the new champions and Martyn Goulding and Agha Zahid had justified all that had been said about their potential abilities. It was later learned that Paignton had easily defeated Sidmouth.

Hiley Edwards first season as captain had seen him as the top scorer in the league for the club with 638 runs. Moore had 555, and with 1299 runs in all games Edwards was second to Ian Moore who scored 1601. With all the team difficulties, and only actually winning two of the league matches, the side had finished in fifth position.

Before closing the memories of this season mention must be made of Devon's last game and of their exploits. Following the defeat of Shropshire Barrie Matthews had ensured Devon's place in the next seasons Nat. West cup competition. For the Wiltshire match, at Bovey Tracey, Devon included Ian Moore after his performances with Torquay. Batting first Wiltshire declared at 214 for 6, whereupon Devon replied with 255 for 2. Wallen had obtained 51 runs in his innings while Folland and Shaw were both not out on 83 when Devon's declaration was made. John Rice, the former Hampshire batsman then hit 121 in Wiltshire's 333 for 7, leaving Devon to chase 297 in two hours and twenty overs. Ray Tolchard and Garry Wallen scored 50 off the first four overs before Tolchard was out for 33. Wallen went on to obtain 70, but Folland did not repeat his first innings batting skills and it was Matthews himself, and Hiley Edwards, who advanced the total with 47 and 42 respectively. With 104 needed off the final twenty overs wickets fell in the fading light and drizzle that had begun. Bovey's Shaw chipped in with 17 and the fast bowlers Martin Taylor and Paul Brown were there for the last over with eleven runs still needed. Three were required off the last ball and Taylor smashed, the only way to describe it, the resulting six. Great entertainment providing one was a neutral spectator or a Devonian!

N.B. (The writer returned to his birth place during the Spring of 1984 to retire and over the years since has missed very few first team games or midweek matches, consequently from this point comments made are based on personal observation.)

After his difficult first season as captain Hiley Edwards was hoping for better things in the 1984 season and an improvement on the final league position. As in every 'closed season' rumours abounded regarding player movement but when the summer came very few were true. Ian Moore had not returned from Australia but Devon's fast bowling policeman Martin Taylor had joined Torquay and Graham Hull had come back from South Devon. On his return to Australia Moore had a letter printed in a paper covering his cricket in the U.K. which caught the eye of two young cricketing brothers. Neil and Bruce Bidgood persuaded their parents they should spend the summer in Torquay and duly arrived at the Recreation Ground. Two happier, fun loving but very serious cricketers could never be imagined and those supporters who were lucky enough to see them play, day after day, still talk about their respective feats even now. Ian Coulton had been on a short tour of Barbados which one hoped had sharpened up his batting, and it did, proving very beneficial during the season.

Following Richard Turpin's performance in the seasons final game of '83, Devon decided to register him when rumours began that Somerset and Gloucester cricket scouts had been "asking questions". He was to celebrate his 17th birthday on the first weekend of the season when he was selected to keep wicket for a Devon X1 against the Devon Cricket League X1 at Exeter. Devon scored 170 for 6 with the young Turpin 21 not out after sharing a stand of 61 with top scorer, his captain, Hiley Edwards. Keith Donoghue, later to prove a Devon stalwart over years, took 4 for 35. The League X1 was all out for 96 and Turpin managed two stumpings and a catch off Neil Wonnacott, Eddie Picton and Agha Zahid. So, without having kept wicket for the club's first team, Turpin had done so for the county!

Having good bowlers available this season Hiley Edwards obtained good league results for the first month's games and then came the almost proverbial cup 'hiccup'. Brixham, who were celebrating their Golden Jubilee that year, did so in style! They defeated Torquay and put the club out of the cup. Martin Taylor scored 57 out of Torquay's 104 for 9 but Brixham passed that total with three wickets in hand.

In a summer of wonderful sunshine there was the first abandoned game, for bad light, against Barton. Torquay had scored 151 for 9 with Martin Taylor once again top scorer with 48 and Barton 110 for 5 when umpires Spencer and Fogwill called a halt to proceedings. Due to the sunshine and drought, water restrictions were put into operation and the groundsman had to arrange for water from the nearby stream to be pumped across to the cricket square. On the 27th August, after the club had played and beaten Sully Centurions, and in those days the evenings were spent in the bar, a thunderstorm broke. Lightning struck nearby cables and the lights went out so candles were hastily lighted while torrential rain fell. Supplemented by the excess rainfall from the Torre Abbey grid, the ground flooded to the extent that the water was quite deep around the pavilion. Not wishing to wade out in deep water everyone stuck to the "liquid" in the pavilion! Once the rain ceased and draining began people were able to wade out the through the side door to the Kings Drive. Several members of the Sully team were down at the ground the next day having refused to believe that play would be possible after that downpour, and were astounded that a game did take place, against the touring Worcester Marauders.

On several occasions during midweek fixtures it was not unusual to see a father and son combination playing. While Dave Perry Senior was happy to help make up a team at the advanced stage of his playing days, his son, Dave Jnr. began developing into a useful quick bowler and the following season actually had games in the first eleven.

August that season saw one game that most members want to forget, although most local cricket lovers, who are not Torquay followers, will ensure it remains in the annals of cricket history. I refer to the return league game against Barton, who were racing away to another league title. Barton had scored 154 for 8 wickets in their forty six overs thanks mainly to Zahid, before he was brilliantly run out by Chris Edwards, when on 79. To Torquay supporters, having beaten Sidmouth and Exeter in their previous games, 155 did not seem an impossible target, until the batsmen went to the wicket. Goulding opened his bowling with the usual pace and hostility but not the accuracy, then he did get a ball through Colton's guard and the first wicket was down for 22, Coulton, 15. Ken Creber, Hiley Edwards, Chris Edwards, Vaughan Hosking and Martin Taylor all came, and went, without troubling the scorers, except to insert the 'duck'! Nigel Mountford did manage two boundaries before being bowled and Malcolm Kingdon became another 'no score' leaving Graham Hull not out. Martyn Goulding had taken 8 for 17 in 10:4 overs, including the hat-trick, in a devastating spell of bowling. True, Goulding was recognised as an excellent Minor Counties bowler on his day, but to take six wickets, all county players, for no runs in eleven balls, was devastating to this watcher. Barrie Matthews, who had gone to the wicket at ten minutes past five, was bowled by Nigel Merrikin for 6, at half past six, having watched the mayhem from the other end. Bruce Bidgood was still at the hospital unaware of the happenings having damaged a finger in taking a catch. "All out for 38", was very soon echoed around Torquay!

At the end of the season Hiley Edwards was able to report a better year and Torquay had moved up the table into the third position. Purely as a personal opinion, the writer feels that had he introduced the Bidgoods into the first eleven earlier in the season, it might have been even better. The individual scores tell the stories of the highly entertaining midweek cricket seen that season with four players topping the thousand runs. Barrie Matthews 1161, Ian Coulton 1293, Bruce Bidgood 1567, and Neil Bidgood 1663.

The Second X1, having won 12 out of the 24 games under Steve Craig's captaincy won their league with one of the strongest second elevens for a long time. Apart from the initial appearances of the Bidgoods, players of the ability of Ken Creber, Colin Davey, Nigel Janes, Derek Merrikin, Dick Lear, Bob Dickinson to call on , just to mention a few, the seconds were a side of experience as well.

As already mentioned earlier, the writer has devoted a certain amount of space to Devon cricket in his Torquay history because of the club's strong connections. This season saw the end of an era, which also needs recording, since few people really understand or appreciate, the time that Ted Dickinson and Barrie Matthews gave to making the county what it became in the cricketing sense. Devon's end to the season was a game against Somerset 2cds at Bovey Tracey which was to see Barrie Matthews play his last game as captain and Ted Dickinson retire as Devon's team manager and chairman of the county cricket selectors. Somerset had declared on 298 for 8 and 203 for 4 while Devon, with 246 for 8 in their first innings, had little time to reply again. Had the game not ended as it did people would have remembered a dull draw, with rain clouds gathering and the odd clap of distant thunder. In those circumstances Matthews decided to open the innings himself, needing nine runs to complete a 5000 total for the County. As soon as he had scored the necessary nine Somerset made to bring on a fast bowler, the umpires in the fading light and drizzle called a halt to the proceedings and everyone made tracks to the pavilion. Less than half an hour later the ground was under water. Barrie had made his Devon debut in 1965 and taken the county to heights only dreamed about in the past. To have won the Minor Counties championship in 1978 and got the county into so many Gillette and Nat West Cup competitions cricket supporters had a lot to thank him for. True he was in a position to be able to give the time to his dedication, as was Ted Dickinson, but how all this could be overlooked in any club publication, defies understanding.

The writer became a club member again at the beginning of the 1984 season and discovered an old pal and his wife, Bert and Irene Schneider, were looking after the bar and catering. Monies from these two sources, and in the old days, gate receipts and scorecards, played a large part in the club's income. Changes brought about by the modern times we live in had necessitated employing people, rather than being able to rely on members. Some of the earliest ladies actually mentioned by name who provided tea were Mrs Snape and Mrs. Whitehead whose husbands have already had mention as club stalwarts. Later Bob and Norah Hill are recorded as running the facilities. While Irene Schneider prepared all the sandwiches and cakes for the players teas, Jane Dickinson and her 'army' of helpers, served refreshments to the public. It is probably difficult to picture now, but such was the business then, that one lady would serve the sandwiches, another the cake, another poured the tea and the last took the money! Always four on duty and after the players had finished their teas the ladies, plus Bert and Irene, Bert's brother Bill, who looked after the car park, Harry and Clara Ball, the club secretary and wife, and quite often John Rossiter who did odd jobs on the score-board, completed the number for a second sitting of tea. Seeing Irene struggling with all that washing up later, the writer popped in to help, and continued to do so for many days before Bert told me to "come in for tea boy" which I did, never realising that one day I would take over completely! The 'behind the scenes' glimpse was quite intriguing, three and sometimes four tables set for helpers after the players had finished, and in those days the players sat at tables with plates and knives for every setting. Lady members who were quite happy to serve at the windows were never seen washing or drying utensils and Bert was needed back in the bar as soon as tea was over. However that indoctrination to the kitchen came in very handy later as, sadly, the Devon Treasurer upset the Schneider's when discussing the accounts for a particular county game and they resigned.

Before the A.G.M. was held the death was announced of a former President and member for forty years, Kenneth Bryant. A wicketkeeper who joined the club from South Devon and became very involved in local politics Ken was another of those councillors who ensured the club always had a fair hearing when sport was under discussion in Council. Another staunch supporter who also died was Charles Jenkins and Mrs. Jenkins donated a bench seat to the club in memory of the happy times she and her husband had together at the Recreation Ground.

The A.G.M. covering the 1984 season held at the Livermead House Hotel, by kind permission of the cricketing enthusiast owner, John Perry, was told by secretary, Harry Ball, that the new nets had arrived ready for the season. He went on to tell members what a success Bill Traylor had been as the midweek match manager and to those who attended every day the reason was obvious. Apart from the frequent availability of those four batsmen, and their thousand runs apiece, the Traylor Brothers Building Co. were at that time employing practically a complete team on their construction work contract at the Toorak Hotel, five minutes up the road. A common sight was to see Bill's son, Paul, leading four, five or even six players down to the ground for the afternoon play where on occasions Bill's brother Dave was already waiting. His master stroke however was when on the rare occasion he was short he had John Millington in reserve. John was a very, very ordinary cricketer but so dependable and he loved the Recreation Ground. Fixture secretary Vernon Goulding had moved out of the area necessitating appointing a new man but other officers remained the same. At the meeting Mr. Ball also had alterations to the Club Rules on the Agenda and one in particular caused smiles from frequenters of the bar. Rule 29 was to read, 'Club to remain open until 11p.m.to agree with the licensing hours', regulars knew this would mean early closing! The other change, 'Dogs, already not allowed in the pavilion with the exception of guide dogs, will no longer be allowed in the enclosure at the request of members'. Kept until a certain captain, Nigel Janes, had an animal and removed the, then permanent, notice.

Before the start of the season League officials met numerous club officers for discussions as many of the "A" League clubs felt that with the expanding number of junior sides they had too much 'say' and the balance of voting was totally unfair. Threats were made regarding a 'break away' league by a number of the senior clubs before proposals were eventually put to League Officials, they called an Extra General Meeting which saved the day.

David Jones was a newcomer to the club and the area, while Pete Socha, previously with Paignton and Barton, who had odd midweek games, officially joined Torquay thus adding to Hiley Edwards bowling strength. Jones had the reputation of having played for Glamorgan 2nds so supporters began anticipating a successful season and especially so when another Bidgood arrived from Australia. Kenneth Bidgood had been so impressed with the tales of his brothers that he decided he too would enjoy a Torquay summer. Sadly he did not enjoy the superb weather they had but, he did carry on the family tradition of scoring runs. By the end of the season, after 32 innings he had accumulated 1250 runs, three centuries and seven fifties, a very useful clubman. Being older, Ken was more mature and very much an adult compared to his 'crazy' younger brothers.

While Edwards was expecting to be without Malcolm Kingdon for some time, he went into hospital for a cartilage operation, it did not work out that way. Kingdon was told after the surgeon had opened the knee it was only inflamed tissue and they were not going to operate further.

Martin Taylor and Pete Socha were mainly responsible for a winning start against Bovey Tracey and then a winning draw in the Sidmouth game. Actually, Taylor was only to bowl 58 league overs for Torquay before being posted elsewhere, as mentioned previously he was in the police force. With Malcolm Kingdon waiting for his knee to heal, Hiley Edwards was once again struggling with his bowling strength. The late May game against Barton at Cricketfield Road saw both Jones and Bidgood called into the first team and the press reminding the club of the last occasion the two sides met! Barton, batting first, had a winning draw, Pete Socha in a long spell of bowling 'sealed' up one end with 23 overs and returned figures of 4 for 83. Graham Hull backed up well with 3 for 50. Goulding did not do as much damage in this game and Hosking and Bidgood were well able to play out the time. However a few weeks later, in the cup match, Agha Zahid got 75 and once more Torquay were out of the competition!

Following two defeats, by Exmouth and Exeter, Torquay then had a brilliant spell, a winning draw at Plymstock which was followed by five consecutive victories. Barrie Matthews had five consecutive seventies while Jones had a not out century and a fifty. There was an upset though, Sidmouth beating Torquay quite comfortably before the return game with Barton. Yet another surprise result later was in store for the supporters, and this time Barton suffered! Batting first they were all out for 64, Malcolm Kingdon 6 for 12 in 18 overs and Graham Hull 3 for 33 in 16 overs. Matthews and Jones lost their wickets for 25 and 18 respectively but there were no more worries and it was an early drink to celebrate a very good win.

Richard Turpin, eventually known throughout the club as Ric, had several midweek games and in a drawn game against the touring Leatherhead side hit a century. He then scored 72, of Torquay's losing total of 172 against Reading. Three successive midweek games kept the scorer busy with Ken Bidgood's personal results, scoring a 92, 124 not out, plus a 50, before taking 4 wickets for 60 in the same game. Mid week centuries were obtained also by Ian Coulton, John Gerard and Scia Scia, a young New Zealand guest player who was in the Paignton side that season.

Despite losing to Torquay by seven wickets Paignton, in their penultimate match, obtained the three points necessary that would ensure they won the league for the first time. Having restricted Paignton to 130 for 8, Torquay lost David Jones for nought but Richard Turpin, called in to replace Nigel Janes, scored 59 and Matthews 25 before Coulton and Chris Edwards passed the runs needed to obtain another victory. Purely for interest, the following day Chris Edwards was the other side of the Recreation Ground playing for the Torquay Athletic against Neath at rugby.

Reviewing the season Hiley Edwards was reasonably pleased to have finished in third place pointing out the club had actually won ten league games, something they had not done before. In the league Barrie Matthews had 696 runs in 18 innings Ian Coulton 423 in 19 visits to the crease while skipper Edwards, with half that number but more 'not outs', had a better average, which always makes statistics very debatable.

Second team captain, Ken Creber paid tribute to the contribution Derek Merrikin made to his side and, while pleased that Nigel Janes had established himself as a first eleven player, said he was badly missed in the seconds. Ken warned that because of the distance he lived from the ground and the travelling involved he would be giving up the captaincy.

To the daily supporter, and observer, it was fascinating to see the progress made by Colts players who found time to play against stronger opposition in the touring sides and, in that season, particular notice was made of Phil Bradford, Sean Kirby, Brendan Scofield and Chris Flanagan. The club were also indebted to numerous youngsters from other teams who came and made up mid-week sides such as Andy Hele, Andy Pugh, Howard Carter and Nigel Merrikin, to name but a few.

In his first season as the Devon captain Hiley Edwards had carried on in the 'Matthews tradition' and ensured qualification for the Nat West competition the following season. The County had finished second in the Western Division of the

Minor Counties League while papers had made great play of his young batsmen and veteran bowlers. Doug Yeabsley had been in his 27th season of county cricket and was still a very effective bowler. One of the 'young' batsmen had been Hiley's own brother Chris, who had himself, as the overage player, skippered the Devon Under 25s against the Royal Navy. The one puzzling factor to a lot of followers was, how the county selectors chose Richard Turpin to keep wicket, while for his club Nigel Mountford wore the gloves and Turpin was played as a batsman! After Devon's last game, at Bovey Tracey, Ken Warren, the county secretary, paid tribute to Agha Zahid, the Barton professional, for all he had done for Devon County Cricket. Apart from his performances for the team he had helped so many younger players on and off the field and would be missed in the dressing rooms. From that season overseas players were to be banned from playing for a Minor County.

One cannot close the chapter on the '85 season without a further mention of Bill Traylor. Throughout the winter of '84/85 he had worked incessantly to make all kinds of stalls and games ready for a new fund raising feature for the club. A 'Fete Day' on the Friday, August 17th. The weather was kind and Bill, backed up by members of his family and a host of club supporters, saw his work come to fruition. The ground was a hive of activity from very early on that morning, the 'official' opening was advertised to be 9:30 but a member of the committee had to be detailed to hold back the 'early birds'. They endeavoured to get to the clothes and bric-a- brac stalls long before the opening time. Pony rides around the ground were very popular with the children and a member of the Traylor family walked miles that day holding the reigns. With such a hot day it was not difficult to get various club members to poke their heads through a board and have wet sponges thrown at them by the hordes of locals and holidaymakers who came. The Fete boosted club funds by well over one thousand pounds but sadly, for the next two years when it was tried, heavy rain within an hour of opening spoilt the day and the venture was dropped.

Before the 1986 season began members were mourning the death of George Brook, a committee member for some twenty five years and a staunch supporter who sat through every midweek game. A retired police superintendent who was very forthright with his point of view in committee, and George hardly needed the loud-speaker to announce daily from the Pavilion steps at three o'clock, "teas are now being served". He was one of the, fast disappearing, club characters that are badly missed today.

The actual cricketing season from Torquay's point of view was one that needed to be forgotten but since it is another part of the history it must be recorded. Hiley Edwards, the captain of the first eleven once again, had a trying time, and one imagines he relished going off to lead Devon and getting away from local difficulties. Non availability, for many different reasons, of first team players, meant promotion through all the teams which resulted in younger players developing more quickly with the experience of playing at a higher level.

Out of the twenty two League games played Torquay managed only four victories and just three 'winning draws' which resulted in a pathetic points total by the end of the season. Throughout the summer supporters were constantly frustrated by events. When the batsmen struck form and provided a good total, the bowlers had a poor day and often did not contain the opposition. If the bowlers 'whipped' out the other side the batsmen often failed to chase quite ordinary totals. The outstanding example was against Sidmouth where Andy Jones and Malcolm Kingdon had bowled all the overs and left Sidmouth on 138 for 7. In their forty six overs Torquay managed 100 runs, and it was widely reported that Barrie Matthews had been the first man to 'hold up his hand' in the dressing room inquest held by Hiley Edwards afterwards. Unusual but Matthews had taken 34 overs to achieve 34 runs!

Other examples of what the long suffering followers went through that season were, against Tavistock, where in a meagre total of 132 the last man, Malcolm Kingdon, had got the 32 !. After taking five of the Exeter wickets for just 18 runs skipper Hiley Edwards himself then held the batting together with 70 not out, enabling the team to hang on for a losing draw. At Barton, the home team had been bowled out for a modest 132 and it was due to the ability of two regular second eleven players, promoted to the first, that Torquay 'hung on' again, at 86 for 8. On several occasions that season Colin Davey and Steve Craig went into the first team and never let the side down, by the end Steve Craig and Paul Traylor were almost part of the first eleven.

One very entertaining day's play was seen when a Gloucester X1 came to the Rec. to play a strengthened Torquay side that included Nick Gaywood and Joey Oliver. Batting first the visitors scored 299 for 9 with Torquay 230 for 9 at the close of play, H.Edwards 41, I.Coulton 40, N.Gaywood 35 and J.Oliver 30.

Colin Davey, who had taken over responsibility for the second's from Ken Creber, had as difficult a season as Hiley Edwards. The continual call for his players to be needed in the first team meant promotion for the senior Colts with Phil Bradford, Nigel Coppen, Brendan Scofield and Sean Kirby going into the Second X1. With the experienced second team players, Davey himself, Derek Merrikin, Ken Creber and Dick Lear the youngsters had every chance to gain valuable knowledge. Obviously they did, since all went on to become first team players in due course. Much of the second team umpiring was done by Bruce Bradford and Ivor Slade. It is interesting to note, over the years, the fathers who gave so much of their time coaching youngsters in the nets and saw their own sons develop. Prime examples of this being Ian Scofield, Bruce Bradford, John Kirby and Ian Western.

Hiley Edwards troublesome club season was, to a small degree, compensated by Devon's performance. Having led the county against their first ever International opponents, Canada, at the South Devon ground in Newton Abbot he also ensured Devon's presence in the following seasons Nat West competition.

The last game of the season took place on the Friday afternoon with the rugby posts already erected. Torquay Athletic were to open their season on the Saturday with a fixture against Headingley from Yorkshire and the visitors asked for a cricket game to be arranged for the Friday afternoon. Happy to oblige the club had a strong side in which Nigel Janes and Barrie Matthews had a 'field day' scoring freely. Martyn Goulding was soon knocking the stumps over and had to be taken off or he would have had all ten wickets! It was an easy victory but Headingley's captain, international Peter Winterbottom, made the Tics pay dearly the next day!

!986 had seen changes come into being that were, over the years, going to affect the club in so many different ways and the ramifications had not really been thought through. Over many years the club had run a Sunday 1st. and a Sunday 2nd eleven with a Third and Third Extras playing on a Saturday. The establishment of a Coca Cola League for the club's third team players changed everything. As the matches for the new league were going to be played on a Sunday it meant there would be no players for the Sunday second side. Consequently, whereas before this time the Corporation would prepare a wicket at the sea-end within a month of the rugby season ending, this was no longer the case and the club had lost another playing area. Initially the secretary, Harry Ball, besieged the Town Hall for permission to use Torre Valley or the Grammar School but other clubs had first call. In reality it meant the end of good cricket on a Sunday at the Recreation Ground, except on rare occasions, purely because the ground was given over to Third team cricket. Twenty years ago members, and other followers of the game, who were not able to attend the Saturdays match, came on a Sunday for a lazy afternoon, tea and a natter in the sunshine with friends. Third and Third Extras players would also wander in to discus their Saturday exploits, if they were not playing in the Sunday Seconds, making the atmosphere one of a real cricket club. Gordon Baker's Third Extras had many games per season at the sea-end with a happy band of 'ex-serious' players who enjoyed going through the motions, and then adjourning to the bar. Roger Wood, John and Clive Haly, Gordon Oliver, John Miles and John Claydon were well supported by youngsters, like the McMurrays, Chris Armes, John Smethurst and others, who could 'save old legs' in the field.

The Colts had an excellent season winning their league and reaching the final of the Under 16 Devon Cup. In the league they lost only one game, and only three of the twenty three played during the season. As previously mentioned, Kirby, Bradford, Coppen and Scofield had played in the seconds while still of the Colts age group.

Nothing at all to do with Torquay! , although quite interesting. The Bovey Tracey team were playing Tavistock in the Devon Cup. Bovey Tracey's last man Steve Taylor, was clearly run out when attempting a third run and everyone headed for the pavilion. The one and only, Gordon Ripley, umpiring, walked to the score board and had it changed from 118 for 9 to 119 for 8! He ruled the third run stood and Taylor was NOT OUT! Nobody had appealed he told the players!

1987

Rumours had circulated around Torquay during the winter months and were confirmed at the Livermead House Hotel when the club's A.G.M. was held in February 1987. J.E.Dickinson, or 'dear old Ted', was to step down as President and K.G. Peppiatt was elected as his successor. Ken had played, and had held various positions within the club, but he was following in the footsteps of the most widely known of Torquay's cricketing fraternity, a hard act to follow. While that move surprised many, Peter Goodrich also resigned as Chairman, after several years in that position he was succeeded by K.V. Hosking. As a committee member in those days, the writer would suggest that despite the numerous arguments he had with Hosking, Vaughan was one of the hardest working Chairman the club has had for a very long time. Unfortunately the hard work was, on occasions, offset by individual action not always discussed, or even known of, by the rest of the committee.

Chris Edwards succeeded his brother Hiley as the first team captain and appointed Malcolm Kingdon as his vice-captain. Dick Lear and Bob Mallon were in charge of the second and third teams.

When the season began there had been the usual movement of players and one, which was very understandable, also disappointed a number of supporters. With the young Richard Turpin developing as he had, Nigel Mountford went back to Bovey Tracey, and while losing a player the club also lost the following of the family. That included the between innings re-marking of the wicket by Nigel's father, Stuart. The Devon spin bowler, Neil Wonnacott, had joined the club, a real country Devonian who, all too sadly, died of cancer within a few years at a very young age. A newcomer to the area, from Lancashire, David Moss also became a playing member. 'Mossy' proved to be a very useful club player and extremely popular around the clubhouse. In addition two Australians arrived, Darren Oliver and Marty Ward. Both were available for most midweek games, while in the league Oliver was a regular first eleven player whereas Ward was more often in the seconds.

After the first two league games were lost, against North Devon and Plymouth, supporters began to wonder if they were in for another poor summer. The faithful were cheered however with a 'winning draw' against Paignton, before suffering another set back against Bovey Tracey. Ironic but true, the main obstacle at Bovey Tracey being a very sound innings by one, Nigel Mountford! Neil Wonnacott's 8 for 77 against Exeter and John Carr's 4 for 50 at Exmouth earned two 'winning draws'. Mention has been made of the strange results against Paignton over the years, and during the 1980s similar remarks could apply to the Barton fixtures. At the Recreation Ground Torquay lost badly when Davidson took 7 for 61 and had the club out for 106. In the return game at Cricketfield Road, thanks to Malcolm Kingdon 4 for 26 and John Carr 5 for 12, Barton were all out for 41 in a complete turn around.

Supporters began to feel somewhat sorry for Chris Edwards, and themselves, since it was well into July before Torquay had an outright victory. The captain had managed to lose the toss on twelve occasions out of the first thirteen, not all on his call of course !, and the toss did make a difference at times.

With the influx of overseas players, our own two Australians and Derrick Perry, a New Zealander playing league cricket for Galmpton, but, in most Torquay midweek sides, the matches witnessed during the week were most entertaining. In addition to the Colonials Bill Traylor had induced several Exeter University students to come down for midweek games and spectators began to wonder when one individual would represent the club in the league. With all the talent on display a certain Tim Lester was outstanding, all too sadly he was eventually 'snapped' up by Exmouth for their league team and Tim became a thorn in Torquay's side whenever we played them. He also went on to play for his home county of Oxfordshire and invariably excelled against Devon. The highlight of the season however was when Gloucestershire came for a benefit game for their Andy Stovold in late June. Torquay strengthened their side with the addition of players that made it a Commonwealth mixture. Cleveland Davidson, playing for Barton, but from the West Indies, was an extra bowler and Chris Yorston, assisting Paignton in the league, but also a New Zealander. Paignton also provided another batsman, Rick Twose, to make up the eleven. Batting first Gloucestershire certainly entertained the crowd scoring 348 for 9 before declaring. Bainbridge with 68 and Graveney 63 treated the bowlers with scant respect and only Davidson with 3 for 68 looked at all impressive. Torquay were all back in the pavilion for 161 with Hiley Edwards on 47, the only batsman able to cope with the county attack.

Late June also saw a very exciting league encounter with Exmouth when, after losing the toss, Edwards was asked to bat. A stand between Barrie Matthews and Hiley Edwards of 91 helped Torquay reach 171 for 5. John Carr and Malcolm Kingdon initially kept Exmouth to 50 from the first 25 overs. However by the time Carr was about to bowl the last over Exmouth needed eleven runs to win. Off the second, third and fourth balls he had the wickets of Tozer, Woodman and Considine leaving Smith to face the last two balls. Carr took 4 for 55, Wonnacott 2 for 31 and Kingdon 1 for 60 in his 23 overs .The thirteen points from the match left Torquay fourth from the bottom and just one point in front of Paignton.

From that position Torquay's season improved considerably and by mid-August they were in the top four, hard on the heels of Plymouth and Barton. Faint hopes were given a hard knock by Paignton, who after scoring over 200 runs for just four wickets then restricted Torquay to 92 for 9, mostly due to the bowling of Vic Macey. A complete thrashing by Exeter then saw ex-colleague Garry Wallen at his best and almost a 'one man team' on the day. Having scored 92 runs he then proceeded to take 7 for 81 in Exeter's comprehensive victory.

After the indifferent start to the league proceedings fifth place was all the supporters could expect. Neil Wonnacott had taken 47 league wickets while both Hiley Edwards and Barrie Matthews each scored over 600 runs. In all games Matthews had yet again totalled over 1500 runs and the Aussie, Darren Oliver, over 1000.

In appreciation of his service to the club, as player and committee man for thirty years, Leo Matthews was asked to raise a side to play a club X1 on Sunday 23rd. August. He paraded, Barrie Matthews, Alan Smith, Jack Davey, George Cowan, Dave Traylor, Vaughan Hosking, Bob Dickinson, Dick Lear, Ian Scofield and Mike Pavey. The club, in honour of Leo's services, fielded an almost complete first eleven which was consequently far too strong for a team that were rather past their best. Ian Coulton, 69 and Ian Osborne 65, were mainly responsible for enabling the club to declare on 241 for 5. When Chris Edwards had Matthews and Traylor back in the pavilion for 18 and 39 respectively the 'writing was on the wall', with the 'backbone' of the batting gone, only Cowan and Davey were able to obtain double figures so the celebrations began rather early in the bar.

On the writer re-reading this history he feels an explanation is due regarding overseas midweek players. Mention has been made of Roger Mann and his exploits when playing for Paignton, as a younger man (no pun intended!). Later very involved with the Galmpton club he did, with his world wide contacts, bring over young cricketers who wanted to experience the conditions in this country. They were to be employed in his business during the mornings and played cricket during the afternoons. It meant league cricket for Galmpton at the weekend but thankfully Roger Mann also enrolled them with the Torquay club, and hence their midweek availability. It is applicable at this stage of the history, since the 1988 season was memorable for the midweek cricket, and those fortunate enough to watch every day will never forget. Mr. Mann had again brought back Derek Perry who was also joined by a Tasmanian, Richard Bennett. Both these players scored three centuries during their games for Torquay but were actually bettered by Nigel Janes, who captained most of the matches and had four 'tons' to his credit. Winning 24 of the 39 midweek matches Janes was 'noted' for the future. Despite the exploits of the players mentioned games were not a 'three man show' and hard working Bill Traylor saw to it that strong sides were fielded each day. Chris Jones, David Moss, David Perry and Alec McMurray were amongst many others who performed superbly that year while Barton Sewell, Arnie Searle, Terry Hubbard, Neil Davey, Rod Gibson and the Evans boys came from as far away as Exmouth and Hatherleigh to support Traylor.

The author will never forget Derek Perry, and not purely because of his cricket ability! After tea one day he came and asked for a favour, was it possible to have some brown bread sandwiches on the tea tables? From that day on each table had a plate of the bread requested, but until D.P. spoke out it had always been white bread! Very remiss of the caterer!

The 1988 season will be remembered by so many different people for many different reasons. New faces at the club when play began included Paul Brown, who had already played for Devon, mostly as a bowler but was a hard hitting batsman. Serving as a policeman it meant he often got moved around the county, as had Martyn Taylor, and hence the different clubs they both eventually played for. John Stables and Steve Broomhall were also two new players, John Stables had experience with Nottinghamshire 2nds while Steve Broomhall had played midweek for Torquay during the previous season when he had been one of the Galmpton 'imports'. Chris Edwards again took on the mantle as skipper, supported by Malcolm Kingdon. Secretary Harry Ball was one of those who did not look back on the season with happy memories having initially had to undergo an operation. Then part way through the season his wife Clare had an accident in their garden and fractured her femur, this left her crippled for weeks and Harry missing, day after day, so much of his beloved cricket. Mr. Ball's life revolved around the cricket club and to a degree the Sports Council, rarely missing a midweek game and knowing the numerous members by name. One of the 'old school' style of secretaries who kept the President and Chairman on their toes, and at Committee meetings was very much in evidence.

The opening league game of the season was at home to Exmouth and it was not enjoyable watching for a Torquinian, all out for 111 runs and the visitors knocking them off for the loss of just one wicket. A journey to North Devon resulted in a losing draw and was followed by a home game, with Barton, where another defeat was suffered. Worse was to come as the team travelled to Plymouth where neither skipper Chris Edwards or Paul Brown put in an appearance. Since Bill Traylor was present, to watch his son Paul play, a little 'arm twisting' was induced and he made up Torquay's ten man team which managed to score 169 for 7. John Stables score of 63 was the main contributor to a total that was insufficient to prevent yet another defeat.

Following the non appearance of Chris Edwards and no contact reported, whereas Paul Brown had advised he had been called for police duty and had been unable to play, this was the main business of a Committee meeting on the Monday night. Members were told there had been no contact with Edwards and a new captain should be appointed. Most of the committee pointed out that, as vice-captain, Malcolm Kingdon should take over but he was reluctant to do so, pointing out Chris had appointed him and not the players. Hard as the meeting tried to persuade Kingdon to take over he stuck to his point and wanted a 'players meeting'. Since several of the players were not available during the week arranging a meeting was a non starter. A side had to be selected for the next league game and, after much discussion, one committee member asked the Chairman to skipper the team. Other committee members violently opposed the request as he was already captain of the seconds and had given up his position in the first eleven. The discussion went on for a long time with other individuals beginning to press for the Chairman to consider the position of captain. Eventually Malcolm Kingdon and chairman Hosking went on 'walkabout' around the ground, while the rest of the committee discussed the problem. After what became a rather heated discussion a vote was taken but not before pencil and paper had to be found, so many refusing to vote with a show of hands! The result was close, but by a single vote the captaincy passed to Chairman Vaughan Hosking once again.

Delving into the facts before publishing this history, the writer is utterly convinced that if the members had been informed of the truth Torquay would not have lost a valuable captain and player, and later, who had been dedicated club members. Had the committee been told that Edwards had apologised before their meeting, explained he had celebrated his birthday too well on the Friday evening and had not even got home that night, regained his senses far too late to get to Plymouth on the Saturday, it is very possible he would have lost the captaincy. However to be told the Committee no longer wanted to see him on the ground, and he would not be welcomed at the club was an untruth. The writer for one bitterly regrets how this whole matter was handled and that the committee had not been kept completely informed of all that had transpired.

After such an upset early in the season it is little wonder that it took so much time for the side to settle, two of the three games won actually came in the last month of the season! Finishing in 8th position in the league was once again disappointing but more and more sides were now geared up for league cricket. With just a little luck, or as one wag put it "different captaincy", two of the four 'winning draws' should have been victories. With 646 league runs to his credit, including two centuries, Hiley Edwards was by far the most prolific scorer, while in all games Nigel Janes had 1863, Richard Bennett 1249 and Ian Coulton 1168. While many individuals had a great season mention must be made of a third team player, Alistair McMurray. He had several good bowling performances when playing midweek and was promoted to the second eleven. In his first match he took 8 for 23 and held his promotion to that team for the rest of the season.

However the 'highlight' of the summer was the match between Devon and Nottinghamshire in the Nat West Cup on the 22cd of June. Much hard work had seen stands erected wherever possible to accommodate several thousand spectators, with numerous sponsor's tents also sighted in advantageous positions. With the weather playing its part the crowds arrived and Nottinghamshire began batting. At 97 for 3 and with only twenty five overs left many Devonians began to feel a little optimistic regarding the home county's chances. Torquay's fast bowler, Paul Brown, had a good opening spell without any luck, while the three wickets that fell were one apiece for Roger Twose, Mark Woodman and Tony Allin. However, with former England favourite, Derek Randall, and team captain John Birch together, the picture changed rapidly. At the end of the 60 overs, and an undefeated partnership of 205 runs, the Notts total was 302 for 3 and spectators had seen a brilliant 149 not out from Randall. Mark Woodman was Devon's most impressive bowler on the day with 1 for 39 from his 12 overs. Devon quickly lost Richard Twose for one and Nick Gaywood for nine. Rice and Wallen were each dismissed in their twenties while Hiley Edwards only scored four. Roger Twose, at that time on the Lord's ground staff, had a 56 to his credit before Paul Brown and Richard Turpin played out time with both undefeated at 67 and 29 respectively, in a total of 238 for 6. A days cricket in the club's history that members who saw it will never forget.

After thirty years with the Torquay club Barrie Matthews was asked to chose a side to play Torquay's first eleven in appreciation of his service to the club. Ted Dickinson and Len Leworthy were to be the umpires. Matthews called on so many of the near veterans who had been such a force in his Devon days and they were delighted to come from far afield for their ex-captain. Included were Garry Wallen, Dave Traylor, Peter Anderson, Clive Wallen, Vic Macey, David Post, Bob Coombe, Paddy Considine, Peter Socha and Sean Kirby. Batting first Torquay totalled 179 for 6 even though Considine had taken the first four wickets for 60, showing he still retained a lot of his bowling skills. Ian Coulton was top scorer with 69. After showing odd flashes of the powers they once had, Matthews eleven were all back in the pavilion for 153, unable to cope with the present day Devon bowler, Neil Wonnacott, who finished with figures of 6 for 70.

Rather sadly some senior players, and other individuals who should have known better, were involved in belittling and childish behaviour within the pavilion towards the end of the season. These happenings cost the club dearly before the beginning of the 1989 season.

While the following is not directly related to Torquay's history it did give "food for thought" to the Devon captain, Torquay's Hiley Edwards. There are times when every captain has to give thought as to how he can win. Near the end of this season Dorset and Cheshire were engaged in a Minor Counties match. Dorset were desperate for points and Cheshire were apparently holding on for a draw at 92 for 6, a long way from the 201 they needed to win. Cheshire were on top of the group while Dorset needed points to qualify for the Nat. West the next season. Dorset's captain, Reverend Wingfield-Digby, suggested to Cheshire that if he arranged for them "to get back into the game", they could then make a true match of the contest. Cheshire agreed, whereupon Calway, obeying his skipper the Reverend, bowled 14 wides in an over which were all allowed to go to the boundary for four. Another boundary in the 20 ball over had 'given' Cheshire 60 runs and they then began the chase for victory. It was not to be and they were beaten by 19 runs. Devon Secretary, Geoff Evans was quoted as saying, "we are one of the potential losers since we are still fighting to qualify". An illustration of a devious mind, captain or Reverend ?

Long before the start of the 1989 season the usual rumours were circulating regarding players movement and by the time of the 'nets practice' a number were confirmed as true. To the writer the saddest happening was the departure of the Edwards Brothers who had left to join the Paignton Cricket Club, not purely because of the loss of their abilities but because of the way they had been treated. In Hiley Edwards case in particular, some 17 seasons, several as the captain and 16,000 runs should have seen a very different parting of the ways. Chris had been a very popular member of the club and for one whole season had played practically every day of the week. The juvenile behaviour of those who caused the move never admitted their stupidity, although they must have realised it.

At the age of 23 Nigel Janes became the youngest captain Torquay had ever had but those who had observed him closely, especially during his midweek exploits, knew of his desire, and attitude, to the game. He had already done his 'home work' during the winter to attract players of his own ilk, from Barton, Terry Farkins and Peter Lucketti, from Paignton Rick Twose, and David Goulding from Babbacombe. Chris Healey and Martin Ellacott, previously with Plymouth, were to join the club and Brendon Scofield was back from a season's experience in New Zealand. Craig Vertongen from New Zealand was another batsman to join the club and supporters were anticipating an interesting season.

When the season began the first thing every captain had to do was to apologise to visiting sides for the diabolical state of the ground. The National Round Table Conference had been held in Torquay and the entire rugby ground, and some twenty five yards of the adjoining cricket outfield at the sea-end had been covered in a huge marquee during the celebrations. To erect such a structure heavy cranes had gone over the ground which necessitated sixty tons of top soil having to be brought in afterwards to fill in ruts and cracks. As a result of this the usual cricketing area was not available until well into July. The fact that it was another season of lovely sunshine was also a factor that caused difficulties, as the top soil did not bed in quickly on the dry surface. Once again pumping equipment had to be hired to obtain water from the stream for treating the actual wicket, as the hose pipe ban was in force.

Under the leadership of Nigel Janes all the new faces quickly moulded into a good team and had an excellent season. Commencing with a winning draw at Exmouth the side went through the league season undefeated and actually finished as runners up in the league. Initially Malcolm Kingdon missed May and part of June, due to an ankle injury, while the first actual victory of the season was only obtained when he played at Plymouth, at the end of June, and had a haul of eight wickets. Throughout the 1989 season Kingdon, Scofield and Goulding became the mainstay of the bowling and together bowled 797 league overs, taking 145 of the 173 wickets that were taken. Nigel Janes, with a young team around him, had concentrated on their fielding and fitness, both of which helped the bowlers and spectators saw many great catches that season. Net practise too was a lot more frequent than for many years, while the new bowling machine the club had invested £1500 in, was, night after night, back in the pavilion having the battery recharged after the evenings practice. When the committee first discussed having a bowling machine Harry Ball, club secretary, spoke firmly against same saying," he could not see who would set it up and return it to the pavilion each night". The following year he complained about the high electricity bill which was the result of the continual battery charging! We did 'pull his leg'.

The Torquay Cricket Club - A Potted History Of The Club From 1851 to 2004

Winning nine games out of the last thirteen saw the team finish second to Barton, who again won the league, and by a twenty point margin. Torquay in turn were twenty two points ahead of third place Plymouth. Twose and Coulton scored 834 and 613 runs respectively in the league, while in all games both exceeded a thousand, as did Nigel Janes with 1778 runs and Craig Vertongen 1264, who both had two centuries each.

David Moss who skippered the Second X1 throughout the season was delighted with his 'troops', as they had won their league with a record total of points. The 'icing on the cake' came when they went on to beat Barton in the final of the Narracott Cup. Chris Healey, Chris Jones, Mark Ferguson, B.J.Sewell, Rob James, Craig Vertongen and Vaughan Hosking were the mainstay of a strong side. The team were further supported with backing from Paul Traylor, Phil Bradford, John Pearce, Nigel Coppen and Steve Craig. Both Bradford and Traylor registered their maiden centuries for the club that season.

Bruce Bradford, who had nurtured the Colts from the time his son Phillip had begun to play, literally saw all his dreams come true. Under captain James Alford, the U17s South League and the Torbay North League were both won, while the U16s Cup was another trophy that came to Torquay. Numerous lads of that era came all the way through various teams, including Alford, Rawson, Smethurst, Jeffery, Lear, Heal and Sewell.

Midweek cricket was again of a very high standard and so many players were able to make themselves available. 27 of the 37 games played were won, thanks in no small measure to Gary O'Sullivan, another of the Australian imports at the Galmpton club. In 19 innings he scored well over nine hundred runs which included three centuries and four fifties. Numerous first eleven batsmen who were often available included Nigel Janes, Ian Coulton, Rick Twose, Barton Sewell, Chris Jones and Dave Traylor. The bowling strength too was formidable with Rob Stewart, Neil Wonnacott, Vaughan Hosking, Alec Mc Murray and Brendon Scofield frequently seen in action. 1989 saw the beginning of another era during the season, the commencement of the scoring activities of Nick Evanson. This young man took over the unenviable task of succeeding Esme Kingdon in the score box and, in due course, he became fully qualified with his framed certificate proudly hanging in the pavilion.

Mention must be made of the catering that season, initially in the capable hands of Pam Cook, with her husband Paul running the bar, but it was panic stations however, when Paul was taken ill at the end of July. After a lot of arm twisting Barton Sewell was persuaded to take over the bar even though he said he felt more at home on the other side of it! , and really was there to play cricket. Over many, many years the club had been fortunate in that players' wives, daughters and girl friends of players, plus friends of wives and lady members had spent their summers ensuring, that when the men came off the field that teas were waiting. The Thompsons, Snapes, the Dickinson 'army', Traylors, Lears, Merrikins, Halys and numerous others who gave so much of their time, and over many summers, saved the club a fortune. In the changing times it was a chore the club had to pay for and where could they find a replacement for Pam at such short notice? Fortunately retired male members stepped into the breech and they did the buying of the necessary foodstuffs every morning before preparing all the required teas for the players, and at that time numerous spectators. Much to the amazement of a lot of holidaymakers who came to the window for their refreshments there wasn't a female in sight in the kitchen which caused a number of comments. There are many less spectators now than there were even ten years ago and a row of deckchairs across the west side of the ground is no longer seen. The catering profits for the club varied between £2500 and £5000 a season then, thanks to all those previously mentioned. A useful income that was taken for granted by so many.

The 1990s

After his highly successful season Nigel Janes again took up the captaincy role in 1990, whereas Steve Craig had the difficult task of taking over David Moss's winning warriors.The club had lost the services of Brendon Scofield, who had gone to Essex in an effort to break into the professional ranks. Fortunately Paul Harding had come to live locally, the club, and especially the batsmen, knew his capabilities from facing his bowling when playing against his former side at Plymouth. Two young Australian players had joined Torquay, Steve Veneris and Andy Lade who, while not quite as experienced as the usual overseas players, did prove useful as the season progressed.

The league fixtures began with an away win at Braunton, where Paul Harding took 4 for 48 and Rick Twose began his season with a good 70. A losing draw against Bovey, despite Kingdom's 5 for 80, was followed by a defeat by Exeter. In a very mixed season there was another setback against Plymouth where Ian Coulton scored 42 not out in the 92 the whole team scraped together. There were still double week-ends then and very few supporters were optimistic regarding the away games with Exmouth and Paignton. However there was quite a surprise in store for those who did follow the team to Exmouth. Chasing 218 for 8 ,Terry Farkins and Rick Twose were in brilliant form, Twose 84 not out and Farkins 101 not out, had a third wicket partnership of 191 to win the game. Playing at Paignton, another 60 not out from Twose was a big factor in one more victory. Nigel Janes felt that losing the toss on eight occasions at home, plus the poor timekeeping by a number of players, may have had something to do with the results. In his next period of captaincy players were at the ground for the time he stipulated! With eight of the eleven away games won however, the whole season was rather mystifying. Mention must be made of Roger Twose who had odd games for Torquay when home from Warwickshire, where he was at that time mainly a second team county player. A brother of Rick Twose, he was very instrumental during that season in the defeat of Barton, taking 5 for 32 in a hostile spell of accurate bowling. A certain Ray Sloane, who had played for the rugby club that year, came across the Recreation Ground and joined the cricket club part way through the season. He bowled quite well in second team games and in a number of midweek matches, which resulted in his being selected for the first eleven to go to Sandford. After taking 4 for 32 and helping to ensure another victory that was the last time he was seen. The writer made visits to his flat in order to trace his whereabouts but his co-tenant said he had just vanished, a real mystery man and neither the cricket or rugby club ever heard of him again.

Radley Gibson, a local well known sportsman employed by the Brittanic Assurance Company persuaded his firm to sponsor a cup to be played for annually between

Barton and Torquay. This inaugural season the cup was won by Barton with their professional, Anjum, doing the initial damage with a fine 82. Martin Powell then bowled out the mainstay of Torquay's batting strength taking 4 for 20. "Puff" Gibson as he was affectionately known organised the day superbly with good prizes for the draw, the teams well looked after and even "bottles" for the umpires.

The big game of the season was the Nat West against Somerset on Wednesday June 27th which once more saw stands erected to accommodate the huge crowd, sponsor's tents in situ and refreshment marquees. Neil Stanlake, the Community Policeman covering the area at that time, often popped in during the midweek afternoon games for a 'cuppa' and asked that a meeting be arranged with the club Committee. This was done and Stanlake plainly told the meeting, "that only club members and their guests were to be served drinks at the bar during the Nat West game". Since the rugby club was to be open as well, the same restrictions would apply, and specific instructions were given that neither club could sign in as "temporary members" any of the general public attending the match. Both clubs were told that plain clothes police would be in attendance to see that the rules were observed. The day prior to the match Neil Stanlake was back again, to remind and reiterate, all that had been previously said.

On the 26th June, the day prior to the big game, the Herald & Express had front page news headlines, regarding the game being 'dry' for 3000 of the expected 5000 crowd! The club chairman, Vaughan Hosking, was quoted as saying "he had hoped members of the public would have been able to enjoy a drink, because they would have been signed in as temporary members". That after both clubs had known for a month the restrictions that were to be enforced, and yet the cricket officials had done nothing to ensure that ordinary spectators would be able to have a beer if they required one!

On the actual day officials on duty at the rugby club did all that they had been requested to do to remain within the law, but it was not the same with the cricket club. No one seemed to know if it was 'the call of the cricket' or sheer incompetence on the part of those involved, but sadly, it was to cost the club dearly before the start of the following cricket season.

A huge crowd saw the Devon captain, Hiley Edwards, win the toss and ask Somerset to bat. Cook and Roebuck opened the innings and 79 runs were on the scoreboard when a mix up saw the former run out for 42. Roebuck was caught and bowled by Mark Woodman for 43 and then it was panic in the kitchen! Rain stopped play at 128 for 2, well before the expected interval and spectators were looking for lunch! Afterwards the carnage began, while some three years earlier Devon had been 'savaged' by Worcestershire in a limited overs game Somerset put that experience into history. In their 60 overs the Cidermen hit 413 for 4 and Chris Tavare had 162 off 132 balls, while Rose had 110 in just 40 deliveries. Devon were bowled out for just 67 runs with only Keith Donoghue showing any fight with 18 not out,

Somerset's Dutch bowler, Roland Lefebvre, returned figures of 7 for 15 from 9:3 overs.

Late in the season Michael Dean joined the club, he was a young bowler from the Midlands, whose family had come to live in the area. Dean was to prove a very useful acquisition and a popular person in the club house. He actually had a 4 for 39 bowling spell in one of the three league matches he participated in before the season closed. Nigel Janes was more than disappointed to finish fourth after the side had been in the top three for much of the campaign. He announced he was off to Australia for the winter and, since he would not be in England when normally a captain would be 'working behind the scenes' for the following season, he was relinquishing the captaincy. While Malcolm Kingdon and Rick Twose were in the League's top ten for bowling and batting respectively, B.J.Sewell won the League second team batting averages with 57:3. Second team captain Steve Craig was unusually frank in his assessment of the season which was presented at the A.G.M. and went on, to say, "How can bowlers perform if simple catches are dropped and lazy misfielding results in their figures taking a battering".

At the end of the 1990 season there was a happening in the "B" Division at Bradnich that must be recorded since it had repercussions that certainly affected the Torquay Club 'history'. Galmpton had managed seven points for a losing draw which retained their then second place in the league table. The League Management Committee decided that the Galmpton ground was not up to the standard of "A" Division requirements and they did not get the promotion they deserved. Alternatives were suggested but to no avail and Roger Mann resigned from Galmpton in protest. He eventually joined Torquay before the 1991 season began with the fortunate result that his wicketkeeper son, Justin came with him. Peter Lucketti, who had kept wicket, had gone off to Manchester during the previous season and the young second team keeper, Nigel Coppen, had taken over the duties behind the stumps. With the season about to start Coppen was now off to college. Not only did the club have a new wicketkeeper but the young fast bowler who had joined Galmpton from Kingskerswell, Ian Baker, was coming as well as Andy Thomas. The hard hitting batsman, Garry O'Sullivan was returning from Australia for another season in England and he had been joined by two New Zealand players, Craig Ross and Graham Patterson. With six new players the captain, Ian Coulton and second team skipper Barton Sewell, were both eager for the season to commence with the talent they could see available for selection. In addition to the new faces Nigel Janes had returned from his winter in Australia.

Early in April the repercussions of the club ignoring Neil Stanlake's warnings took place when, following a court case, the Torquay Cricket Club's liquor licence was taken away. Pathetic excuses were made to the court by individuals but the secretary, Harry Ball, did admit " there had been a degree of incompetence , not on the part of the club, but on the part of certain members"!

Numerous letters appeared in the local press against the police but the writers were in complete ignorance of the warnings the club had received. This writer was quite amused eventually when the police, through Chief Supt. Colin Moore, replied to the newspaper critics in cricket phraseology. "The cricket club did not heed the umpires warning and were caught out, the rugby club kept a straight bat and turned non members away"! So with a new season in view and a fantastic array of talent it was 'soft drinks' only. The whole incident was rather sad for the club but it was disgraceful incompetence by those who were supposed to be looking after members interests.

When the season got under way the strength of the talent within the club was quickly evident and certain individuals were on top of their form immediately. Gary O'Sullivan had 117 out of a total of 198 for 2 in the first league game at Exeter, even though only a winning draw resulted. Victories over Plymouth and Seaton were thanks to the bowlers Dean and Patterson who were recording figures of 4 for 22, 4 for 23 and 4 for 33 regularly. Dean actually had five wickets to his credit in successive games, but he had fewer opportunities when Ross recovered from his early injury. During the first half of the season Ross and Patterson whipped out Paignton at Queen's Park for 78 and then O'Sullivan got 60 not out in the winning total of 80 without the loss of a wicket. Mention must be made of a lost game against South Devon. Torquay managed only 128, with 71 of the runs scored by Gary O'Sullivan. Ian Gore had a superb spell of fast bowling for South Devon and took 7 for 60 after which Hall with 103 not out, saw South Devon to a winning total of 129 without losing a wicket.

The Brittanic Cup game, played at Torquay was won by the home team and again the Australian O'Sullivan scored another century in Torquay's 185 for 5 before taking 3 for 29 in his bowling spell. The Barton team were all out for 152 and the 'man of the match' award was very quickly, and easily, decided in favour of Gary O'Sullivan. Due to his performances in the Devon League Gary O'Sullivan was chosen to open the batting in the Inter- League Final against the Western League which was held at Bath. He had yet another century to his credit, 145 not out off 129 balls, but despite that effort he found himself on the losing side!

Before the end of the season the absence of Nigel Janes was very noticeable and his athletic fielding was certainly missed.

Even finishing the season with victories over Tiverton, Paignton and South Devon, Torquay again finished second in the League, three points behind Exmouth. The last game away to South Devon was actually a 'praying' affair, praying Torquay could get all twenty points but praying too that Paignton could stop Exmouth's advance for the title. South Devon scored 224, with Ian Gore getting 143 and Mike Dean taking six wickets for 54 runs. Skipper Ian Coulton opened with Rick Twose and the two passed the home total without the loss of a wicket, Coulton 101 and Twose 93.

Torquay had done all they could and as the local cricket correspondent wrote at the time, "a performance which stamped them as champions in class if not in name". Exmouth's tight bowling had kept Paignton's batsmen to 137 for 9 and that total was passed for the loss of only one wicket.

So ended an exciting season, supporters had memories of good batting, and bowling, both in the league and mid-week matches, and fine performances by so many different individuals. When the dedicated scorer, Nick Everson collated all the statistics Gary O'Sullivan had scored over 800 league runs, and in all matches for the club had totalled 2321 runs. Michael Dean had taken 40 league wickets in his first full season, closely followed by Craig Ross with 38. Dean had also represented the Devon Under 19s during the season. Although five players, excluding O'Sullivan, had scored centuries in the midweek matches, no other batsman had totalled a thousand runs. While so many of the first team bowlers had also played during the week the one who had caught the eye of most supporters had been Tim Jeffery, and his 5 for 17, in a Sunday game, ranked along with another Sunday 'king', Andy Thomas and his 6 for 15 in 5 overs. Chris Healey who captained the Sunday First X1, was well supported by the overseas players that season and won eight of the twelve games the team played. It should be explained that overseas players, who often participated in the midweek matches, sometimes liked to see the surrounding countryside and Sundays was very often the day they elected to do so.

Mention has been made of the various players who came and helped the club fulfil its commitments for midweek games and this season was no exception. An Australian was the 'overseas player' for a club in Somerset and he had brought over his wife and two sons for the summer. They came to explore Torquay for a day and eventually discovered the cricket ground as they walked the sea-front. That was the beginning of their visits to the sea-side. Jim Rennie made arrangements to play the next mid-week game and eventually came for seven matches during the season. His two sons also played in six of the games, with the younger one thrilled to be playing with his father in another country. All three were more than useful players and fitted in well with the midweek contingent. Only those readers who have experienced sport in Australia will realise the Rennie's comments after the first match, when they discovered the bar was only providing soft drinks!!

Before detailing the 1992 season the writer takes leave to refer in some depth to the shock announcement of Malcolm Kingdon's leaving the Torquay club. From the time the writer returned to his roots the Kingdon family had been very kind in so many ways, and he was privileged to what might be described as 'inside information'. The family had been bitterly disappointed that Malcolm had not taken over the captaincy after Chris Edwards departure and yet, had the full story been told, Edwards would have still been there. Throughout the '91 season the 'inside story' of each Saturday game was told by Bert Kingdon to the writer as he wound up the pavilion clock on Monday morning, a job that he has been done throughout summer and winter for many years and is still being attending to now(2004). Medium pacer, son Malcolm, christened in the local press by David Thomas as "sultan or king of swing", had been with the club some twenty years but through that season had mentioned to his father 'strange happenings'. Told in the dressing room he would be opening the bowling from the sea-end, but on the field was first change at that end. On the occasions he did open the bowling he was taken off after a very short spell while previously he had very often bowled throughout the innings. Dropped for the game at Plymouth he was told 'spin was needed' and yet the spinner who replaced him did not bowl at all in the match. Malcolm Kingdon took his family on holiday in Cornwall and undertook to be back for the Saturday game, which he was. He left his wife and children there to enjoy the Saturday before they made their own way home and he left very early to get to the game but was never asked to bowl an over. The final indignity was to be dropped for the last match and not even be chosen for the second eleven without any explanation. He sat watching the Torquay first team play at Newton Abbot where they defeated South Devon. These 'snippets' are not widely known, but were part and parcel of the reasons the club not only lost a great stalwart, but a whole family. From the days of Malcolm playing in the Colts mother Esme was scoring, and eventually, it was a full time occupation for her. She did every midweek game, as well as the League, and the Sunday first elevens. Those members 'close' to the action know that Esme often helped out behind the bar when things became hectic, that Bert took home the balls after a game to polish and clean, thus ensuring a good supply for midweek and third team matches. It was not only the balls that were carefully looked after but the stumps had to be cleaned as well, plus heavy bails were always available on a very windy day.

Dear reader, it is small wonder that the family were made Life Members for the work they all put into the Torquay club and such a tragedy they were lost through poor man management.

While the departure of Kingdon to Paignton was disheartening, the news that a fast bowler, Pietrus Stefanus De Villiers was joining Torquay was very uplifting for supporters. This Springbok cricketer, after injury, had been advised to get in a seasons action to see if he would be fit for the forthcoming Test Series, with his contacts Roger Mann had secured De Villiers services for Torquay. While one man does not make a team, newspaper comment of the time inferred it might, Fanie as he became known, pronounced Farney, certainly attracted the supporters. It was a most popular signing and his friendly character endeared him to all, while his other assets were that he brought his wife Judy, and young daughter of some three months. While bowler Paul Harding had left to join Kingskerswell another bowler, Bob Learmouth, had joined Torquay from Tiverton. Rumours existed regarding Nigel Janes, but, as he did not appear to have signed for any other club, hopes were high he would come back. After skippering the seconds so well Barton Sewell had moved up to become vice captain in the first eleven, leaving Vaughan Hosking to take over his old position as skipper of the second eleven.

The league season began with a home game against Seaton and with Torquay including De Villiers, their first club professional in almost twenty years, there was a larger attendance than normally. Barton Sewell scored 76 of Torquay's 197 for 9 and then the expectations began. De Villiers first five overs cost him two runs and he had clean bowled Jenkins. Mike Dean, who had opened the bowling with Fanie, had to leave the field with a groin strain and those present were delighted to see Nigel Janes come on the field as the substitute. At the halfway stage Seaton's score was only 39 and a second wicket had fallen, that was as a result of a fantastic catch by Ian Baker, off a very poor ball by Tim Western that was destined for a boundary. De Villiers returned to bowl when Seaton were 111 for 5, and although Cottam hit the first ball for six that was to be the end of the run- making. De Villiers eventually finished with 6 for 33 in his fifteen overs and five balls with Seaton all out for 117 and Bob Learmouth having 2 for 60.

With such a beginning captain Ian Coulton was eagerly awaiting the rest of the season and yet, hard to believe, only one more victory was to be achieved by the time the season was half way through. Paignton were beaten at Queen's Park where De Villiers took 8 for 35 to reduce the home side to 94 all out. Coulton himself obtained half the necessary runs to win in the total of 97 for 2. What might have happened had Kingdon still been with the club, to close up one end while Fanie was bowling at the opposite, is open to conjecture but, with Dean on the injured list, the overall bowling attack was inconsistent. A loss was sustained at Exmouth, where only Sewell with 50 showed any form, and the Torquay total was passed with the loss of three wickets. Tim Jeffery was included in the first eleven at Sandford, and took 5 for 59 when a winning draw was obtained, retained for the Plymouth match he then had 3 for 36. Fanie De Villiers had scored 50 in the Plymouth match as well as taking 4 for 74 but, the overall total had not been big enough to give the bowlers much of a chance.

Mention must be made of one midweek game against the tourists Evercreech. A fellow Transvaal team mate of Fanie's popped into the Rec. for a game and had quite an afternoon. The story goes that when he was asked what he did the reply was, "well I bat and bowl a bit", and he most certainly did! 101 not out and a few cheap wickets showed what Brian Van Onselen was capable of and it was a pity he only stayed for one game.

The second half of the season was a complete change around and the captain felt it was partially due to the fact that the toss was more in his favour. The team went on to record seven outright victories and only lost two games. It is surprising that so many Torquay captains have, over the years, felt that the sequence of winning or losing the toss, irrespective of the weather, has affected results. What was certainly much more noticeable to the researcher was the fact that when Dean was fit again, he certainly played his part when asked to bowl later in the season. Also Twose, Bradford and skipper Coulton scored runs more consistently. De Villiers eventually took 89 league wickets in the season and some spectators felt that the figure might have been even more had the slips judged the pace of the ball off the bat and corrected their catching positions. With Phil Bradford and Tim Western holding their places in the first team and Tim Jeffery's occasional appearances, supporters tended to feel that the future of the club was looking quite healthy with younger players making the grade.

What Ian Coulton must have felt after such a superb end to the season one can only wonder but the early season results cost him dearly. Exmouth were more than forty points clear of second placed Paignton who in turn, even though defeated by Torquay twice, were eight points above our third position.

Vaughan Hosking had seen his second eleven finish their season at the top of the league despite the number of his side who had made first eleven appearances. A 19 year old from New South Wales, Mike Gerits, was one of the stars in his side and managed an average, in League games, of over 83 runs. He had also taken 33 wickets and was ably supported by John Pearce, Derek Merrikin and the skipper himself Hosking. In a season when only one overseas player was allowed in the first eleven Gerits was a class act in the seconds, and so richly deserved a first team place.

Having won through to the semi-final of the Devon Senior Cup Torquay eventually met their match in the form of the Plymouth club. Having lost and had a losing draw in the league, anticipations of a victory were not high and there was not a lot of support at Sidmouth. All out for 92, with B.J.Sewell 17 not out and Phil Bradford 15, Plymouth scored the necessary runs with the loss of six wickets. Then, right at the end of August, after all the hard work that had gone into the organising it, a game against an Old England X1 was completely rained off.

Following the end of the season at the League Awards Dinner Vaughan Hosking, with his 6 for 14 against Brixham took the May, Premier 2nd.X1 award, while Fanie De Villiers carried off the June, July and August awards for the Premier 1stX1, his figures being;

June 8 for 35 runs against Paignton.
July 8 for 36 runs against Seaton.
August 8 for 12 runs against Tiverton.

While the 1992 season saw the club able to entertain visitors again, with the bar operating, the sad thing was that within a month of opening the steward had to be dispensed with. The details of the dismissal are not relevant to this history, however, the lesson to those on the committee who are responsible for appointing such people, certainly is.

Season after season the local cricket reporters have tried to analyse Torquay's chances in the league prior to the commencement of play. After finishing in third position with the assistance of Fanie De Villiers the "scribe" was quite careful with his prediction for 1993, despite the arrival of a number of new players. The Chairman had heard that a new student at Exeter University, Alan Jones, was an Under 19 England and Glamorgan 2nd. team player and moved to obtain his signature. Julian Wyatt an ex-Somerset opening bat and change bowler had also joined the club along with three Australian youngsters. Jason Foster was from Adelaide and was reported to have been in the South Australian squad as a teenage opening bowler. Charlie

Amos, at eighteen years old, was a qualified coach and while Jason Fairbrother was from Victoria he held a British passport, so was not classed as an overseas player. This was the season the league brought in the rule that only one non English player was allowed in a team.

There had been rumours of another batsman Phil Blackmore joining the club, but in the first league game he was on the other side, batting well for South Devon. Torquay's batting strength was evident from the start with a total of 201 for 1, Coulton declared with Alan Jones 105 not out and both Coulton and Bradford getting well into the forties. Despite the extra overs at the captain's disposal the Newtonians were in little difficulty and when stumps were drawn were 154 for 4, Blackmore 73.

At the end of just one week there was shattering news from the Recreation Ground, Rick Twose had sent in his resignation and was joining his old club Paignton, just three years after he had left there. The press reported he had said, "I joined Torquay to play on a good wicket but, a few issues I do not agree with have been building up, and they outweigh the benefits of the wicket."

During the early months Ian Coulton chopped and changed his bowlers as well as batsmen. He said he felt Foster in particular was bowling well without any luck, the Jones 'boy' did not appear to need luck since he was continuing to hammer out the runs, 89 not out in the defeat of Brixham and 72 not out against Exeter. In both of these games John Pearce and Bob Learmouth bowled well, the former 4 for 21 and 4 for 60, the latter 5 for 36 and 3 for 30. Both Phil Bradford and the teenager Guy Sewell were in and out of the first eleven with the continual changes. Barton suffered another defeat when John Pearce took 7 for 74 after Julian Wyatt had hammered a not out 70. At Paignton however Ian Coulton had reason to appreciate what the club had lost with the departure of Malcolm Kingdon. In his 'old style' Kingdon bowled his 23 overs for 49 runs and took 5 wickets, leaving Torquay 'hanging on' at 94 for 8 and most fortunate not to lose that game.

As mentioned during Rick Twose's time at Torquay, there had been occasions that his brother Roger had also assisted Torquay while home from Warwickshire. While Torquay were beating Barton, Roger had come home and offered to play for Paignton against Brixham. The captain of Paignton said "thanks, but no", whereas Brixham's Andy Pugh welcomed him with open arms and with an innings of 87 he helped Brixham to an eight wicket victory, against his brother's team.

Peter Roebuck became the third Devon captain in as many years and was not slow in recruiting his fellow ex- Somerset team mate, Julian Wyatt, for county duty from Torquay.

With all the overseas talent able to play together in midweek matches, against the tourists, there was some very good cricket played, which helped the daily supporter somewhat after the rather disappointing league performances witnessed. The initial anticipation most spectators had for a successful season gradually disappeared as the league season went on, and then came another shock! Michael Dean left the club to join South Devon, a talented bowler who had represented Devon at Under 19 level felt he was not getting the enjoyment out of his cricket that he had in the past. It also left the club in a difficult position since his father was a most able and conscientious secretary. Yes, Arnold resigned at the next A.G.M. and now, having returned to live in Devon again, is seen occasionally at Torquay games. Dean eventually took up employment in his homelands and began playing again for Sutton Coldfield. He achieved his goal of playing in a Cheltenham & Gloucester Trophy match for a Warwickshire Board X1 against Herefordshire and in 2003 was still in the Sutton 1st X1.

Jason Foster did take 4 Barton wickets for 55 but their Graham Wilson had seen Torquay all out for 152 with his 8 for 43. Losing the last league match of the season to the local rivals meant the club had to settle for fifth place in the league table. Some small compensation went to Ian Coulton on the Sunday when, at Exmouth, he lifted the Devon Cup. Playing against Exeter in the semi-final both teams scored 127 in their allotted overs but, Torquay had only lost six wickets, as opposed to Exeter's nine. Against Braunton in the final, Torquay batted first and totalled 134 for 9, Bradford 34, Western 31. Tight bowling by Learmouth 3 for 26 and Foster 3 for 28 kept Braunton to 126 and Torquay had won by eight runs.

Before completing remarks on this season mention should be made of the Sunday 1st. X1, which under the leadership of Justin Mann only lost two games. So many of the first eleven made themselves available for Sundays, which in retrospect now (2003) is quite amazing, but it did help in the advancement of the younger players. Jason Foster scored a couple of centuries, and at Tavistock Phil Bradford had a hundred off fifty balls. Whether it was the winning or the man management, (no pun intended) but the team were a happy side. Neil Matthews let it be known, at the seasons end, that he would be leaving the area to take a business post in the North Midlands.

The 1994 season should really have been filmed and the tape played on 'special evenings' in the clubhouse. Thanks to certain individuals working extremely hard throughout the winter months, and some even before the end of the previous season, it really became memorable. Not only were Torquay to host the Minor Counties X1 playing against the touring South African team but an Old England X1 had also agreed a fixture. Under the leadership of Jim Parks the 'old timers' match gate receipts were to be divided between the Institute for the Blind and the Sports Foundation. John Childs, the England and Essex bowler, was in his benefit season and since he had begun his career at Kingskerswell, and then South Devon, he had decided a game locally would be ideal. This match was to be played in a manner of the 'old days' when top cricketers would tour the country and play any twenty two, as mentioned in the beginning of this potted rambling. Childs promised to bring as many of the Essex X1 as possible to play 22 of the Torquay club and the home side were to ensure the presence of a bookmaker so that bets could be made regarding individuals. In addition to these games Vic Marks was to bring an England X1 to play a Somerset X1 in aid of Neil Mallender's Benefit and the Children's Hospice at Fremington, the game being sponsored by the St. Regis Paper Company. All this, as well as the usual midweek touring sides, made it a season to look forward to.

After news of the games came the surprises of player movement. Probably the biggest being the arrival of Haydn Morgan from Barton. The press invariably referred to Morgan as "A young opening batsman for whom big things are forecast". Mike Pugh, who had scored a lot of runs for Abbotskerswell, had joined but Rob Learmouth had left the club. Jason Fairbrother was to have another season at the Recreation Ground and three new overseas players were at the club's opening night. Tim Bower, a quick bowler from Tasmania, Peter Hendle from New Zealand and Chris Bossano an eighteen year old from South Africa. The latter is still in this country playing county cricket for Derbyshire (2003). It is fair to say that expectations were not high after the previous season's fifth position but, with the influx of new players, supporters were hoping for better things.

Those who went across to Exmouth for the opening league game were in for a miserable afternoon, 15 for 3 in no time at all. Jones and Pugh, 72 and 37 respectively, did get the total to 151 for 7 but it was never enough against a side of Exmouth's class and their batting strength. If that was a bad start the following week at Bovey Tracey was worse, all out for 95 was unbelievable, but true!

Winning three games in succession saw the side in a more comfortable position but when the inconsistencies returned the number of team changes that took place were not all due to non availability, and puzzled spectators more than somewhat. The cricket reporter had a field day when second team bowlers were selected for the first eleven again, after being discarded as veterans. "Experience is needed", was the headline. Skipper Coulton really suffered with his own injuries and while out of the team, Justin Mann had to take charge for several weeks. By the end of July Torquay were one position from the bottom of the league and relegation was a real possibility. The numerous team changes had not seen the desired effect, so after meetings and discussions drastic action was taken. Supporters suddenly saw in the press that David Lawrence the ex-England and Gloucestershire player was being brought in for the last month. 'Syd', as he was affectionately known, had to retire from county cricket because of knee trouble and supporters were divided as to the wisdom of this move. No one wanted to see the club relegated but there were those who were very much against Lawrence's inclusion.

In his first game at Seaton he took two wickets for twenty six, while comments to the effect that "he softened up the batsmen for the other bowlers" were heard. The mere fact that for a change so many batsmen scored runs, 234 for 5, which gave all the bowlers real time to obtain opposition wickets was ignored. In the following double week-end the umpires actually "ordered" Lawrence out of the bowling attack, because of his follow through, and that caused more than a little discussion, even on the national radio. His six games for the club saw him take thirteen wickets and his mere presence in the team appeared to bring out the best in others. From the very real possibility of being relegated Torquay eventually finished in seventh place. With the unexpected victory over Braunton in the last game of the season Torquay not only hauled the team to the more respectable position but also made it Exmouth's title for the fifth successive year. Braunton, who had led the table nearly all the season, had a twenty point lead over Exmouth when this last game started. Holding Torquay to 181 for 2 the Braunton side thought the total well within reach of their batsmen. Tim Bower, 5 for 51, and Vaughan Hosking, 4 for 25, proved how wrong they were and Exmouth 'pipped' them at the post!

While The Old England X1 were good entertainment, the Aussie exile, Jason Fairbrother, was the most delighted of the players. Forever talking about his bowling he was looking forward to going back to Australia and telling them how he had three internationals for just eighteen runs, Luckhurst, Jones and Lever! Nigel Janes, 50 and Phil Bradford 48 were the batsmen to see Torquay home to a rather hollow victory.

On the day before the South Africans arrived at the ground the setting looked a picture with all the stands, marquees and sponsors tents in place. Sadly, torrential overnight and morning rain completely spoiled all the hard work of the organisers. The club phone rang all the morning with probable spectators enquiring about the chances of play. There was panic in the kitchen since, as the rain eased, the umpires came and asked for an early lunch! Very difficult in those days with such limited facilities in the kitchen trying to work to a timetable. Wandering around the pavilion talking to old friends was Fanie De Villiers, having a rest after having to do so much bowling in the Leeds Test match after Allan Donald got injured. Play got underway rather late and the South Africans were 185 for 7 at stumps, Cronje 47 and Cullinan with 68 were the only two batsmen to show any form. The second day they batted on to reach 249 all out ensuring the game would fizzle out into a draw. There was time for the Minor Counties to face 46 overs before the close of play during which time 145 runs were scored for the loss of two wickets. Due to the morning rain on the first day, and the tourists making little attempt to really make a game of the proceedings, the attendance was most disappointing, but very understandable.

One man who did have a quiet laugh was the caterer. Roger Mann, who had done so much work regarding the whole organisation of the event, had warned him that one of the South Africans was a Muslim and would need Al-hal killed meat. A butcher was found after much chasing around the town, who supplied same and the said meat was cooked separately for this one individual. When the 'special' was placed before him he enquired for the tomato sauce and each day he emptied the entire contents of the container over his special meal! (a memory for the caterer!)

After his quiet beginning Tim Bower was one of the few who did play consistently well as his eventual 59 league wickets showed. Haydn Morgan, Phil Bradford and Julian Wyatt were the batsmen to stand out.

Only Wyatt managed a century, against Exmouth, although there was much sympathy for Morgan who, against Braunton on the last ball needed two for his ton. He scored one and remained 99 not out.

Ian Coulton was a very disappointed captain at the end of the season, Bovey Tracey had knocked Torquay out of the Devon Cup and the league position was the lowest for many years. When he presented his report for the season at the Annual General meeting, Coulton was very forthright and critical of the whole club. Some of it quite fair, but other points totally unfair as he made comments regarding the second X1 when they had actually finished runners up in their respective league. He resigned the captaincy which was to pass to Nigel Janes.

Captain of the Second X1 that season, B.J.Sewell, as stated, led his team to the runners up spot in their league and in his report he pointed out the contribution from the overseas players, Chris Bassano, Peter Hendle and Jason Fairbrother. All three were better than the normal second team players, but the skipper was honest enough to admit that three local lads had been deprived of the opportunity of playing for the club, whereas it should have been developing such individuals for the future.

While the following page of Torquay's 'hidden history' is slightly out of sequence the seed was sown following a cricket season. President Gordon Oliver was having a drink with Ian Western, which was not at all unusual! However, the result of their conversation certainly was.

Ian Western had a playing career with Chelston and South Devon but had eventually followed his son, Tim, to the Recreation Ground where smooth talking Chairman Hosking had persuaded him to take over the captaincy of the thirds and do some coaching for which he was so well qualified. Time and time again however, Ian Western was noted as knocking out runs for the second X1 under Hosking's leadership! Oliver was the spokesman for the Devon Conservative Group on Economy and Europe and explained to Western the numerous educational contacts in the area of Baranya in Hungary and the lack of sporting links. How much drink was consumed is not known but a suggestion was put to Ian W. that he should visit the area and attempt to introduce cricket! No small undertaking, since Ian did not speak Hungarian and the people had no idea of what the game was all about

Working 'behind the scenes' Gordon Oliver then arranged that Western, and wife Sandra, were invited to the Devon County Council 'Chairman's Supper Party' in the November, when there were also present a number of teachers of English from the very part of Europe that had been discussed. One individual, Victor Csongor, spoke at length with Ian Western about the game, the planning and necessary organisation to persue the idea further.

Early in 1995 Ian Western received a letter from the Devon County Council asking him and his wife to go to Hungary in September, travel and accommodation would be provided. So far, so good, but then the hard work began. A little money would be provided for playing equipment but not sufficient, so numerous old colleagues had to be 'chased' for bats, pads etc. that were no longer being used. During the July a lecturer from the Janus Pannonius University was visiting schools in Somerset, so a meeting was arranged to discuss the intended programme. Later the official interpreter for the Baranya County, Robert Marcz, was in England and he agreed to convert a few simple cricket rules into the Hungarian language. The next problem to be overcome was that all the playing kit, purchased and cajoled from friends, had to be transported to Hungary. The Grenville Yeo organisation of Barnstaple took schoolchildren to Budapest and after discussions with them that was the main part of the journey covered, although further arrangements had to be made for ensuring it eventually reached Baranya.

The actual story of the trip and subsequent sessions out there are 'books' in themselves. Sufficient to say that local radio and television covered the venture and Ian made further trips accompanied by son Tim, Mike Pugh and Matthew Hunt, all of whom are qualified coaches, and umpire/organiser Ken Jeffery. With these extra coaches more schools were catered for and the highlight of the visit was the tournament, to see which team had learned the most. The Devon Cricket Association provided caps for the children, oh yes! , there were girls as well as boys participating. In the August of 1999 a group of Hungarian children came across to Torquay to further their cricket education and were accompanied by four of their teachers.

An episode rarely mentioned, but a fantastic undertaking, by a staunch clubman.

At the beginning of each season the movement of playing personnel has been mentioned and during the 1990's some of the biggest changes amongst the club officials also occurred. While in earlier years there had been a Ladies Committee this decade saw Sally Craig became the first lady member of the Management Committee, and the following year she took over the duties of Secretary. Chairman, Vaughan Hosking decided at the end of the 1997 season that it was time to step aside and concentrate more on his rugby, off the field activities, which would occupy him twelve months of the year. His deputy, Stephen Craig took over as Chairman with Ian Western as Vice-Chairman. Gordon Baker, after many years as the club treasurer, resigned in 1992 and, until Robert Dickinson took over the position in '96, the club actually had an 'outsider', Len Clissold, fulfilling the duties. Harry Ball, who had been such a hard working and dedicated secretary for so many years was persuaded to become, Hon. Club Manager. It is impossible to describe to those who did not know Harry, just how much of his life he devoted to the club. He made it his business to know the members and that the Club Rules were strictly adhered to when he was in office. The hours spent at the Town Hall on behalf of the cricket club or the Sports Council, he rarely talked about, and only a few people appreciated his dedication to the position. His embarrassment when the club were taken to court over the drinks fiasco was something the author will never forget. Ian Handley was succeeded by Sally Craig and Colin Dayment was to occupy the secretary's role as the club went into its 150th year.

Changes in playing personalities before the 1995 season, when Nigel Janes took up the captain's reins again, saw the departure of Julian Wyatt to Tiverton Heathcote and the arrival of Mohammed Amjad, a Pakistani bowler, from the Midlands. Matthew Hunt and Marcus Green, from South Devon and Cockington respectively, added to the batting strength while Australian Mark Bailey was yet another new face. Jeremy Batty, an off spinner on Somerset's books, had signed to play for Torquay when not needed at Taunton, while Ian Baker, home again after his wanderings overseas, was available to play. Janes told the press he was hoping that Ian Coulton had put a bad season behind him and he was expecting big things from both Tim Western and Guy Sewell.

Whatever was to come during the season supporters were delighted with the first game, a home encounter with Bovey Tracey. Batting first Haydn Morgan showed he had benefited from a season in New Zealand with an excellent 102, ably supported by Western 37, Sewell 25 and Batty 25 not out, the total was 224 for 4 when the overs ran out. As Bovey had attracted Donohue and Tall, Devon County all rounders, plus South African batsman Moffat Billy, the tea interval was full of conjecture as to what might happen. Mark Bailey did the initial damage to the Bovey batting taking 2 for 23 while Jeremy Batty removed the danger man Donohue. When Amjad came into the attack the middle order and later batsmen departed very quickly and Bovey were all out for 109 with only Mark Gribble 41, at all comfortable. In his debut Amjad had taken 6 for 29 against one of the teams that had been tipped for the title.

A comfortable victory followed at Plymouth, where Ian Baker took the bowling honours with 4 for 16 while Morgan, with a 79, saw Torquay through to a total of 133 for 1. Nigel Janes policy was for Haydn Morgan to keep his end going and the other batsmen to get after the runs, he also promised they would not be dropped for a low score on odd occasions. Morgan certainly kept his end going with good scores week after week. Other than two 'losing draws' the first half of the season went as Janes had hoped for. After the losing draw with Tiverton, when only 178 for 6 was recorded chasing 203, Janes felt the chasing had not been hard enough and Ian Coulton went back to the Second X1. Only once in the first half of the season did all the players get to the wicket and that was during a tied game with Sandford at 132 runs for each team.

Even at the halfway stage cricket followers, throughout the county, were saying the title race was between Exmouth and Torquay. In Torquay's side everyone was contributing to a string of victories, including a young Andy Bertram, brought into the side against Seaton, and taking two of the first four wickets for just eighteen. Whatever Nigel Janes decided things went his way, after Amjad and Batty had reduced Plymouth to 150 for 9 the captain decided he would open the innings. He did so, with Batty, who went on 62 while Janes himself was 53 not out in the winning total of 151 for 1.

While the supporters enjoyed a wonderful cricket season it was not confined to the league, the Devon Cup had been just as exciting. In the first round South Devon had been defeated, a young Guy Sewell had scored 110 out of Torquay's 264 for 8 and Haydn Morgan, excelling with the ball, took 4 for 32 in South Devon's 148 all out.

Morgan was the centurion with 158 out of 279 for 2 in the next round against Buckfastleigh, who could only reply with 147 for 7. Then it was down to Plymouth where the home side could only muster 120, which presented no problem to Tim Western and Haydn Morgan who passed it quite easily. At Exeter the home side had no answer to a total of 242 for 7 which saw Torquay having to face the old foe Barton, in the final at Bovey Tracey. That was to take place on the Sunday after the last league game of the season.

When that time arrived it was a very sad weekend for the Torquay supporters. At Exmouth the home side had a thirteen point margin in their favour and while their captain talked about a 'normal game' it was anything but that. Exmouth's skipper Chouhan did not have to win the match to win the title, so he, as a good captain should, played it to the benefit of his team. Torquay won the game, but lost the title by four points. Chouhan having declared Exmouth's innings closed on 178 for 3, twelve overs before the allotted number ran out, deprived Torquay of any possible chance of further bowling points, which in effect finished the title race. Torquay's eventual victory, after such a wonderful season, meant nothing as regards the league.

To have gone through the league season without losing a game but to find the title remained in East Devon was most disappointing but, worse was to follow!. In the Cup Final, at Bovey Tracey on the Sunday, Barton scored 240 for 4 and had Torquay all back in the pavilion for 135. Whether it was a reaction from the Exmouth experience one will never know, supporters could only offer condolences to all the players who had given their followers such an exciting season. One's sympathy went to Nigel Janes who had lost out again, missing the league title on the last day of the season, as he did when previously captaining the team.

JANES TROOPS SUCCEED

A 14 YEAR WAIT OVER

After the undefeated season of '95 supporters expectations were high for the new campaign. The new opening bowler was an Australian, Neil Hancock, and nobody realised what an effect he was to have on cricket throughout the County, and for years to come. Ryan Horrell, after a successful season for Devon and Braunton, joined the club and was to be the replacement for Amjad who had returned to the Midlands. Versatile Ian Bransdon came to the Recreation Ground from Barton while Kevin Barrett arrived from Plymouth. Bransdon proved to be a very useful all rounder and as a change bowler often broke stubborn partnerships. Barrett, a student at Durham University, had topped the league batting averages the previous season with 69. Shane Mitchell and Steve Short were two further new players who had signed for the club. Janes did have one worry, his wicketkeeper, Justin Mann, had broken his leg playing football and was unlikely to be fit for some time.

The league season began with an away game at Barton and batting first Torquay were all back in the pavilion for 147, the main contributors to that total being Morgan 45 and Bradford 44. During the tea interval there was much discussion among the supporters as to whether the total was enough. Even though Ryan Horrell began his Torquay career with 5 for 38 Barton hung on to finish on 103 for 9. In the first season of, fifty over league cricket, Torquay had began with a winning draw on the ground of their keenest rivals. Steve Craig was promoted from the second eleven to keep wicket in this particular game.

Contact had been made with Richard Williams, or 'Reggie' as he was known far and wide, a wicketkeeper batsman with Gloucestershire and he had signed to play when not needed by his county. At the last moment he was required so Craig continued behind the stumps in the next game against Paignton.

Losing the toss at home to Paignton and asked to bat first Torquay were all out for 204, with Tim Western making 76 before being the first of three run outs. A young Chris Read, later to go on to play for England, made 47 but Paignton were all out for 159, bowling honours went to Bransdon 3 for 19 and Horrell 3 for 38. The last two games in May were abandoned because of rain, at Bovey the home side having already been bowled out for 143, with Neil Hancock taking 5 for 57.

Having the luck of the toss in six consecutive weeks, Janes saw eighteen or nineteen points added weekly to the growing total. At Exeter, where there was a late start because of the rain, Horrell 3 for 10 and Hancock 3 for 17 saw the home side all out for 82. 'Reggie' Williams, with 31 runs out of the 83 for 4, then saw Torquay safely to victory. The Braunton game at the Rec. should be remembered for Haydn Morgan's exploits. He was the sixth bowler asked by the skipper to 'turn his arm' and then took 3 for 24, to leave Braunton on 149 for 9. With Tim Western he then opened the batting and proceeded to smash 88 runs in a stand of 150 to win the game.

Throughout the first half of the season the Torquay side all went to the wicket on only two occasions, at Barton and Paignton. Morgan, Western, Barratt, Hunt, Pugh and Mitchell kept supporters happy with their run getting while all the bowlers were taking wickets. At Sidmouth Ian Baker had an opening spell of 1 for 17 and when he later returned he took a further 3 for 1 to add to his afternoon performance. Morgan had a hundred against Sandford and Barrett made a century in the match at Exmouth.

The captain's luck changed in the second half of the summer and he only had the advantage of the toss on two occasions. Interestingly there was a tied game with Paignton, 197 each with 5 and 6 wickets apiece, neither side getting the two hundred batting bonus point, even with so many wickets in hand. The double weekend, against Budleigh and Tiverton saw both games washed out after only a few hours play. Unfortunately, in each instance, Torquay had been asked to bat, while they did not have the time to acquire batting points, they were long enough at the crease to lose two and four wickets in the respective games. At this time Exmouth had finished one of their games and picked up the full twenty points. The nine point margin Torquay had, when previously Tiverton had surprisingly beaten Exmouth, meant that Janes was once more 'looking up' rather than 'looking down'.

Having been put in at Sidmouth Torquay were 215 for 6 at the end of their overs, Mike Pugh having 'retired hurt' and been taken to hospital, while Haydn Morgan's father, John, came on to the field as the 'twelfth man'. Horrell 3 for 33, Bransdon 2 for 9 and H.Morgan 2 for 16 saw that Torquay obtained the winning points by bowling Sidmouth out for just 131runs.

It was another 'two- horse race' for the title and once again against Exmouth. These 'scribblings' cannot give enough credit to the entertainment the team provided that season and all the score cards should have been printed and displayed to show the effort put in by every one who represented Torquay. Janes always insisted on good fielding, the practise put in during training had paid dividends with amazing run outs and brilliant catching. With the penultimate game washed out at Sandford, the title was at stake in the last match. This was to be at the Recreation Ground and against Exmouth. Excitement, expectations and anticipation were all very high with more than a few nerves on edge. The league title had been 'snatched away' at the last minute on several occasions and was it to happen on our home ground!

Captains and leaders are fascinating people to those who study them, one has to be one's own man and, after studying a problem, have great conviction in one's action.

Before this last crucial game Nigel Janes astounded most people, but not those who knew him. While Mann's broken leg had been healing, as already reported, Craig, Williams and even Janes himself had kept wicket at different times. Once the leg had healed Justin Mann had been chosen to be behind the stumps for eight successive matches, but, he was dropped for this crucial game. He had not been called upon to handle a bat in any of those games and careful analysis of the byes conceded were noted before the recall of batsman keeper Williams, on the adage of 'always playing ones strongest side'.

Janes was lucky that the Exmouth captain called the toss incorrectly, and was quickly told to bat. In the first over Ian Baker had Lye caught by Nigel Janes, which was a great beginning. Neil Hancock, not to be outdone, bowled Baggs and then Cruft, before Baker had an lbw decision against Small. It was 26 for 4 when Nick Folland arrived at the wicket, with Wood, and then Proctor, the score rose to 96 for 6 before Folland himself was sent to the pavilion, caught by Barrett off Horrell's bowling. Rhodes and Pritchard added twenty apiece but all out for 144 made the tea interval a happy time for the Torquinians. Morgan and Barrett opened the innings but after 24 runs were on the score board the former was out, and on his way back to the clubhouse with 16 runs to his credit. On the same total Folland caught Barrett off the bowling of Proctor and those of 'little faith' were beginning to wonder! Reggie Williams and Matthew Hunt settled in and took the score to 70 before Williams was out for 25. It then became 77 for 4 with Mike Pugh bowled for 2. Exmouth were making a fight of it but, this was to be the year the title came back to the Recreation Ground. Tim Western stayed with Hunt to see the score reach 118 and his own tally 17 before captain Janes arrived at the wicket. Cracking three fours in the twenty balls he faced, Nigel Janes was out to win the title in style. Matt Hunt 56 not out and Nigel Janes 13 not out saw Torquay finish the game with a flourish.

The writer had tea in his car on the other side of the ground and had seen Justin Mann sitting in his vehicle watching the game. One could understand the bitter disappointment at being dropped but the team spirit had been great until then. The captain had felt it was for the good of the side, as well as the club, to replace Mann by Williams, who was, after all, a first class counties player. With the mind 'drifting', as the crumbs accumulated, he wondered too how Shane Mitchell, Marcus Green, Guy Sewell and even James Duder felt, since all of them had played a part in the season's success but had not been included in the final eleven.

The Devon Cup was of second consideration to the league from the very beginning of the season, but Sidmouth were well beaten in the first round when Haydn Morgan scored 101, Tim Western 50 and Neil Hancock 59 not out. Sidmouth could only muster 138 against the bowling of Shane Mitchell 2 for 13 and Marcus Green 3 for 18. In the second round, away at Plymouth, the home side were 149 with Horrell, Hancock and Bransdon each taking three wickets. Torquay were 152 for 2 with Western 67 not out.

However that was the end of cup success since Bovey Tracey came to the Recreation Ground and, after scoring 209 for 6, had Torquay all out for 185, with only Kevin Barrett showing any kind of form with a solid 50.

Reflecting on the season that the league title had been reclaimed the writer must mention the difficult first game of the second team. Playing at home against North Devon the skipper was faced with fielding just six players in addition to himself. Whether through force or coercion but Paul Cook, the previous bar steward, Roger Biddick, very much an extra third team player at his age, Bernard Phillips, no cricket player but over from the King's Bowling club to watch and an unnamed Colt were quickly found suitable clothing and 'pressed into service'! To learn the composition of the side, after following the first team, it was more than a surprise to hear they had actually won, and also obtained the full twenty points! Following this incident captain Vaughan Hosking was fortunate that Barrie Matthews, out of the game for some two years, became available and Ronnie Owen returned to the area from Lancashire. Matthews cracked over five hundred league runs later that season, and retained his position in the slips!

Ryan Horrell, Matthew Hunt and Kevin Barrett all played for Devon during the season while youngsters Arron Williams, James Toms and Oliver Pitts had represented Devon in the U 12s and U13s age groups.

Naturally after such a successful season Nigel Janes retained his position as captain and he was as determined as ever to emulate Exmouth with 'back to back' league titles. In the shuffle of players during the closed season, Janes, and the club supporters, were more than disappointed to learn that Neil Hancock was to remain in England but, not with Torquay. Ex-Torquay player, Phil Bradford, who had a season or so at Brixham was taking over the captaincy at Buckfastleigh and Neil Hancock was to also play for that club. Another ex- Torquay player, Guy Sewell, was making his way out into the countryside to play for Buckfastleigh. Haydn Morgan had been given a contract by Somerset and would only be available occasionally, but a new teacher at the Paignton Community College, Mark Tamplin had joined Torquay and was reputed to be an all rounder from South Wales. The not unexpected, but rather disappointing, move across to Paignton by Justin Mann allowed Andy Hele to join the club and to take over the wicket keeping duties. Craig Wiseman, a young Australian left arm pace bowler was the replacement for Hancock but Janes did express fears that Morgan's bowling might be missed more than his batting. Mark and Simon Edwards, sons of the former Torquay and Devon captain Hiley Edwards, had joined the club both having represented Devon up to U 18 level. Rumours abounded regarding members of the Needham family joining as several had played in midweek matches during the previous season.

While the papers described it as a 'makeshift side', Torquay picked up the maximum twenty points in the first league game at Instow, against North Devon. Neither Ian

Baker nor Matthew Hunt had been able to travel so Mark Edwards and Shaun Needham were both selected in their respective places. Janes won the toss and asked the home team to bat. Mike Pugh actually opened the bowling and in his five overs took 1 for 18. Wiseman started his career with the team taking 3 for 18 and Horrell 3 for 20 with the result that the home side were all out for 125. Haydn Morgan, not required by his new masters at Taunton, had a not out 70 in the 128 for 3. Next was a home game against Tiverton Heathcote and, with Nigel Janes not available, Mike Pugh took over the captaincy. Steve Short came into the side to replace Mark Edwards but none of the bowlers were seriously troubled by the batsmen and, with wickets falling regularly, Tiverton were all back in the pavilion for 152. Tamplin and Western, with 40 and 55, gave Torquay a great start but, five wickets were lost in obtaining the necessary runs. Stuart MacGill, playing for Tiverton, scored 53 and took 2 for 56 in this game, but few of those who saw him play that afternoon realised that by 1999 he would be in the Australian Test squad.

Having the luck of the call on the first seven occasions saw only one defeat, and that was at the Recreation Ground, against Budleigh Salterton. Asked to bat, the visitors did with a vengeance, and had 217 for 9 by tea. Torquay were all out for 111. The result really was a shock. At that time, 47 games unbeaten was the longest run in league matches. It had been August 1994 when Barton had accomplished the last victory over Torquay, however, it is worth noting that Budleigh that season where led by Peter Roebuck, ex-Somerset, who took 3 for 28. The team also included Bobby Dawson, who had seasons with Gloucestershire and eventually succeeded Roebuck as the Devon captain. He contributed 130 not out and took 3 for 19, while Cowley, an ex Hampshire spinner, had 4 for 24.

There was just one more defeat before the halfway stage of the season was reached, and that was against Exmouth. Once more the visitors were asked to bat and when Ryan Horrell had them back in the pavilion for 172, with a personal seven wicket haul for fifty-six, no one realised what was to come. Tierney took 3 for 17 and Woodman 4 for 32 as the Torquay wickets fell and only Kevin Barrett, with a score 21, seemed able to cope with the bowling. All out for just 101, so on the two occasions all the eleven players had gone to the wicket Torquay lost, whereas in other games the batsmen had all shown form, thus avoiding the necessity of the tail-enders having to bat. Nigel Janes decided in the Barton match, at the Recreation Ground, it was time he had an innings and actually opened the batting. Barton had been restricted to 153 for 8 with Ryan Horrell taking 2 for 29 in an 18 over stint. Janes twenty three runs were the next highest score behind Hele's 78 not out, clobbered against his ex-colleagues in yet another win.

The return match against Tiverton was away, and was the only loss suffered in the second half of the season. Winning the toss, the home side decided to take first knock and with Ryan Horrell having a five wicket haul, for just thirty six runs, it meant things were looking quite good chasing a mere total of 114. However, as always in most sports, and especially cricket, there were more surprises to come. Matthew Hunt scored 27, Nigel Janes 23 and 'Mr. Extras' 23, but then the other nine players only managed thirty nine runs between them, to leave the total three runs short of the target. Stuart MacGill again! 5 for 50, and Torquay's ex-colleague, Julian Wyatt, 4 for 26, ensured the visitors had a miserable journey home, but it had been quite a game.

Richard Merriman had arrived to join the club just prior to the last double weekend of the season, he was stated to be a Minor Counties player who was settling locally and taking up a teaching post. Janes put him straight into the first team and kept him there for the last three games. Having lost to Exmouth earlier in the season and the points totals being very close, the return match was of great importance to both sides as there were only a few games left in which to decide the title .Exmouth were two men short when Janes won the toss, so, he decided to bat and make the most of things before those players arrived. 145 runs were scored before the first wicket fell and Torquay reached 214 for 9, with Craig Wiseman 76, Kevin Barrett 66 and Mike Pugh 37. Ian Baker, who had been getting some unfortunate publicity through the season, took his first wicket, that of danger-man Small for a duck.An opening bowler who had not taken a wicket by August was open to criticism, but, people did not realise how many games Baker had missed. Steve Short, who had been called into the team at the last minute on the previous Saturday, was retained for this match. He bowled 18 overs and took 4 for 77, which was a prodigious effort by who was essentially a second team player. Short had occasional outings in the first X1 but until then had little experience of bowling against batsmen with the ability of the Exmouth men As the Exmouth total rose nearer to the Torquay score the tension grew amongst the supporters, neither side could really afford to lose.At 199 for 7 and five overs left it looked as though the visitors would win, but there was yet another twist to come. Mark Woodman was run out off the last ball, trying to get one run for a tie, and their total of 213 for 9 left Exmouth with 11 points and Torquay 15 for the winning draw.The game had provided plenty of excitement for the spectators but it was not quite the result either captain really wanted.

Having come away from Sandford victorious, where Ryan Horrell and the retained Steve Short spun their way through the home batting, while Craig Wiseman hit 64 of the 160 runs needed to win, it was across to Barton for the final game.The full twenty points were necessary to ensure the 'back to back' title Janes, and his team, desperately wanted, while the supporters too could also be included in that desire.As has been already mentioned Barton are one of those teams who often spring a surprise and, irrespective of what went on in the dressing rooms, nerves were tingling around the ground. Janes called incorrectly when Jim Parker tossed the coin and was asked to bat. Throughout the season the supporters never knew who would succeed 'on the day' but they had grown to have faith that somebody would. Craig Wiseman, opening with Kevin Barrett, saw his partner out for 13 then both Haydn Morgan and Matthew Hunt went cheaply.Andy Hele contributed 30 before Wiseman himself went for 60 and 140 was on the scoreboard. Richard Merriman added 34 before being smartly run out. Mike Pugh and Sean Needham both lasted long enough to just get in to double figures before Farkins took both of their wickets. The skipper himself was run out for 15 and it was 200 all out, but actually one of the better scores on that ground during the season. Craig Wiseman, after his good innings, opened the bowling with Hunt but came in for harsh treatment and was taken off after four overs. Hunt had nine overs, getting the wicket of Terry Farkin, and only conceding 13 runs. Ryan Horrell bowled three consecutive maiden overs and then clean bowled Pugh. Cowley who was normally noted for his big hitting fell to Horrell for just five runs and then the procession began. Steve Short had joined Torquay from Abbotskerswell as a second team batsman who occasionally 'turned his arm', now took the applause of the Torquay supporters with three quick wickets. With the tail end batsmen in it was a case of could Barton save the game? , practically every ball was treated with a straight bat by Parker and Lievesley. An occasional single was scampered until the latter was eventually bowled by Steve Short. Barton's captain Jim Parker, together with Mike Pedley, prolonged the inevitable for some eleven overs during which time Janes brought back Hunt for an over, and Morgan for two. Halfway through the forty fourth over Ryan Horrell found a ball to clean bowl Pedley, and then the celebrations began! It is impossible to describe the emotions, none of the players, and very few members, had been ever been involved in 'back to back' league titles in the modern era. Apart from the joy of seeing the team win 'back to back' titles it was also very emotional as, having achieved that goal on the very ground where the Torquay Club had its original beginnings, and against what many members consider, the club's keenest rivals.

The bowling figures that day of Horrell and Short were truly remarkable and they were backed up with some excellent fielding. Ryan Horrell, 17:3 overs, 9 maidens, 4 for 18, ably supported by Steve Short's wonderful spell of 11 overs, 6 maidens, 5 for 8.

Having accomplished his goal Nigel Janes relinquished the captaincy as he was living and working in Bristol and uncertain how often he would be available to play in the future. To follow two successful seasons was going to be a difficult task. The departure of so many of the players who had made that piece of club history was a warning in itself to supporters regarding too many expectations of the season to come. Vice-captain Mike Pugh had returned to Abbotskerswell and had taken Marcus Green with him. Ryan Horrell, who had travelled from North Devon each week-end, left Torquay and joined the Braunton club while Haydn Morgan was preparing to settle, permanently, in New Zealand. There were worries too regarding the fitness of Matthew Hunt who, at different times, was plagued by shin-splint niggles. The one plus was a newcomer, a bowler from New Zealand, Emmett Craik, and at that time no one realised what a 'plus' he was to prove. Popular throughout the club Emmett was wholehearted in all he did on the field. Wicketkeeper Andy Hele was the person who took up the reins for the season and he was very realistic when he discussed the situation with the cricket correspondent of the local press. He pointed out that there were experienced players in the side and they would help to bring on the promising youngsters, but it definitely would be a season for consolidation.

The opening game against Sandford tended to show spectators what the team were to experience for the season and a losing draw was not too disappointing. Emmett Craik took 3 for 30 while Steve Short, continued where he left off the previous season, and had 4 for 47. Everyone was pleased to see Tim Western hit a good 78 since the club needed him to overcome the inconsistency that appeared to affect him the previous season. Against Bovey Tracey, who eventually totalled 223 for 7, five bowlers had been tried when Hele asked Merriman to turn his arm. Previously considered a batsman and a very neat fielder, he went on to take 4 for 71. When Torquay's innings began only Kevin Barrett, with 47, appeared able to cope with the Bovey bowlers and the last pair at the wicket were hanging on grimly for what was to be a losing draw when the overs were completed.

Against Barton, Emmett Craik bowled very well, finishing with 4 for 50 and giving the team a target of 187 to chase. Over tea the Torquay supporters felt there was a fair chance of obtaining the runs but only Barrett with a half century in the eventual total of 169, looked at all happy batting. Before May was halfway through Andy Green sought permission, and was able to join Torquay from Paignton. Another quick bowler who, on his day, was useful but on others could be quite wayward, however, he did add to the overall bowling strength. Of all the places to record a first victory very few supporters would have expected it to take place at Exmouth. Batting first, Barrett and Merriman each had over forty runs to their credit, and were followed by Western and Hunt with each getting 71 in the final total of 215 for 5. The bowlers really had something to play with and, since Emmett Craik was injured, Louis Visser, a young South African in the second team was taking his place. Visser's 3 for 43 and Andy Green's 3 for 56 helped with a most unexpected, but very welcome victory. The following weekend it was the Paignton 'derby' game at the Recreation Ground and having had the visitors all out for 216, Emmett Craik 4 for 44, it was developing into an interesting encounter when the rains came, finishing any further action. Kevin Barrett 56 not out and Matthew Hunt 57 not out, were really going well in Torquay's 117 for 1.

After the halfway stage of the season Ian Baker took more of the bowling honours but both Craik and Short had certainly played their respective parts in keeping the club's flag flying. The most remarkable game of the whole season was the Queen's Park encounter with Paignton. Andy Hele won the toss and, despite the overcast conditions, which spectators said 'would be meat and drink for Malcolm Kingdon', he decided to bat. How right they were! Ex-colleague Malcolm Kingdon, bowled 21 overs and had 8 wickets for 36 runs. Tim Western played a patient, and what was to prove a priceless, innings of 43 runs and had a stand of 27 with James Duder, which was also to be vital. The latter, a lad who had promised so much had not fulfilled his potential, but on that day really did show what he could be capable of. Nigel Janes diligently played thirty five balls and was still out for the proverbial duck. Torquay were all out for 90 and Paignton had an extra five overs to chase a seemingly very small score. What the tea room was like during the break heaven alone knows, one can only repeat what Andy Hele told the press. "It was very quiet at tea as we were all devastated, after winning the toss. We had a good talk". There was a lot of talk around the ground, but mostly by the Paignton folk! Torquay's followers were very subdued and understandably so. However, it was a cricket match and as everyone knows cricket is a funny game. Paignton were as much at sea trying to bat as Torquay had been. Quick wickets went down and Paignton were 23 for 3, and then a little later 35 for 8. Woodcock played a ball into his stumps but the bails remained in situ, by this time it was excitement for the Torquay supporters, at least until Stuart Lott put Steve Short's bowling away for two sixes!, and then the worried looks returned. Ian Baker clean bowled Lott however, and Kingdon did not last long, which left Torquay the winners. Neither side had scored a hundred runs, 90 to 68, and yet it had been a most interesting afternoon for any cricket fan, and truly fantastic if one supported Torquay!

The writer had a very difficult job convincing John Pelosi that the result was true when he phoned his Saturday night report to him !, how can people leave before the end ?

Mid-August saw the last of the double weekends as the league were to abolish them the next season. Andy Hele led his team to two victories in those matches and picked up thirty-eight points out of the possible forty. Kevin Barrett was in sparkling form with the bat scoring 85 not out and a 65, while Hele himself had contributed 39 and 42 to the two winning totals. Whether the captaincy had affected his play or not was a matter of conjecture, but there was only one of the Andy Hele 'special' innings during the season, a 66 at Seaton. In both matches Ian Baker and Emmett Craik were the most successful bowlers.

After a rather torrid season, for his first year as captain, Andy Hele had a very easy victory at the Recreation ground in the last game. When Budleigh Salterton arrived spectators could hardly believe their eyes. So many of the players looked as though they were expecting to play the Colts, they were so young, whereas the older looking gentleman was not a parent on a day out, but 'a well over 60 years of age', Ron Tyler. Batting first the Budleigh team were all out for 99, Kevin Barrett 4 for 36 and Emmett Craik 3 for 39 being the bowlers mainly responsible for the low total. Torquay got the runs with the loss of two wickets with Shaun Needham hitting eight fours in a very quick forty four not out.

Following a season where Andy Hele had been under a lot of pressure it was still a surprise, to a number of supporters, that he did not resume the captaincy for the '99 season. He had said prior to the beginning of the season, "mid-table and consolidation", which was exactly what he had achieved. Under Hele's leadership certain youngsters had certainly developed, their first team experience with his guidance, had seen an improvement in their general play and that had to be for the good of the club in the future. Mention has been made of Steve Short on several occasions and during the season he had also been played as an opening batsman in the first eleven. A very versatile player, who arrived at the club as a second team player and became an almost indispensable member of the first eleven.

Mike Pugh, following his one season back at Abbotskerswell, returned to the Recreation Ground and actually took over the captaincy. He was certainly fortunate with the prevailing circumstances in that Emmett Craik returned for another season, while Phil Bradford and John Dupree joined the club from Buckfastleigh. Rather unfortunately the Bucks had been relegated after the previous season's results. While Bradford had been known as an attacking batsman when he had been with the club, after his seasons at Brixham and Buckfastleigh, bowling had become his forte. Dupree was definitely a first team player with batting and bowling skills, that the club, and Pugh were to appreciate during the season. In addition Matt Swarbrick, a Dorset opening batsman, had joined the club which gave Pugh a squad that he felt could make a big impression in the league.

Following Phil Bradford's experience of leading the sides at Brixham and Buckfastleigh he was persuaded to skipper the seconds and his expertise was a great help to the younger players, that was when he was not helping out the first X1! For too long aging veterans had been in charge and had not really allowed the youth to develop in the second team.

Away to North Devon in the first game Torquay batted first and had 195 for 8, thanks in the main to a completely fit again Matthew Hunt with 70 not out, and Shaun Needham with 48. Hunt then took 4 for 16 and John Dupree 3 for 10, which had the home side all out for 76. A second victory did not look very likely when Torquay were 77 for 5 against Bovey Tracey but out to the wicket strode Andy Hele to have one of his 'specials' with boundaries galore. Wickets fell at the other end and he was left to face the last four overs with a former Colt, Jason Westcott, who had graduated under his captaincy the previous season. Westcott did not score and Hele added 26 in the last over finishing on 86 not out. The total of 187 for 9 ensured a winning draw since only Bradford, with 3 for 10, was in form with the ball.
A losing draw at Sidmouth was the only blot in the first half of the season while outright victories were obtained against Exeter, Seaton and Barton. Against the latter Emmett Craik had a five wicket haul to have the Cricketfield Road boys out for under a hundred.

Swarbrick was not seen during the second part of the season but with the addition of Ben Passenger, an ex Gloucestershire U 19s player, occasional games by Nigel Janes and Phil Bradford drafted into the senior eleven, Mike Pugh kept the pressure on all the opponents. But for the fact there was a blip Pugh might very well have had a title credited to him. Having obtained a winning draw away at Exmouth, when the skipper had top scored with 79, Pugh was also the best batsman with a 64, when the return match took place at the Recreation Ground. This time however it was a very different story and Exmouth passed the target of 169 for the loss of only one wicket. Beating Paignton had seen Torquay go ten points clear of Exmouth in the league and had given supporters high hopes that another league title might be in the offing! However another hiccup occurred at the Recreation Ground, there was yet another losing draw, against Sidmouth, which left supporters wondering at the inconsistency of certain players.

Going across to Barton for the last league game of the season Pugh's luck with the coin calling deserted him and he was asked to bat. With so many batsmen scoring runs, Western 54, Hunt 36 and S.Needham 33 the declaration came on 201 for 7. Mike Pugh said to the press, "it is slow and low here and if you want to stay in you usually can" which was exactly what Barton managed to do after some early shocks. Andy Pugh had 51 not out for Barton, in their overall total of just 108 for 6. With the fourteen points Torquay obtained from the game and Exmouth picking up twenty, from their win at Tiverton, Torquay were once again second in the league title race, this time by a margin of six points.

Into the Year Two Thousand

Having come so close to winning the title Mike Pugh continued as the captain for the start of the twenty first century. Popular Emmett Craik was available for yet another season but, rather disappointingly, John Dupree had decided he was going to join Bovey Tracey, after just one summer of showing Torquay what a useful team member he was.

Although the first game, away at Plympton, resulted in a rather easy victory it did cause a few 'flutters' amongst the travelling supporters. Emmett Craik bowled Torquay into a winning position with 5 for 28 in Plympton's all out total of 87, and in doing so obtained his one hundredth wicket in the Premier League. Torquay lost four wickets far too cheaply and it was only when Andy Hele and Marcus Green came together, 24 and 29 not out respectively, that the points were secured. The first home game followed and with some excellent batting, especially by Tim Western with 84, the scoreboard read 237 for 8 at the end of the allotted overs. During the tea interval expectations of a good result, in Torquay's favour, were prevalent amongst the home supporters but there was even better batting to come! Mention has already been made regarding Neil Hancock and his influence on Devon cricket, and at this time he was playing for Sidmouth. He hammered 129 not out from the Torquay bowling and the visitors won by five wickets. So much for expectations! With the next two games rain affected Kiwi Craik was most upset, having batted and scored a great 93 against North Devon, the weather prevented him bowling and thus killing his chance of any wickets. In the Seaton match he had taken 3 for 20 in the total of 133, and had no chance to bat. However it was the captain who felt that the rain had deprived the team of an almost certain twenty points in each instance!   Skipper Pugh, was delighted by the result of the game at Exmouth, the home side were all out for 164, Craik returning figures of 4 for 50, and his batsmen then obtained the necessary runs with the loss of seven wickets.

The first half of the season finished with the home 'derby' against Paignton and what a match that turned out to be! Batting first Paignton made 125 runs with Ben Passenger taking 4 for 35 in his best spell of bowling, and Phil Bradford 4 for 38. Torquay had included in their side a fourteen year old Grammar School pupil, Liam Rice, who was looked upon as a very promising spin bowler for the future and probably the youngest player to ever be in the first eleven. At tea it looked as though the bowlers had done the hard work since 126 did not look a big target. However the 'old days' returned!, with Malcolm Kingdon bowling at the sea-end, as he had for years in the past for Torquay, and once more taking wickets 'old memories' were stirred. A stupid run out from a silly call was the start, followed by batsmen trying to knock the cover off the ball even before they had the measure of the bowling, saw wickets begin to tumble. Certain spectators were swearing as they sat around the boundary watching the mayhem. Steve Short kept grafting away and eventually accumulated twenty runs before he was out. Schoolmaster Passenger and his young pupil were left at the wicket with only bowler Ian Baker to come after them. Passenger was dropped, not a difficult catch and Torquay supporters were relieved. He then went on to finish with 24 not out while pupil Rice scampered the odd single and also finished on 7 not out as the winning runs were finally made. It certainly was exciting cricket but one did wonder what the hell was going on with some of the Torquay batting, the situation had called for concentration and patience. Team manager John Morgan walked some miles that day!

Mention of the team manager, an appointment which John Morgan had held for years and still does as this is being scribbled, although mention has been made that he is likely to become chairman of selectors next season. In the writer's opinion John's presence has helped the side in so many ways. Drinks are now swiftly placed around the boundary in reach of thirsty bowlers at the end of their over, helmets are always available when batsmen or close to the wicket fielders require same. John is quick to see a field change is needed, or some other requirement in tactics, and gets a message to the captain, even on occasions carrying out the drinks during a break to pass on a subtle hint. However over the years too many aspects of his activities appear to be taken for granted and few of the club's officers helped with the tasks he once did. Once upon a time the boundary rope was collected and stored safely after some thirty yards were cut off the first night it was left out. Even after being on the go all the afternoon Morgan had to rely on Colin Dayment or other individuals who helped him with that chore. In recent times the rope goes out for the first game and is left there, much to the annoyance of the Corporation grass cutters who are not keen cricket fans.

Mention must be made of Ben Passenger's first appearance for Devon, against Wiltshire, in a game at Exmouth. With his first ball he had a wicket and after nine overs his figures were 1 for 6, later he was brought back for another spell and finished with 2 for 21.

The year 2000 saw the introduction of a Mid Week cricket league but it did not catch the imagination of the average follower of the game. Business, or work commitments, meant players were not always available and lack of, or very little publicity, did not help the possibly interested spectators. Noted in the writer's diary were Torquay getting well beaten by Barton even after Phil Bradford had taken 4 for 23, the batsmen had been unable to score a hundred. Losing to Chelston but just managing a winning draw against Abbotskerswell. In the modern world innovations need careful thought and execution, not rushed into just because it "might help the bar takings".

By July Mike Pugh knew he had troubles to overcome as Emmett Craik had a severe groin problem. To lose one's main bowler at that stage was a huge blow and it was not surprising that only two games were won during the second half of the season. Those happened to be against the two bottom sides, Seaton and Cornwood, where the batsmen had been chasing totals exceeding 250 and getting them. Western, Green, Barrett and Hele really were batsmen in form during those two games. Sadly no one was in form at Exeter, although Kevin Barrett did manage 32 out of the 89 the whole team recorded, but Exeter obtained the necessary runs without losing one wicket. The August of that season will either be forgotten, by Torquay supporters, or remembered for evermore by other cricket lovers. With Emmett Craik gone, Andy Hele absent from the team on his honeymoon, and Ben Passenger off on holiday, Pugh's problem was fairly obvious to all. The last game of the season, away at Queen's Park Paignton, was an absolute disgrace to the club, and another of those instances where the man management skills of the club's officials were shown to be sadly lacking. Ones sympathy went out to Mike Pugh and the six players who supported him playing in an arena where they pray for Torquay to fail anyway. Irrespective of the excuses that were trotted out, it was diabolical on the part of the club, to ask any captain to represent it with just six players. The captain, plus his six should never be forgotten. It should have been foreseen that with the weddings arranged for later and the holiday period, there would be players missing at the end of the season, but still insufficient players had been registered. Pugh had to open the bowling himself and had the amazing figures of 4 for 81 in a total of 309 for 5. Picture the wicketkeeper and bowler dear reader, and then visualise the amount of field to be covered by the other five players! After their exertions in the field Tim Western 33, James Boase 28, Andy Hele 52, and Mike Pugh 27 helped the total to reached 171 and saw Torquay finish fifth in the league table. Liam Rice, Tim Robinson and Arron Williams also had an afternoon of cricket they are not likely to forget.

Over many years there have been numerous changes at the Recreation Ground and reference has already been made to several, including that there was also a time when the area was locked up at night. Gates the Corporation employees use to go into the Kings Drive are now never closed, let alone locked, giving free access to the public and their dogs. This being irrespective of the fact the Recreation Ground is noted in the Environmental Handbook as a completely 'dog free zone'. The resultant consequences are that very often there has to be a 'clean up' operation for some individual. Chairman at the time, Vaughan Hosking, persuaded the Devon Council to change the Falkland Road entrance to nearer the Torre Abbey traffic lights, thus enabling cars to enter clear of the actual cricket field and park more adjacent to the Pavilion. The change enabled players to have a shorter journey with their cricket "coffins" to the pavilion and is ideal when the weather has been 'summer like', but it does cause problems after heavy rain. In recent years no grass wicket for practice has been rolled out, whereas that was standard procedure once upon a time.

Very, very sadly Mike Pugh resigned the captaincy at the end of the season, and after the Paignton fiasco it was understandable, feeling that the lack of commitment to support his, and John Morgan's input, was insufficient for him to complete the three year programme he had mentally planned. Certain individuals had a good season in their own speciality with Tim Western outstanding with his batting. Two centuries in the league, plus three other innings in excess of fifty, emphasised his return to form and the consistency he could produce. The development of various younger players was noted in the different teams including James Toms, Aaron Williams, Liam Rice, Oliver Pitts and Jason Westcott.

With the county and the country in the grip of a foot and mouth epidemic the league officials decided there would be no promotion or relegation for the 2001 season.

The supporters were eagerly anticipating the 2001 season which was going to celebrate the 150th.year of the Club's foundation. Individuals had worked hard throughout the winter to ensure attractive fixtures and others devoted to time produce a booklet to celebrate the occasion. Sadly, this was a beautifully presented item but in many ways terribly short on the factual history of the club and the men and players who had made it.

Prior to play commencing both the players and umpires were having to read the new laws that Lord's had brought into being, some making good sense while others appeared to be rather unnecessary. Locally, the Devon League had also specified that 120 plus overs was to be replaced with a 110 over match with the team batting first to have the benefit of 60 overs to encourage more sides to bat first.

Ben Passenger took over the captaincy from Mike Pugh and while there had been numerous rumours throughout the winter months, regarding players that were leaving, the only significant departure was that of Kevin Barrett. In the previous season he had played occasionally following his release from a contract at Surrey, but had not been regularly available. The overseas player who arrived at the Rec. was Craig Adlington, another New Zealander, who actually turned out to be quite an all-rounder, including being able to keep wicket when necessary.

Minus Pugh, Baker and Short for the first game of the season, away at Exeter, the home side inflicted a heavy defeat and obtained the necessary runs to win the game with just the loss of one wicket. Only Andy Hele with 66 and Marcus Green 55 showed anything like resolution against the bowling of Price. When Exmouth came to the Recreation Ground for the first home game, skipper Passenger was pleased to see his team at full strength. Batting first and having 250 for 9 on the scoreboard, Adlington 64 and Western 60 being the main contributors, Passenger then took 3 for 41 and Baker 3 for 48 to help reduce the visitors to 185 all out. On the Sunday, in the Devon Cup, it was Western 95n.o. and S.Needham 52, who boosted the total to 240 for 7. That total was far too many for Tavistock, who could only muster 179 while the best of the Torquay bowling that day was by Marcus Green who finished with 4 for 41.

While there had been odd midweek teams which had included David Needham and up to three of his four sons in the side, the match against Plympton included three of the four sons, Shaun, Matt and Chris, in the first eleven for a league fixture. All three took catches to help reduce the home side to 201 all out, and assist Steve Short's bowling figures of 4 for 40. Torquay's batsmen passed the total with the loss of six wickets, thanks to Tim Western 48, Andy Hele 58 and Shaun Needham 41.

Once again the Paignton encounter at Queen's Park was a match to have the supporters talking for a week. Having won the toss Ben Passenger decided to bat and then, must have wondered "what on earth was happening". At 35 for 6 it looked like 'a bad day at the office' type of happening and the supporters who had made the trip were certainly an unhappy bunch. Thankfully, Mike Pugh and Andy Hele batted sensibly, and getting 46 and 34 respectively, helped to take the eventual score to 159 all out. With Bill Athey, the ex-England player in the Paignton side, as well as the South African, Jacques Rudolph, later to play Test cricket for that country, it did not look a big total to chase. However it was a day when Ian Baker enjoyed his tea, and, really was on form. Passenger and Baker struck early, and then Baker had Athey caught with just 27 runs to his credit. Superb fielding saw Shaun Needham run out Farkin and Marcus Green brought off one of his special catches to dismiss Griffiths, by which time it was a question of "could Paignton hang on?" They could not and were all out for 90, Ian Baker having taken 4 for 22 and showing once again to be a very useful bowler on his day, Steve Short supported him superbly, returning bowling figures of 3 for 18.

A great shock awaited the side that went to Sidmouth in mid-June, and it was shell-shocked supporters who made their way home later. Unbeaten after that opening day defeat by Exeter, and Sidmouth not having won a game, no one was prepared for what happened that afternoon. Torquay were bowled out for just 98 runs! Sidmouth got the necessary runs and only lost two wickets in the process. Ben Passenger actually took the two wickets for nine runs but at the other end, amongst some poor bowling figures, Chris Needham bowled a thirteen ball over!

Ben Passenger however, was pleased in July, when he was told that Matthew Hunt had asked to come back to the Rec.. Studying at University had restricted his opportunities to play and when he was able to he had joined the Exmouth club, so to see him return was great news. Young players such as James Toms, Oliver Pitts, Aaron Williams ,Tim Robinson and Liam Rice had been given opportunities in the first eleven but, not always at the right time and, on occasions, too many at the same time, so another experienced player was most welcome.

Throughout the season Torquay, Bovey Tracey and Sandford had each occupied the top spot in the league at different times but a surprising Recreation Ground defeat by

Sandford shook some of the 'faithful'. Having Sandford all out for 148 and cruising along at 110 for four, home supporters were anticipating another victory, but it was not to be. A batting collapse saw Torquay reduced to 135 all out and a defeat by thirteen runs. By August five points separated the same three, well clear of the fourth side, but there were frustrations galore for skipper Passenger. At Barton, where the home side had been bowled out for 164, Torquay were 81 for the loss of three wickets when rain stopped play. Without consultation with the two skippers, the umpires eventually called the game off, whereas both Andy Pugh and Ben Passenger wanted to continue. Both captains felt the game could have been won by either side. Even worse for Passenger was the cancellation of the trip to Sandford for the return game, heavy rain had washed out any hopes of play.

So with two league games left, one of which was against contenders Bovey Tracey, the supporters realised everyone was in for a nerve tingling finish. Batting first Bovey Tracey had 251 for 8 at the end of their allotted overs, thanks to Neil Davey 63 and Colin Mortimore 54 n.o., while Ben Passenger had taken 4 for 77. Torquay had 205 for 8 when stumps were pulled, with Matt Hunt 82 n.o. and the club having had the worst of the drawn game. Sandford had also drawn their game but, because of a fraction of a point difference, had taken over the top spot in the league. The last match was away at Cornwood, who had occupied the bottom of the table for most of the season, and consequently anticipation was high as regards getting a good result. Passenger and his team knew they had to get the full twenty points and hope that Barton could frustrate Sandford in some way. Even though it was a very interesting situation for the last game of the season Torquay had very little support on the Cornwood ground and the committee were conspicuous by their absence. When Cornwood were 93 for 6, and the grouse, from the local estate, were walking the boundary as they fed, the signs were in favour of Torquay. However that changed more than somewhat when the latter batsmen went after the runs, and the grouse had to run for cover. When the overs were completed Cornwood's score had advanced to 246 for 9, thanks to a magnificent knock of 103 by Jamie Pfeiffer, even though Ben Passenger had returned excellent bowling figures of 6 for 72. Torquay's batsmen never looked like approaching the required total and when the skipper went to the wicket to join Steve Short it looked odds on that Cornwood would actually win. Staying together for some eighteen overs, Ben Passenger 39 n.o. and 'Shorty's' 30 n.o. took the score to 174 for 8 to obtain a losing draw and yet another second place in the league. After such a superb spell of bowling and following that by a very stubborn stand with Steve Short, Ben Passenger joined Nigel Janes, Ian Coulton and Mike Pugh as captains who, in their first year in charge, finished the league in second place and missed the title by narrow margins.

After all the publicity regarding the 150th anniversary of the club's foundation there was only one special match, and that took place on the Sunday May 27th against Somerset County. Peter Anderson, the ex-Torquay player, and currently chief executive of the Somerset club, brought down a side to play twenty two of the Torquay club. On September 29th an Anniversary Ball was held at the Riviera Centre where the guest speaker was Fannie de Villiers, the ex- South African test player and the former, for one season, Torquay professional.

Having finished in second place there were expectations in some quarters regarding the possibilities of winning the league in 2002 and it certainly proved to be an interesting season. After a number of years living, and marrying, in New Zealand, Haydn Morgan was back and ready to play. Since he was a useful bowler, as well as an opening batsman, supporters felt he would more than offset the loss of Steve Short who had left to join South Devon. Craig Adlington, officially qualified by residence, was available again, while a New Zealander, Mike Baumgart, had been brought over to play. After a season playing for Plympton Kevin Barrett had rejoined Torquay and Danny Johnson had left South Devon to come to the Recreation Ground. The one sad departure was that of Aaron Williams who had left to join rivals Barton. Williams had come through the junior sides, captained the Devon U 16s and, while he had an odd first team game, he felt he would get more opportunities elsewhere. Thus once again, showing how difficult it is to keep ambitious youngsters happy in a successful squad. The new league ruling this season was to see both sides having the same number of overs, 55 each, rather than the 60 – 50 that had been so unsatisfactory.

Starting the summer with an away trip to Exeter those supporters who did not make the journey wondered what on earth was going on when they heard the tea-time score! Western Australian, Chris Rogers, Exeter's overseas player for the season, had rattled up 154 in a total of 282 for 6.(A very interesting lad later to come back and play county cricket) Thanks in the main to Barrett 59 and Hele 33 Torquay hung on at 192 for 9 to get a losing draw. A complete turn around in the next match saw Shaun Needham in great form with 115 n.o. and Torquay's score reach 238 for 7. Ian Baker with 3 for 40 helped to reduce Exmouth to 185 for 8.

The first victory was obtained at Paignton where, after the rain, the game was reduced to 45 overs a side, following the delayed start. Paignton lost eight wickets in getting 151 and Torquay had to bring on their 12th man, Justin Yau, after Phil Bradford slipped in the wet outfield and injured his ankle. Danny Johnson had 3 for 40 and was the best of the bowlers. Torquay, in their turn, found batting difficult and also lost eight wickets in getting the necessary runs to record their victory. Rain did more than spoil the game against Plympton where Kevin Barrett had scored 45 and then had taken 2 for 8 against his ex-colleagues when play was stopped. Mike Baumgart recorded his fourth consecutive 'duck' in this game.

Losing badly against Sidmouth, and then Barton, where Shaun Needham had 24 out of a total of 77, and Barton's bowler Ahmed took 7 for 28, Torquay suffered a further humiliation against Sandford. The team were bowled out for 79 in 34 overs, with only Haydn Morgan showing any resistance and scoring 43 not out, of the pathetic total. Things were beginning to look very bleak indeed at that stage of the season. Although restricting Bovey Tracey to 150 with the skipper taking 4 for 27,

Ben Passenger saw his side hanging on at 143 for 9, thanks in the main to Tim Western with a stubborn 42. A victory was obtained eventually, after some six games, against Cornwood. Both Ian Baker and Ben Passenger bowled well on this occasion resulting in respective figures of 6 for 60 and 3 for 61. Mark Baumgart, after so many poor innings, found the bowling of Cornwood to his liking and actually accumulated 62 runs.

Part way through the season schoolmasters Ben Passenger and Andy Hele were taking a Grammar School squad of cricketers to the Caribbean which meant the club were minus a captain and a wicket keeper! Following such a number of lost games the club were languishing at the wrong end of the league table and at the end of July yet another loss was experienced in the last over at Plympton. Having scored 183 for 9 Torquay needed the bowlers to really perform and they really did begin well, having the first five batsmen back in the pavilion for 97 runs. However, from that point the tempo changed and the batsmen began to get the measure of the bowling. Runs were accumulated by the Plympton batsmen but the wickets were no longer being taken, as they needed to be, and the required total to win was actually passed in the last over. Discussions amongst the supporters questioned the captain's commitment to his position when they learned he was to be missing again for yet another wedding!

It was almost unbelievable that the bottom three in the league included Torquay and Exmouth who, year after year, had invariably been so much nearer the top. The beginning of August saw Baker and Passenger back in the side for the match at Barton, "two first team bowlers again" supporters were heard to say! The return of the captain and Baker to the bowling attack did not prevent Barton from knocking up the considerable total of 207 for 7. Following a rather indifferent display by most of the batsmen, the two bowlers were together at the wicket to play out the last over of the game when Torquay were hanging on, at 164 for 9. The eight points gained in that match really were precious for the Torquay club. Fellow strugglers, Exmouth, were found to have been well beaten by Bovey Tracey, to such an extent that they had only picked up a single point. As there were only two games left to play in the league the odds were quite short as to who would be relegated along with Cornwood. One of Torquay's remaining games was with the possible champions, Bovey Tracey, who were in contention with Exeter and Sidmouth for the league title. Bovey Tracey came to the Recreation Ground and their intention was fulfilled as they easily beat Torquay, obtaining the full twenty points which took them to the top of the table and left Torquay with just four points from the game.

Torquay's last match was against the side that could not avoid relegation, Cornwood. Thankfully a very easy victory resulted, batting first Cornwood were bowled out for the lowly total of 84 runs, with Ben Passenger returning the excellent figures of 5 for 10. However the Cornwood bowlers gave the home supporters a few shocks as Torquay lost three wickets before Tim Western 23 and Craig Adlington 24 not out, made the runs which saw that very necessary win attained. Even though nine times champions Exmouth beat Paignton they were still relegated. While no club has a right to a permanent place in any league most cricket followers were sad to see Exmouth drop out of the Premier Division with the ground and facilities they have at the Maer. Alternatively as one 'wag' was heard to say, "better them than us"!

Mention must be made of the Torquay Second X1, who won their particular league and promotion back to the Seconds League where they belong, under the direction of Neil Matthews. With the experienced players and promising youths, which every club needs, the side were strong in most departments being frequently called on to bolster the firsts because of the various reasons of non-availability. With the first team experience of Phil Bradford, James Toms, Tim Robinson and all the Needhams it was no surprise to see the development of the youngsters throughout the season in that side.

Matthew Hunt, who opened for Devon was singled out by the retiring Devon captain, Peter Roebuck, as, "the discovery of the season batting consistently with a common sense unusual amongst Devonians", the last three words, in the author's opinion being completely unnecessary! However, in fairness to Roebuck, it must be said he had been a superb captain for the county, after his career with Somerset, and four successive Minor Counties Championships will take some living up to for his eventual successor.

THE END OF AN ERA

During the 'closed season' the club lost its best known and most respected member, Mr. Torquay Cricket, Ted Dickinson. While much has been written about him in this book, relating to cricket, he was a dedicated sportsman in so many other fields. He had played county cricket for his beloved Leicestershire and professional soccer for Derby County, where an injury cut short his career. Like so many cricketers he took up golf, and became a county player, while hockey eventually became the winter sporting pastime after his football injury. Proficient at that as well, he also played at county level for his native Leicestershire.

The writer first met Mr. Dickinson when he opened a sporting outfitters shop in Belgrave Road, almost adjacent to the butchers shop my father managed. In the following forty odd years, throughout hundreds of conversations, I learned something every time we spoke. Not always sporting, but relative to life and living, with Ted's outlook on same.

Player, Chairman and President of the Torquay club in turn, his biggest frustration was after his stroke in the late 1980s, which affected his speech, and he was no longer able to make his views known at the A.G.Ms. Bert Kingdon and the writer frequently met Jane and Ted in Hoopers for coffee on a Wednesday morning and, while Jane talked with her lady friends, cricket was the topic of our conversation. In the latter years however Ted was armed with a little note pad on which he scribbled what he could not put into words.

Cricketers and sportsmen from far afield attended Ted's funeral to pay their respects and display the affection they had for this sporting legend. David Post gave a superb eulogy during the service which everyone present fully endorsed.

This page has been devoted to J.E.Dickinson's memory since the 150 Year booklet would have ignored his fantastic contribution to the club had it not been for a mention by Wilfred Hore, the longest serving club member, to whom local history is part of our heritage and should be remembered.

The Second Millennium Continued

Prior to the start of the 2003 season youngsters, Mickey Wilkinson and Justin Yau had more than their fair share of cricket experience. In a West of England party of promising young cricketers, they had been on a tour of the West Indies and then, in a Devon U15 squad, had toured South Africa. These two trips, coming after the Grammar School cricket tour of the Caribbean, showed the benefits to be had when youngsters really concentrate on the sports they take up. The tours were a great cricketing experience as well as being educational. They had spare time for leisure activities and sightseeing, as well as their cricket games.. The writer has pointed out, time and time again, at A.G.Ms, both at the cricket and rugby clubs, neither Committees' advertise what dedicated coaches, in their respective sports, do for the benefit of the town's local youngsters in either field.

Following a season where the club just managed to hang on to premier league status there were a few changes in personnel before the commencement of the 2003 games. Sadly, wicket-keeper Andy Hele returned to the Barton club, over a misunderstanding which should never have arisen. There was an internal upheaval at Bovey Tracey during the closed season, despite their winning the league for the very first time in their history. Wicket-keeper, Peter Lucketti, left there and joined Torquay thus answering the question that had been posed when Hele departed, "Who would be behind the stumps?". Danny Johnson had returned to South Devon and a new overseas player from Sri Lanka appeared. Sanjeewa Arangalla was reputed to be a bowler who also batted. Ben Passenger retained the captaincy amid rumours that it would be his last season at the helm.

After the usual 'friendly' games, at the end of April, the season was due to commence with a home match with Sandford but heavy rain made the encounter a non starter. It was the only Premier League game not to take place that day! So the club started the season with just six points. However, Matt Hunt quickly had the chance of batting and playing, for Devon on the Sunday at Exmouth, and scored 84 against the M.C.C. Disappointingly the victory over the M.C.C. did not help when the county then played Lancashire in the C and G Trophy competition. Consolation for local supporters was the fact that although losing badly, Neil Hancock, with a 'typical Hancock innings' of 73, won the Man-of-the- Match award, despite being on the losing side. Irrespective of his Australian background Hancock is a popular character throughout the cricketing fraternity of the county.

Losing the first league encounter, and at Paignton of all places, left supporters once more wondering about the season ahead. Simon Edwards and Neil Hancock each made 53 in the home side total of 215. Mike Pugh with 52 and Phil Bradford 33 were the only batsmen who really got to grips with the bowling. The sad weekend continued on the Sunday, at the Recreation Ground, when Exeter came and knocked the club out of the Devon Senior Cup.

The home game with North Devon had a delayed start due to the heavy rain and when it did commence the umpires had reduced the overs to 32 per team. Mainly due to the bowling of Phil Bradford who returned figures of 4 for 42, the North Devon team were reduced to 143 for 8 at the end of their allotted overs. Tim Western 63 n.o. and Shaun Needham 51 n.o. took Torquay to 144 for 2 and ensured the club of 18 points. After collecting further totals of 18 points, from each of the games with Abbotskerswell and Plympton, heavy rain certainly saved the club from defeat against Barton. The visitors had scored 257 runs for the loss of just five wickets after an explosive 118 from Cowley. Torquay's early batsmen, apart from Western with 33, made no impression, and with eight wickets down supporters were anticipating a defeat. Justin Yau and Peter Lucketti played carefully, and sensibly, and the total gradually increased. As the storm clouds gathered and the rain finally arrived, two game saving innings came to an end with the young lad 25 n.o. and the 'young old timer' 20 n.o.

At Sidmouth Marcus Green and Haydn Morgan took the bowling honours with 4 for 48 and 4 for 60 respectively. The total of 215 was quite a good figure to chase but there was the bonus of five extra overs if needed. With James Toms hammering a good 84, (he should have made it a century!) and Tim Western 37 the team were given a great start and obtained the required runs with the loss of just five wickets. After the way Hancock had treated the club, during the years he played for Sidmouth, it was a great feeling to come back from there with the twenty points. Following their off the field troubles, and the departure of so many players, Bovey Tracey were having a difficult season but they made it very hard going for Torquay on their home ground. Ian Baker, 4 for 23 and Haydn Morgan 3 for 39 reduced Bovey to 131 all out and most of the many supporters who had followed the team to Bovey were expecting an early finish. It was not to be and although Torquay won they had lost eight wickets when the winning runs were hit, the top scorer being Haydn Morgan with 27.

Having been knocked out of the Devon Cup by Exeter, supporters were hoping the team could put that behind them and play up to the form they were capable of when the respective sides met in the league match. Western made a good start with a solid 47 but at 100 for 6 few watchers were happy. Lucketti was sent in earlier than usual and accumulated 17 runs off the 70 balls he faced. However, while he remained at the wicket, first with Green who made 43, and then Bradford 32 n.o. they eventually got the total to 201 for 8. No 'fairy tale ending' however as Exeter reached a winning score with the loss of five wickets. Away at Sandford Torquay put 223 for

9 on the score-board, thanks mainly to Haydn Morgan's 91, and although at one time the home team were 141 for 6 they went on to pass the required total with the loss of eight wickets. Marcus Green 4 for 60 was the one bowler to find any form. The return game with Paignton did keep the majority of the spectators at the ground until the end. Those who went home early certainly needed some convincing of the result when friends' phoned later. Batting first, Torquay's score of 176 all out looked very inadequate, although later Shaun Needham's 49 really did prove to be the innings of the day. Paignton were going along quite steadily with wickets falling, but runs accumulating, when Bradford and Green took over the bowling. In an amazing spell with the ball Bradford had 3 for 24, and Green 3 for 60, leaving Paignton all out for 152 and Torquay with another nineteen points in the bag.

Kevin Barrett came into the team for his first game against North Devon at Instow. Torquay had 220 for 8 on the score-board after their allotted overs with Western and Green scoring well with 53 and 49 respectively. It was a 'nail biting' time as the home team crept nearer and nearer to the score but eventually the overs ran out leaving North Devon on 218 for 6. Green had been the best of the bowlers with 4 for 43. The following week everyone was looking forward to an 'old boy's re-union' against Abbotskerswell. So many players in both teams had, at different times, been members at either of the clubs. However it was only a meeting in the bar as heavy rain put paid to any play whatsoever!

August was a nightmare for the supporters, weakened sides were fielded due to more weddings, which resulted in the club followers having to witness defeats by Plympton, Barton and Exeter. A victory was obtained, against Sidmouth where Phil Bradford had a 'five wicket haul' for 43 runs. The game against Bovey Tracey saw some heavy scoring by both teams and a winning draw, as regards the allocation of points. Batting first Torquay had 283 on the board when their overs came to an end and Matthew Hunt had a superb 121 to his credit. Just to prove it was a lovely afternoon for batting the Bovey Tracey opener, Neil Davey then scored 105 for his team and the Torquay bowlers suffered just as Bovey's had done.

With so much potential talent in the team it was another disappointment for the club's supporters to see the side finish in fifth position in the league, below Paignton and fifty six points adrift of leaders Sandford. Marcus Green, with amazing bowling performances throughout the season, and in all aspects of play certainly earned his title, 'Player of the Year'.

On the social side it had been a season almost recapturing the club house atmosphere of some years ago. Odd evenings after mid-week games, players and spectators had remained in the bar to enjoy the music that had been thoughtfully organised by respective match managers who were 'new blood' on the committee. What had been widely advertised as a 'Special Evening' was not completely ruined by the weather either, even though it could not take place in the outside enclosure. The organisers, quickly recognising that with the inclement weather, the entertainment could not be held, even in the Pavilion, arranged for it to be held in a nearby Hotel. While the attendance suffered somewhat, more monies were raised for club funds purely by certain individuals' ingenuity.

A widely advertised function, for Sponsors, Life Members and Vice-Presidents held once a season, prior to a 'derby match', did not take place and caused more than a little embarrassment. It was a superb day, brilliant sunshine, Life Members arrived early to chat to old friends and the hard working fund raisers were there to welcome the Sponsors. The game itself, after the advertised lunch, against old rivals around the Bay, Paignton, invariably attracted people that had not been seen all the season. Then the whispers began, "There is no Lunch"! "Who cancelled it?"! Comments that were heard would fill another book, but no, not in this publication, dear reader!

To see ex-players treated in this manner, after they had been made Life Members for all they had done for the club, was so sad but it was even worse for those who were supporting the club as sponsors. If this was not bad enough the annual match between the President's X1 versus A Colt's X1, always looked forward to because of the social atmosphere and the number of parents who put in an appearance, did not take place in 2003. The game was cancelled, more than twenty four hours before the scheduled starting time, according to the groundsman. A weather forecast was not 'promising', but things changed and it turned out to be a lovely evening!

REFLECTIONS

So, as the 2004 season begins I am going to settle back in my chair and enjoy the cricket, I hope!, while soaking up the sunshine. Researching and reading over the last three years to gather the information related, has given me enormous pleasure and even more of an insight into my club and my town. My sincere wish is that numerous other people will also get some pleasure from ploughing through my ramblings, and somewhere, there is that person who will have sufficient interest in the Torquay Cricket Club to keep the story ongoing. With the modern age of technical advancement and computers it should be an easier and a quicker task. Whoever takes it on I wish them fun and enjoyment.

Chairman at the time, Vaughan Hosking, promised me a new Pavilion within five years!, that was in 1992 and I told him, and the assembly at that A.G.M. in the Livermead Cliff Hotel, it was a "pipe dream" and would never happen in my lifetime! However, there does seem to be a change taking place in the management and the introduction of a programme this season, not just a score sheet, is a big plus for the present Committee. I doubt whether the old social days will ever return to the Pavilion since the "drink and drive" mentality is no more, thank heaven! Oh yes! In the past years many a member has staggered from the pavilion bar, to their car, and then driven home. I am certain that with the co-operation of the caterer, Social evenings can occur again, albeit in a different way. Last seasons musical evenings were enjoyed by the tourists for example and, had there been meals available! Certain touring sides in the past always headed for one of Barry Matthews numerous bars where they knew they could get a good steak. A letter to the tourists, or a phone call to the hotel where they are staying, to check what they are planning after the game is all that is needed. Of course it means "someone has to do it" but that is the essence of a club, all pulling together. Midweek fixtures must be given more attention, young players should be encouraged to play whenever possible. They develop more quickly when playing in a better standard of game than in their usual weekend league. Good Sunday fixtures and midweek matches saw the development of such players as George Emmett, Barry Matthews, Hiley and Chris Edwards, Ian Coulton, Phil Bradford, Nigel Janes, Malcolm Kingdon, and many, many more who were not content to just drift from Saturday to Saturday. In recent years few first or second team players have supported the club to entertain visiting teams, many of whom have been coming for decades. A sad reflection on the lack of club spirit unfortunately.

Good luck and happy reading.

GALLERY

TORQUAY CRICKET CLUB.
GRAND FÊTE
In celebration of the Opening of the New Ground,
AT CHAPEL HILL CROSS.

THE Committee beg to announce that it is intended to OPEN the NEW CRICKET GROUND, on MONDAY, 16th of AUGUST, 1852, when a Match will be Played between the

THE OFFICERS OF THE GARRISON, AT PLYMOUTH, AND THE TORQUAY CRICKET CLUB.

By the kind permission of Col. FRAZER, the SPLENDED BAND the 35th Regiment will attend, and Perform choice Selections of the most admired Music, commencing at 3 o'clock.

AN ELEGANT AND SPACIOUS MARQUEE,
the Floor well Boarded. will be erected, and towards Evening thrown open

FOR A SOIRÉE DANSANTE.

LADIES' PATRONESSES.	STEWARDS.
LADY YARDE BULLER,	L. PALK, Esq.
MRS. PALK,	R. S. S. CARY, Esq.
MRS. CARY,	H. C. M. PHILLIPPS, Esq.
MRS. HARRIS, *Rooklands.*	CAPT. STORY,
MRS. STORY,	CAPT. PHILLIPPS,
MRS. BELFIELD LOUIS.	F. M. LYTE, Esq.

Ladies' Tickets, 4s., Gentlemen's 5s. including Admission to the Ground.

Admission to the Ground, 1s.—Tickets to be obtained of the Secretary, Committee, and at the Libraries, Torquay.

A Special Train will leave Exeter, at 8·20 A.M., calling at all Stations, and arriving at Torquay, at 10.

Also a Special Train from Plymouth, at 8 A.M., calling at Ivybridge, Kingsbridge Road, Totnes and Newton, arriving at Torquay, at 10.

These Trains will leave Torquay, at 9·20, P.M.

REFRESHMENTS WILL BE PROVIDED ON THE GROUND.

W. H. KITSON, Secretary.

Torquay Cricket ground from a print believed to be
around 1860 showing Windmill Hill in the background.

Published by G. Daimond, Newton Abbot.

Torquay C

Lithographed by Newman & Co. 48, Watling St. London.

t Ground

TORQUAY CRICKET CLUB.
GRAND FÊTE
IN CELEBRATION OF THE
OPENING OF THE NEW GROUND
AT CHAPEL HILL CROSS.

THE COMMITTEE beg to announce that it is intended to OPEN the NEW CRICKET GROUND on MONDAY, the 16th of AUGUST, 1852.

A MATCH will be played between the Officers of the Garrison of Plymouth and the Torquay Cricket Club.

By the kind permission of COLONEL FRASER, the BAND of the 35th REGIMENT will attend and perform a choice selection of the most admired Music.

An elegant and spacious MARQUEE (the floor well boarded) will be erected, and towards Evening will be thrown open for a

SOIRÉE DANSANTE.

The list of Ladies Patronesses, and further particulars will be duly announced.

W. H. KITSON, Secretary.

Torquay, 2nd August, 1852.

The 1905 First XI

G. Crockwell
Sandiford (pro)
A.N. Other   T.A. Codner   E.E. Speight   J.N. Leleu   W. Stuckey (umpire)   C.G. Deane
C.W. Robinson   B.L. Gerrish   J.F.W. Little   E.B. Fulham   S.G. Crockwell   H.F. Grahame

The Pavillion - Pre 1906

Rebuilt After The 1906 Fire

Teas In The Early Years At The Recreation Ground

Using The Rugby Clubs
Facilities The
Tourists "Old Collegans"
Batsmen Take The Field

The Torquay Pavillion - Built 1936

"No Play Today" - August 1938

George Emmett

1940 - Torquay & District XI and A R.A.F. XI

Recreation Ground - 1951

A Torquay XI 1938

Unveiling the clock and tablet in memory of the club members killed in WWII.

TORQUAY CRICKET FESTIVAL

RECREATION GROUND (opposite Station)

S E P T E M B E R   6 t h — 1 2 t h ,   1 9 5 8

YOUR ONLY OPPORTUNITY TO SEE FIRST CLASS
CRICKET IN DEVON

School Parties specially catered for

**Reserve your seats now from Dickinson Sports, 40 Torwood Street,
Torquay**

Price 5/- per day or 25/- for six days, including admission to ground
Ordinary admission to ground 2/6 per day, 1/6 children
1/- and 6d. after tea interval

Saturday, Monday, Tuesday, September 6th, 8th, 9th

North v. South

NORTH—R. T. Simpson, (Capt.) (*Notts.*) ; D. Brookes, K. Andrew,
M. Allen (*Northants.*) ; D. Kenyon, M. Horton, G. Dews (*Worcs.*) ;
R. Illingworth, B. Stott (*Yorks.*) ; C. Gladwin, L. Jackson (*Derby*)

SOUTH—C. Ingleby-MacKenzie (Capt.) (*Hants.*) ; J. Robertson,
F. Titmus (*Middx.*) ; G. Lock, K. Barrington (*Surrey*) ; D. Halfyard (*Kent* ; G. Emmett (*Glos.*) ; N. Thompson (*Sussex*) ; A. Watkins (*Glam.*) ; M. Tremlett, H. Stephenson (*Som.*)

Wednesday, Thursday, Friday, September 10th, 11th, 12th

England XI. v. Commonwealth XI.

ENGLAND XI.—R. T. Simpson (Capt.) D. Brookes, D. Kenyon,
K. Barrington, B. Stott, R. Illingworth, G. Lock, F. Titmus, K.
Andrew, C. Gladwin, L. Jackson

COMMONWEALTH XI.—V. Jackson (Capt.,) W. Alley, C. McCool,
J. Manning, J. Livingston (*Australia*) ; F. Worrell, G. Sobers, C.
Smith (*W. Indies*) ; G. Fuller (*S. Africa*) ; Hanif Mohammed
(*Pakistan*) ; H. Stephenson (*Commonwealth XI.*)

Hours of Play : 11.30 a m. to 6 p.m.   **Umpires : Messrs. Buller and Price**

**Why not make up a party through your local Coach Proprietor, or
British Railways ?**

Licensed Bars under the direction of J. Sorrell, Standard Inn,
Devonport

Luncheons, Teas and Refreshments under the direction of
Austin's of Exeter

BELLAMY, PRINTERS, TORQUAY

Devon and Pakistan Teams - 1954

The Australian Touring Team of 1968

The Torquay Cricket Club - A Potted History Of The Club From 1851 to 2004

At The "Sea End". A Brockman Cup Game About 1948

A Torquay Ladies XI
A. Scofield   P. Sangster   R. Fredman   J. Mathews   V. Haydock   P. Dickinson   J. Barker
P. Twose   S. Lear   S. Mathews   S. Mathews
P. Dunkells

Torquay 1961
P.Anderson   B. Bettesworth   J. Fox   B.Williams   D. Post   I. Scofield   A.N. Other
C. Greetham   R.Matthews   P.Twose (Capt)   B.Mathews

Coldwell Cup Winners
T. Holloway   B.Bettersworth   G. Baker   G. Patel   A. Rich   R.Williams
Mr Murray-Watts making the Presentation

A Second XI in 1958
V. Tucker   K. Peppiatt   G. Baker   R. Stainton   T. Gardiner   A.N. Other   R. Haly
M. Simpson   G. Collings   K. Gale   S. Swift   J.White   W.Traylor

A Second XI 1970
R. Lear   D. Post   A. Rich   R.Stainton   G. Baker   P.Goodrich
B. Stone   J.Nevill   R. Haydock   B.Westcott   B. Bettesworth

3rd XI in The 1970s
E. Kingdon   R. Biddick   C. Johnson   R.Harvey   R. Lear   L. Mathews   C. Haley   J.Vasey
B. Kingdon   V. Goulding   K.Creber   J. Haly   S. Smith   D. Merrikin

Two Great Captains of
Torquay and Devon

Barrie Matthews (Left)
and
Hiley Edwards

A Devon XI - 1974

R. Haly J.Tolliday G.Wallen B. Harriot I. Roberts B. Coleman J.E. Dickinson J. Childs
P.Anderson P. Dunkells R.Staddon B. Matthews (Capt) M.Wagstaff M. Goulding

Torquay 1970's

K. Peppiat K.Warren M. Kingdon N. Mountford B. Hatchett C.Wallen E. Kingdon B. Hill
D.Traylor M. Goodrich B. Matthews V. Hosking H. Edwards G.Wallen J. Gerard

A Torquay First XI
A. Smith B. Sambrook G. Gardiner H. Edwards B. Matthews M. Goulding
M. Goodrich V. Hosking D. Traylor R. Tolchard

L. Leworthy T. Dickinson R. Tolchard B. Stone P. Dunkells A. Smith B. Sambrook P. Hobbs
D. Traylor H. Edwards V. Hosking P. Goodrich B. Matthews G. Wallen

1988 - XI

E. Kingdon J. Stables S. Broomhall P. Bradford J. Pearce N. Coppen N. Wonnacott
M. Kingdon I. Coulton C. Edwards H. Edwards P. Traylor

E. Kingdon N. James I. Osborne N. Wonnacott I. Coulton J. Carr S. Craig
M. Kingdon H. Edwards C. Edwards B. Matthews D. Oliver

Torquay 1st XI - 1992
N. Evason T. Weston J. Mann M. Dean I. Baker R. Learmouth H. Ball (Sec)
C. Healey R. Twose F. De Villiers I. Coulton B.J. Sewell P. Bradford

Narracott Cup Winners - 1989
A. McMurray C. Vertongen R. James M. Ellicott J. Pearce M. Ferguson C. Healey
P. Bradford D. Moss S. Craig S. Kirby C. Jones N. Coppen

A Colts XI With Ian Scofield

M. Westcott   S. Toley   D. Penny   N. Elliot   R. Turpin   W. Daniels
B. Scofield   P. Tree   P. Traylor   S. Kirby   A. Merrikin

John Kirby (Coach)   C. Corline   J. Lear   J. Alford   T. Rawson   P. Smethhurst   N. Coppen
S. Kirby   P. Bradford   C. Armes   S. Tapley

Ian Westerns first visit to Hungary.

Highlight of Ian Westerns second visit to Hungary.

Graham Gooch leads out the Essex XI (v. Torquay) during the Cricket Festival, August 1994

League Champions

Scorer N. Evason   M. Pugh   I. Bransdon   M. Hunt   I. Baker   K. Barrett   N. Hancock   R. Williams
H. Morgan   T. Western   N. James   R. Horrell   J. Morgan

INDEX

Butler, H., 22
Butler, G.S., 40, 41,42,43,44,46, 48,49,50,51,53,54,55,56,57,58, 59,62,63,64,65,66,67,68,69,70, 72,73,75,76,78,94,100
Butters, L., 65
Byfield, G.R., 79
Cahn, Sir Julien, 46,47,50
Calland, A., 114,120
Calway, J., 179
Cameron , R., 156
Campbell, M., 45
Campling, F.S., 51,53,54,55,57,58,64
Carpenter, J., 5
Carr, J., 174,175
Carter, R., 94
Carter , H., 170
Cary, R.S., 1
Cassells, P., 74,114,140
Cath, H., 74,75
Caunter, General, 34
Chamberlin, N., 101
Chappell, G., 116
Chappell, I.M., 118
Chatton, 34,36,44
Chavasse, H., 119
Chave, E., 68
Cheadle, Rev., 22
Cheeseman, B., 68
Chesterton, A.H., 73
Chick, D., 119
Childs, J., 137,192
Chouhan, 198
Christie, Agatha, 19,124
Christie, O., 102
Clake, Mrs. M., 132,144
Clake, E.G., 132,144,152,162
Clarke, W., 3
Clarke, C.C., 59
Clarke, B., 92
Clarkson, T., 109,110,111
Claydon, J., 173
Clissold, L., 196
Cliverd, M., 163
Close, B., 93
Cockayne, R., 22
Cockrayne, C., 119
Codner, A., 24
Colby (R.A.F), Ac., 60
Coldwell, R. J., 82

Coldwell, L., 133
Cole, D.V.H., 63,65,69,70,71,76, 77,79,80,81,82,85,86,87,88,89, 93,94,95,100,101,117,118,121, 133
Cole, C., 121,122,125,126,128, 129,130,131,136
Collins, G., 86
Collyer, F., 148
Comber-Higgs, E.D., 64
Compton , D.C.S., 56,60
Conan-Doyle, Sir A, 23
Congdon, B.E., 148
Conley, J., 72
Connolly, A.N., 118
Considine, P., 134,155,161,175,179
Constable, B., 77
Cook, P., 181,182,184
Cooke, P., 88
Coombe, R. "Bobby", 96,97,105,107,142,152,155,179
Cooper, F., 65
Cooper, E., 83,91
Cooper, W.V., 107
Cope, C., 104
Coppen, G., 79
Coppen, N., 173,181,185
Cottam, R. (Bob), 144,147,149,189
Coulton, D.J., 47,50
Coulton, I., 162,165,166,167, 170,172,176,178,179,181,183, 185,186,189,190,192,193,195, 197,215
Cousins, F., 52
Cowan, G., 130,136,176
Cowdrey, M.C., 72
Cowley (Jnr) 205,221
Cowley (Snr), N.G., 203
Cowper, R.M., 118
Crabtree, K., 102
Craig , S., 135,144,149,172,181, 183,185,196,200
Craik, E., 205,206,207,208,209,210,212
Crang, A., 68
Crapp, J.F., 73,84,86
Crawley , L.G., 59
Craxford, F., 135
Cray, S.J., 79,81,83

Creber, K., 125,129,131,135, 137,140,142,147,162,163,166, 167,170,172
Crinje, H., 194
Cripps, A.B., 78
Crockwell, S.G., 21,22
Crockwell, G., 34,36,39,44,47
Crossley, J., 74
Crowdy, C.W., 18,20
Croxford, F., 65
Cruft 202
Cullinan, M.R., 194
Cullis, P., 130
Cummings, Alder., 33,35
Curtis, R., 15
Curtis (R.A.F.), Ac., 62
Daniel, J., 119
Dare, R., 85,87,88,89,90,91,92
Davey, C., 167,172,173
Davey, A.E., 59,68
Davey, N., 176,215,222
Davey, J., 176
Davidson, C., 174,175
Davies 75
Davies, L., 107
Davis, Rev., 13
Dawes-Dingle 91
Dawson, H., 63,80
Dawson, R.I., 203
Dayment, C., 197,211
De Villiers, P.S., 188,189,190,194,216
Dean, T., 76,77,82
Dean , M., 185,186,187,189,190,192
Dean, A., 192
Deane, C.G., 27,29,30
Dear, C., 33,50,52,62,64,66,67, 70,71,73,75,77,78,80
Dempster, C.S., 50
Dews, G., 93
Dexter, E.R., 106,120,122
Dickinson, J.E., 67,68,69,70,74,75,76,78,79,80, 81,83,87,89,91,92,94,95,97,98, 99,100,101,102,103,106,107, 108,110,118,119,126,134,136, 137,151,160,161,167,173,174, 179,220
Dickinson, R., 131,167,176,197
Dickinson, Mrs. J., 69,137,

167,182
Dineley, A.G., 21,22,24,27,30,62
Dobson, W.S.,
27,28,29,33,34,36,42,44
Dobson, L., 64
Dobson, A.W., 71
Doidge, F., 123
Dollery, H.E., 77
Donaghue, K., 165,185,197
Donard, A., 194
Dooland, B., 84,86
Doshi, D.R., 157
Doughty, D., 104
Douglas, Miss, 108
Douglas, J.W.H.T., 108
Drennan, R., 65,66,68
Duder, J., 201,206
Dunkells, P.R., 112,114,121,122,
123,128,130,139,163
Dupree, J., 209,211
Dymond, R., 1
Eager, E.D.R., 89
Easterbrook, G.H.L., 36
Edmonds, G., 84
Edrich, E.H., 62,65
Edrich, W.J., 56,58,59,60,62
Edrich, G.A., 62,65,75,81
Edwards, I.J., 68
Edwards, Coun., 90
Edwards, P., 161
Edwards, J., 5
Edwards, J.H., 125,128,130,132,
133,136,138,140,141,142,143,
145,147,148,149,151,153,155,
156,157,158,159,160,161,162,
163,164,165,166,169,170,171,
172,174,175,178,179,184,203
Edwards , C., 145,148,153,158,
159,160,161,162,163,164,166,
170,171,174,175,177,178,179,
180,187
Edwards, M., 203
Edwards, S., 203,222
Edwards (N.Z.), G.N., 148
Ellacott, M., 180
Elson, A., 109
Ely, Alder., 75,77,78
Ely, P., 62,63,75,100
Emmett, A., 44,48,67
Emmett , G.M., 42,44,46,48,
49,50,54,62,63,73,79,83,84,85,

85,90,93,97
Emmett, R., 44,56,57
Emmett, D., 108
Emmett, S., 44,48,67
Evans, G.R., 150,179
Evans, T.G., 85
Evanson, N., 181
Evenett, J., 134
Fairclough, H.D., 73,75,79,80,
81,82,83,84,87,93,99
Farkin, T., 180,183,205,215
Featherstonhaugh, B., 83
Felce, Ald. F., 111
Fellowes, Col., 17,21
Ferguson , M., 181
Flack, B., 148
Flanagan, C., 170
Flemming (RAF) 62
Fletcher, C.,
135,137,141,142,143
Fogg, T.H., 21,24,26,27
Fogwell, Mr., 162,166
Folland, N.A., 160,164,202
Ford, M., 34,36,43,44,45,48
Ford, D., 5,33
Ford, C.W., 59,65,68
Fortesque, W.B., 11,13
Foster, M., 133
Foster, J., 190,191,192
Fox, J., 113,115,117,118,119,
120,134
Fox, W., 158,159,161
Fredericks, R.C., 133
Fredman, B.,
101,105,125,126,145
French, W.T., 47,59
Friend, T.,
114,119,120,130,138,153
Fulcher, E.A., 24
Fulham, E.B., 24,25
Fyfe, Capt., 3
Fyfe, 2
Gale, K., 100,104,112,115
Gale, R., 116,133
Gamble, F.C., 57
Gardiner, G.,
134,138,139,141,143
Gardner, F.C., 77
Gardner, Mrs., 80
Garlick, R.G., 65
Garnham, M., 133,134

Gaywood, N., 157,172,178
Gerard, J., 102,144,156,158,170
Gerard, R., 151,162
Gerits, M., 190
Gerrish 25
Gibbs, A.G., 64
Gibbs, L.R., 114
Gibbs, L.R., 133
Gibson 15
Gibson, R., 176,183,184
Gibson, S., 161
Gilligan, A.H., 60
Gimblett, H., 76,79,82,89
Girdlestone, Rev., 68,85
Gladwell, C., 77
Gladwin, C., 84,93
Goddard , T.W.J.,
61,62,70,73,79,80
Goodrich, P., 94,99,102,104,111,
112,115,117,124,125,130,174
Goodrich, A.L.,
89,90,91,102,103,106,118
Goodrich, M., 102,107,112,114,
120,121,122,124,126,128,131,
133,136,138,139,141,142,143,
144,145,148,149,150,152,153,
155,156,157,158,159,160
Gore, I., 186
Goulding, V., 147,155,168
Goulding, M., 126,128,129,130,
137,139,147,150,152,153,156,
160,161,162,163,164,166,169,
173
Goulding, D., 180
Gower, T., 48
Grace, W.G., 7
Grace, E.M., 7
Graveney, D.A., 175
Graveney, T.W., 73,79
Green, M., 197,201,205,210,
211,212,213,214,215,221,222
Green, A., 207
Green, J., 5
Green, B., 156,157
Greener, F., 68
Greetham, C., 107,113,115,116,
117,118,119,120,133
Gregory, G., 102
Gribble, M., 197
Grieves, K.J., 75,81
Griffin, B., 30

Griffen, B., 30
Griffiths, P., 161
Griffiths, M., 204
Grimshaw, H., 13
Grogan 21
Groves, C.W., 77
Gunn, J., 47
Gupte, S., 88
H.Grant, C., 52
Haider, M., 95
Haig 7
Haines , D.L., 78,79,80,82,83,
85,86,88,89,92,93,94,95,96,98,
99,103,104
Haines, C.V.G., 63,64,65,66,67
Haines, Mrs.D.L., 103
Halfyard, D., 110
Hall-Plumber 13
Haly, R.J., 47,48,67,78,87,88,
91,94,99,100,101,103,108,111,
113,116,124,137,182
Haly, J., 81,111,129,135,138,
145,173
Haly, C., 81,129,130135,173
Hammond, W.R., 59,60,79,80
Handley, B., 106,109,110,111
Harding, P., 183,188
Harriott, R.F., 135,148,150,153
Harris, H., 68
Harris, L., 68,74
Harrison, E.W., 55
Harry, F., 27
Hart, Capt. M. G.,
53,54,56,61,62,64
Hart, F.W., 85,90,94
Harvey, R., 135
Harvey-Macleay, B.J., 76
Hassan, W., 83
Hatchett, W.
143,145,146,147,152,155
Hawes, A., 5
Hawke, Lord , 17
Hawke, N.J. , 118
Hawkins, P. , 95
Haydock, R., 114,121,131
Hayman, A.R., 36
Hayter, Corp., 61,62
Headley , G. , 84,
Heal, R., 181
Healey, B. , 119
Healey, C., 180,181,187

Hearder, W. , 13
Heath, C., 68,104
Hele, A., 170,203,204,205,206,
207,208,209,210,211,212,213,2
14,216,217,221
Henderson, D. , 110
Hendle, P. , 193,195
Hetherington, H., 75,78
Hicks, R., 50,54,56,57,58,59,
60,62,63
Hield, H.A. , 38
Higgins 67
Hill, Mrs. , 127,167
Hill, R.G. , 142,150,155,156
Hillier 3
Hilton, M.J., 75,76,79,81,82
Hinds, G.W. , 37
Hitchman, A.E. , 77,93,98,101,
102,105,106,107,113,134
Hobbs, P. , 99,126,132
Hocking, D.W. , 59
Hodson, J.H. , 12
Holder, V.A. , 133
Holliday, A.H. , 79,150
Hollies, W.E. , 77
Hollis, G.H. , 74
Holloway, A., 107
Holloway, R ., 136,137
Hook 139
Hooman 21
Hore, W.H., 30,47,133,155,219
Hore, C.W. , 34
Hore, H.S. , 111
Horrell, R. , 199,200,201,202,
203,204,205,206
Horswell, R. , 86,91
Horton, M.J. , 92,93
Hosking, K.V. , 121,125,126,127,
129,130,131,132,133,136,137,1
38,142,145,146,147,149,151,15
2,153,155,158,161,166,169,174
,176,178,181,184,188,190,194,
195,196,201,213
Howard, N. 65,66,75
Hubbard, T. , 132,
142,143,152,176
Hughes, B. , 56
Huish 16
Hull, G. , 146,149,165,166,
169,170
Humphries , N.H., 76,83,93

Hunt, R. , 126
Hunt, C. , 114
Hunt, M.P., 196,197,201,202,
203,204,205,206,209,210,214,2
16,218,220,222,223
Hussain, M. , 83
Hutchinson , Capt. , 8
Ijax, H. , 92
Ikin, J. , 75,81,148
Iles 7
Illingworth, R. , 90,93
Ingleby-Mackenzie, A.C.D. , 93
Ingram, E. , 75
Inverarity, R.J. , 118
Iqbal, M.Q. , 92
Iredale, G.H. , 37,38,40,41
Irish, A.F. , 73,75,79,80,81
Irving , G. , 98,99,100,102,
103,105,107
Jackson, W. , 33,34,68
Jackson, V.E. , 86
Jackson, L., 93
Jackson , P., 73
Jadeja, R. , 145,146
James, R.. , 181
James, N., 162,163,167,168,
169,170,172,173,176,178,180,1
81,183,185,186,188,189,194,19
5,197,198,199,200,201,202,203
204,205,206,209,216
Jarvis 15
Jeffery, T. , 181,187,189,190
Jeffery, K. , 196
Jenkins, R., 79
Jenkins, T., 114
Jenkins, Mrs. , 168
Jenkins 189
Jennings, K.F. , 139
Jennings, G. , 119
Johns, Ald., 52,53
Johnson, C. , 135
Johnson , D., 217,221
Jones, W. , 83,86
Jones, B. , 142
Jones, C. , 176,181
Jones, A. 135
Jones, D. , 169,170
Jones, A. , 191,194
Jones, A. , 172
Jordan, W. , 114,130
Joslin, P. , 56,68,72,76

Milburn, C. , 122
Miles, J. , 173
Miller, F.A, 15,16,19,20
Miller, K.R. , 71
Miller, R. , 80
Miller , Mr. , 162
Millett, F.W. , 118
Millington, J. , 168
Mills, D. , 91,101
Milton, C.A. , 73
Mitchell, M. , 125
Mitchell, S. , 200,201,202
Moffatt, J. , 109
Mohammad, H. , 83,92
Mohammad , K. ,
76,77,79,80,85,87,88,90
Montgomery, S. , 85,86
Moore, I. , 162,163,164,165
Moore, Chief.Suptd. C. , 186
Morgan, H. , 193,195,197,198,
200,201,202,203,204,205,206,2
16,217,222
Morgan, J. , 211,212,213,221
Morkel, D.P.B. , 50
Morrell 37
Morris, C. , 68
Morris, F. , 117
Morrison, J., 23
Mortimore, J.B., 83,84
Mortimore, C. , 215
Moseley, H.R. , 135
Moss, A. , 133
Moss, D. , 174,176,181,183
Motts 50
Mountford, S., 80
Mountford, , 7
Mountford, A., 42
Mountford, W. , 42
Mountford, L. , 74
Mountford, S. , 80,139,145,174
Mountford, N., 139,141,143,
147,149,158,159,163,166,171,
174
Moylan-Jones, R. , 109,139
Muncer, B.L. , 69,171,84,89
Munro, G. , 50
Murray, J. , 133
Murrin, I. , 76
Naran, M. , 148
Narracott, P.T. , 21,22,23,24,27
Needham, D. , 214

Needham, S., 203,204,205,207,
209,210,213,214,215,216,218,
222,223
Needham, M. , 214,218
Needham, P., 218
Needham, C., 215,218
Neville, J. , 142
Newcome, R 153
Newham, H. , 7
Newman, D. , 117
Nicholson , Rev. G.H. , 96
Nickels, W.H. , 43,45,48
Nickels, D. , 66
Norman, A, 127,130,131,133
Norman 86
Northey, Rev. , 21
Norton 148
Odell 7
O'Donoghue, P. , 135
O'Donoghue, W.G. ,
36,38,40,41,60
Old, C.M. , 117
Oldfield, W.A. , 56
Oliver, D. , 174,176
Oliver, R.J. , 50,57,59
Oliver, L. , 63
Oliver, J. , 63
Oliver, J. , 114,117,119,120,172
Oliver, G. , 173,195,196
Osborne, P. , 82
Osborne, M.J. , 114,115,117,118
Osborne, I. , 176
O'Sullivan, G. , 181,185,186,187
Outschoorn, L., 73
Owen, R., 160,161,162,202
Oxley, S., 67,68
Padfield, J. , 97
Palk, Mr., 3
Palk, Sir Lawrence, 3,4,
8,9,11,14
Palmer, 23,25,33
Palmer, C. , 90
Pamplin, R. , 112
Parker, R., 66,68
Parker, J. , 205,206
Parker(NZ), J. , 148
Parkinson, H. , 59
Parks, J.M. , 106,192
Parr, C.S., 34,36
Parry, E. , 96
Parsons, P. , 93

Parsons 7
Pascoe, K. , 68
Passenger, B. , 209,210,211,212,
213,216,218,220
Patch 4
Patel, G. , 98,107,108,112,
113,115,116,121
Patterson, G. , 185,186
Patterson, R. , 22
Pavey, M. , 135
Payne, Rev. , 30
Peacup, S.H., 89
Peagram, H.L. ,
45,47,50,56,59,68,74
Pearce, Capt. , 1
Pearce, J. , 181,190,191
Pearson, D.B. , 89
Pedley, M. , 206
Peebles, I.A.R.., 50
Pegg, A. , 102,109,119
Pelosi, J. , 25,36,207
Pepall, C. , 18
Pepper, C.G. , 105
Peppiatt, K., 88,89,94,112,120,
127,129,135,144,151,174
Peppiatt Jnr., 114,129
Percival 5
Perry, J. , 96,168
Perry, Coun. , 90
Perry, D., 174,175,176
Penny Snr., D. , 166
Penny Jnr. , D. , 166
Pettiford 88
Petto-Shrub 17
Pfieffer, J. , 215
Phadkar, 86,88
Phillips, B.F.J., 203
Phillipson, W.E., 65
Picton, E. , 149,150,152,153,165
Pierpoint, F.G. ,
73,74,76,77,78,79
Pike, W. , 70,71
Pinney, M. , 114,119
Pitts, O., 203,213,215
Place , W., 81
Plumb , G.L., 47
Post , D. , 94,96,98,99,101,
102,103,104,105,106,108,109,
110,111,112,115,117,120,121,
123,179,219
Potts, F.G. , 38,39,40,41,54

Potts-Chatto, D. , 22,30
Poulton, A.W., 68
Powell, M. , 184
Poynder, J.S. , 47,65
Price, H. , 65
Price, T., 128
Price, J.W., 42,46,47,48,49,68
Price, L.P., 47
Prior, J., 117
Pritchard 201
Proctor 202
Pugh, C. , 39
Pugh, B. , 119
Pugh, A.J. , 170,191,206,210,215
Pugh, M. , 193,196,201,202,
203,204,205,206,208,209,211,2
12,214,215,216
Rabukaewaqa 95
Ramadhin, S. , 86
Ramzan, M., 91,92
Randall, D.W. , 178
Ransom, V. , 75
Rasa, J. , 42
Rawlings, W. , 71
Rawson, C. , 181
Read, C. , 200
Reed, R. , 4,5
Reed , A. , 155
Rees-Price, 142,143
Rennie & Family, J. , 187
Rhodes, C. , 47,59
Rice, L. , 211,213,214,215
Rice, J. , 164
Rice, L. , 178
Rich, A. , 107,112,126
Richards, T., 108
Richards, I.V.A. , 135
Richardson, P.E. , 73
Richardson, T. , 114
Riddell, V.H. , 39,41,45,52,53
Riddle, Dr. D.R. , 52
Ripley, G. , 173
Rivers, C. , 21
Rivers , A.S. , 54
Roberts, D. , 59
Roberts, W.B. , 65
Roberts, I. , 137
Robertson, J.D.B. , 83,86
Robins, R.V.W. , 47
Robinson , T. , 213,215,218
Robinson, G. , 61

Roebuck , P.M. , 139,140,185,
191,204,218,219
Rogers, C. , 216
Roost 137
Roper, B. , 135
Rose, B. C. , 139,184
Rosenburg, T. , 68
Ross, C. , 185,186,187
Ross, 66,67
Rossiter, J. , 168
Rothchild, L. , 16
Rowe, G. , 68
Rowe, L..G., 133
Rowley, J. , 71,85
Rowley, Mrs. M. , 160
Rudolph, J. , 215
Russell, 18
Sadler, 50,54,55,56,57
Sambrook, B. ,
109,114,134,137,139,140,141
Sanbrook, S., 102
Sandham, A. , 69
Sandiford 22,23,24
Sangster, M. , 110
Satterley, R. , 114
Saunders, P. , 34
Saville, C.J. , 117
Schneider , A.H. , 167,168
Scia, S. , 170
Scobell, Rev. J.F. , 10,25
Scofield, I. , 108,111,112,114,
115,116,124,125,133,136,145,
149,151,172,176
Scofield, B. ,
170,172,173,180,183
Scott, M. , 114,117
Scott, A. , 119,121
Scott-Smith,, D. , 17
Scourfield, W. J. , 68
Searle, A. , 176
Seldon, R.G. , 47,59,65,66,70
Semmence, D. J. , 104,105,106,
107,108,109,110,111,145
Sewell, G. , 181,191,197,202
Sewell , B.J., 55,111,112,115,
119,122,123,152,181,185,188,
190,195
Sharp, H.P.H. , 69
Shaw 164
Sheahan, A.P., 118
Shears, G., 140

Shelton, Mr., 15
Shepherd, D. , 106
Shepherd , A. R., 36,44
Short , S. , 199,203,204,205,
206,207,211,213,214,215,216
Shorthouse, W., 29
Shorto R.N., Lt. , 44
Shrubb 16
Sibley, A. , 83,101,103,105,
106,109,110,112,113,115,117,
118,102,121,130,131,152
Simpson, Janet, 107
Skelton , I., 73
Slade , I. , 172
Slater, J., 110
Sloan , C. , 111
Sloan , R. , 183
Slocombe, P.A. , 139
Smale, J., 157,158,159,161,163
Smethurst, J., 173,181
Smith , Corp. , 61
Smith , A. , 132,133,136,139,
141,142,143,144,148,149,176
Smith, E.R., 17,46
Smith, W. , 32
Snape, Mrs., 167
Snape, H. , 50,63,70,81,95,100,
102,104,106,119
Sneyd, Mrs. , 104
Snowdon , A. , 71
Sobers, Sir G.S.A. , 93
Socha, P., 152169179
Solanky, J., 117
Soper, B. , 129,136,139
Spencer, , 16
Spencer , , 166
Spry, T.H. , 26
Spurway, , 68
Stables , J. , 177
Staddon, R.C., 139
Staddon (Bovey Tracey) 7
Stainton, R.J., 71,73,104,125
Stallibrass, J.H., 74,77
Stanlake, N., 147,184,185,186
Stebbings, H., 87
Steele, J.F., 153
Steer, K. , 101
Stephenson , H., 86,95,147
Stevens, R. , 57
Stevenson , H., 135
Stewart, R. , 181

Stewart , M. , 126
Stockhill, B. , 104,106,107,110
Stockman, B. , 91
Stoneman 50
Stovold,A.W., 175
Stranger,T., 127
Stuart ,J. , 26
Stuckey, B. , 86
Stumbles, M. , 138,153
Stutchbury,W. , 81
Sullivan, S., 102
Summers, G.F. , 47,50
Surridge,W.S. , 69,77
Suttle, K.G. , 86
Sutton,J., 117,118
Sutton, 76
Swarbrick, M. , 208
Swift, S. , 86,95,100,103,112
Swinburne,J. , 115
Sylvester, R. , 152,153
Taber, H.B. , 118
Tall, D., 197
Tamplin, M., 203,204
Tappenden, F. , 87
Tattersall, R. , 75,76,86
Tavare, C., 184
Tayleur 10
Taylor, Coun., 20
Taylor , M.,
164,165,166,169,177
Taylor, S. , 173
Terry, H. , 21,28,31,33,37
Thomas 71
Thomas, B. , 115
Thomas,A., 185,187
Thomas, C., 187
Thompson, H.H. ,
90,96,98,113,116
Thompson , Mr. & Mrs., 87,181
Tierney ,J.K., 204
Tinley Bros., , 3
Titmus, F.J., 86,88,90
Tolchard,J.G., 95,102,106,108,
109,112,113,114,115,117,118,
119,120,126,153,156
Tolchard,R.C.,102,103,
106,109,112,151,153
Tolchard, Ray , 136,139,141,
142,143,149,150,151,152,153,1
54,157,163,164
Tolchard,T. , 65,99,102

Tolliday, H., 144,152
Tomkin, M., 86
Toms,J., 202,213,215,218,221
Towell, C.T. , 30
Townsend,A. , 77
Tozer, 141,175
Traylor, P., 160,168,172,177,181
Traylor,W.J. , 55,83,87,88,92,94,
97,109,119,129,168,171,174,17
5,176,177
Traylor, D. , 109,114,116,119,
125,132,133,138,141,142,143,
147,158,160,162,164,168,176,
179,181
Traylor Family 182
Treeby, R. , 95
Tremlett, M.F. , 86
Tribe, G.E., 83,86
Troop, Rev.W.J., 98
Trueman, F.S., 122
Trump, G. , 100,101,117
Tucker,V.G. , 89,98,100,102,110
Tucker, Mrs. , 96,113
Tulloh, B. , 107
Turle, G.L. , 65,67
Turpin, Rev. J., 29,30,31
Turpin (Jnr) Ric. , R. ,
163,164,165,170,171,174,178
Turpin (Snr), R. ,
97,125,129,163
Twose, P. , 41,95,99,101,104,
105,110,111,112,113,115,118,1
51,161
Twose, Ric. ,
41,175,180,181,183,
185,187,189,190,191
Twose, Roger , 41,178,183,191
Twose, Mrs. P., 41
Twose,A.V. , 41,95
Tyler, R., 208
Tyson, F.H., 83
Ufton, D.G., 72
Uren, H.G. , 74,83,110
Uren, C. , 125
Uren,W. , 74
Vallis, 58,61
Van Onselen, B. , 189
Varcoe, 76
Vaughan, L., 42,45,46,47,48,
49,50,53,62
Veneris, S. , 183

Vertongen, C. , 180,181
Vincent, S. , 126
Virgin, R. , 126
Visser, L. , 206
W. McKinnon , Mrs. , 46
Wagstaffe, 153,154
Waitt 71
Waldock 113
Waldron, F. , 63,64
Walker, H. , 34,36
Walker 149
Wallen, G., 137,138,139,140,
141,142,143,144,145,146,147,
148,149,150,152,153,155,156,
157,158,160,164,175,178,179
Wallen, C.,
152,156,157,158,161,179
Walsh,J. , 84,86
Walters, Dr. , 28
Walworth, R. , 131,139
Ward,T. , 119
Ward, Dr. , 39,41,44
Ward, Roland,, 53
Ward, M. , 174
Wardle,J. , 93
Warner, Rev. G.T. ,
4,5,7,8,11,13,15,17,21,25
Warner, Rev.W.S.O., 13,25
Warner, P. , 49
Warren, Rev. K. , 131,145,152,
155, 159,160,162,171
Warren, Rev. S.B. , 8
Warrington 133
Washbrook, C. , 81
Wassall 89
Watkins,A. , 83
Watson, G. , 67
Watt-Smith, S. ,
147,149,153,154,155
Webber, F. , 85
Wells, H.S. , 81,88,116,118
Welsh, D., 49
Were,T. , 5
Westcott ,J. , 209,213
Western , I. ,
172,190,192,195,196
Western,T., 189,192,195,196,
197,198,199,200,201,203,207,
208,209,210,211,212,213,214,
217,218,221,222
Westlake,J. , 102

Written by Mr Raymond C. Batten, May 2005
Designed & Published by Hutton Design
Tel: 01083 668718

ISBN 0-9550403-0-2